THE HISTORY OF PHILOSOPHY

THE HELLENIC AGE

THE HISTORY OF PHILOSOPHY

THE HELLENIC AGE

BY ÉMILE BRÉHIER

TRANSLATED BY JOSEPH THOMAS

THE UNIVERSITY OF CHICAGO PRESS
CHICAGO AND LONDON

Originally published in 1938 as Histoire de la philosophie:
L'Antiquité et le Moyen Age. I: Introduction.
Période Hellénique. © *1938, Presses Universitaires de France*

*The present bibliography has been enlarged
to include works listed in the eighth
edition of the French text (Presses
Universitaires de France, 1963)*

International Standard Book Number: 0-226-07217-7

*The University of Chicago Press, Chicago 60637
The University of Chicago Press, Ltd., London*
© *1963 by The University of Chicago
All rights reserved. Published 1963
Third Impression 1970
First Phoenix Edition 1965
Printed in the United States of America*

TRANSLATOR'S NOTE

The Hellenic Age, the first in Emile Bréhier's monumental seven-volume work on the history of European philosophy, is an exposition and a critical treatise on the Pre-Socratics, Socrates, Plato, and Aristotle, the founders of Western thought. M. Bréhier has had many distinguished predecessors among historians of philosophy and particularly in the field of Greek philosophy in which he was a specialist, but his interpretations have a marvelous freshness which renders his work exciting.

The Introduction is an essay on the history of philosophy as such which gives us a perspective of the course of its long history. In the chapters on the Pre-Socratics, M. Bréhier moves with great ease from religion, to science, to politics and shows their mutual bearing on each other. The expositions of Plato and Aristotle are clear and exceptionally easy to follow in spite of their respective complexities of thought and technicalities. Throughout the entire work, M. Bréhier combines exposition and criticism in masterful fashion. He points up the small and big differences in the successive thinkers with great ability. *The Hellenic Age* will surely fulfil a useful purpose for students of philosophy in the English-speaking world.

I wish to thank Professor Thomas R. Palfrey of Arizona State University and Professor Joseph Katz of Stanford University for their generous help in reading the manuscript and making valuable criticisms and suggestions.

JOSEPH THOMAS

CONTENTS

INTRODUCTION

IT HAS seemed at times that the history of philosophy might only be an obstacle to living thought, an embarrassment and a constraint for whoever seeks the truth. "Do not believe in the past!" Emerson has Nature say. "I give you the world new and unworn for the first time. You think, in moments of leisure, that there is enough history, literature and knowledge behind you to exhaust thought and to prescribe your future as well as any future. In lucid moments, you will see that not even a line of it has been written." [1] Words of a conquering pioneer who fears the past may have a secret spite against the freedom of the future. And it was also, in another sense, freedom of mind which Descartes defended against the forces of the past when he rebuilt the edifice of philosophy from its very foundation.

There are, indeed, all too many reasons to fear the past, when it demands to be continued into the present and to be perpetuated, as if duration alone established a right. But history is precisely the discipline which regards the past as such and which, as it penetrates it further, sees in each of its moments something original that is without precedent, never to return. Far from being an obstacle, history then, in philosophy and everywhere else, is a true liberator. It alone, by the variety of views it gives us of the human mind, can root out prejudices and suspend judgments that are too hasty.

But is a general view of the philosophic past possible? Faced

[1] Ralph Waldo Emerson, *Autobiography*, Vol. I.

with the enormous complexity of facts, does it not risk either being very difficult if it does not choose among them and merely yields to the rhythm of a plethora of thoughts, or being superficial if it does choose? It is certain that we cannot represent the past without classifying facts in some way; this classification implies certain postulates. The very idea of undertaking a history of philosophy assumes, in fact, that we have raised and solved, in a provisional way at least, the following three problems:

I. What are the origins and what are the frontiers of philosophy? Did philosophy begin in the sixth century, in the Ionian cities, as claimed in a tradition going back to Aristotle, or did it have a more ancient origin either in the Greek or the oriental countries? Can and should the historian of philosophy limit himself to following the development of philosophy in Greece and in the countries with a civilization of Greco-Roman origin, or should he extend his view to oriental civilizations?

II. In the second place, to what extent and to what degree has philosophical thought had a sufficiently autonomous development to make it the object of a history distinct from that of the other intellectual disciplines? Is it not too intimately connected with the sciences, with art, with religion, and with political life for us to make philosophical doctrines the object of a separate inquiry?

III. Finally, can we speak of a steady evolution or progress in philosophy? Or did human thought, from the beginning, have in its possession all possible solutions to the problems it raises, and does it afterward only repeat itself indefinitely? Or do systems supersede one another in an arbitrary and contingent way?

We believe that there is no rigorous solution to these three problems, and that all the solutions that have been suggested contain implicit postulates. Yet, it is necessary to take a position on these questions if we want to deal with the history of philosophy. The only possible course is to disentangle very explicitly the postulates contained in our own solution.

I

The first question, that of origins, remains without adequate solution. Along with those who, with Aristotle, make Thales in the sixth century the first philosopher, there were already historians in Greece tracing the origins of philosophy back beyond Hellenism, to the barbarians. Diogenes Laertius, in the preface to his *Lives of the Philosophers* speaks of the legendary antiquity of philosophy among the Persians and Egyptians. Thus, since antiquity, two theses have faced one another: Is philosophy an invention of the Greeks or a heritage they received from the "barbarians"?

It seems that the Orientalists, as they unveil the pre-Hellenic civilizations, such as the Mesopotamian and Egyptian, with which the cities of Ionia, cradle of Greek philosophy, had been in contact, have decided in favor of the second of these theses. It is impossible not to feel the kinship of thought between the well-known thesis of the first Greek philosopher, Thales, that all things are made of water and the beginning of the *Poem of Creation,* written some centuries earlier in Mesopotamia: "When the sky above was not named, and when the earth below had no name, from the primordial Apsu, their father, and from the tumultuous Tiamat, their mother of all, the waters mingled in one." [2] Texts like these suffice at least to show that Thales was not the inventor of an original cosmogony. The cosmogonic images which he was perhaps the first to define had existed for long centuries. We suspect that the philosophy of the first physiologists of Ionia may be a new form of an extremely ancient theme.

The most recent studies in the history of mathematics have led to a similar conclusion. As early as 1910, G. Milhaud wrote: "The materials amassed in mathematics by Orientals and Egyptians were decidedly richer and more important than was generally suspected even up to a decade ago." [3]

[2] Louis Delaporte, *La Mésopotamie* (Paris: La Renaissance du livre, 1923), p. 152.
[3] Gaston Milhaud, *Nouvelles études sur l'histoire de la pensée scientifique* (Paris: F. Alcan, 1910), p. 127.

Finally, the work of anthropologists on more primitive societies introduces new data which further complicate the problem of the origin of philosophy. In fact, we find in Greek philosophy intellectual traits which have their analogy only in a primitive mentality. The ideas which the first philosophers used, those of destiny, justice, soul, god, were not notions which they created or elaborated themselves; they were common ideas, collective representations which they found. These were notions, apparently, which served as schemata or categories to understand external nature. The Ionian physiologists' idea of the order of nature, as a regular grouping of beings or forces bounded by the sovereign destiny, is based on the transfer of the social order into the external world. Philosophy was perhaps, in its origin, only a sort of vast social metaphor. Facts as strange as the numerical symbolism of the Pythagoreans, who said that "all is number," would be explained by this form of thought which a German philosopher recently called the "morphologico-structural thought" of primitive peoples and which he opposed to functional thought based on the principle of causality. As the North American tribe of the Zuñis makes a division of seven in the village, in the regions of the world, in the elements, and in time, corresponding to the division of their race into seven parts, so the Pythagoreans or even Plato in the *Timaeus* continually invented numerical correspondences of the same type.[4] The resemblance in the *Timaeus* between the intervals of the planets and the musical scale seems completely arbitrary, and its logic escapes us quite as much as that of *participation,* studied by L. Lévy-Bruhl in his work on primitive mentality.

If such is the case, the first philosophical systems of Greece would not be original; they would only be the elaborated form of a much more ancient thinking. It is, no doubt that at this stage of mental development one should search for the true origin of philosophical thought or at least of one of its aspects.[5] Auguste Comte was not

[4] Ernst Cassirer, *Die Begriffsform im mythischen Denken* (Leipzig: B. G. Teubner, 1922).

[5] On this question, see the very striking book by F. M. Cornford, *From Religion to Philosophy* (London: E. Arnold, 1912). Cf. E. Bréhier, "Une nouvelle théorie sur

mistaken in seeing in what he called fetishism the root of the philosophical representation of the universe. Now that folklore and studies of non-civilized peoples have given us a more exact and positive knowledge of the cast of mind of primitive peoples, we realize more clearly how much of it survives in the more advanced metaphysics of the Greeks.

Thus the first "philosophers" of Greece did not really have to invent; they worked upon representations of a complexity and richness but also of a confusion which we can scarcely imagine. They did not so much have to invent as to disentangle and choose, or rather the invention was in this discernment itself. We would understand them better no doubt if we knew what they rejected, rather than what they retained. Moreover, we see now and then the suppressed representations reappearing; and the underlying primitive thought makes a continual effort, which sometimes succeeds, to overthrow the barriers which contain them.

If, in spite of these remarks, we make our history begin with Thales, it is not because we deny the long prehistory in which philosophical thought was developed; it is only for the practical reason that the epigraphic sources for the Mesopotamian civilizations are few in number and difficult to get at. And it is also because the sources on primitive peoples cannot furnish us with indications of what primitive Greece was like.

The question of frontiers in the history of philosophy, related to the question of origins, cannot be solved with any greater precision. It is undeniable that, in the countries of the Far East and especially in India, there has been a real flowering of philosophical systems at certain periods. But the problem is to know whether the Greco-Roman and then the Christian world, on the one hand, and the Far Eastern world, on the other hand, have had a completely independent intellectual development. In case they have, it would be permissible to leave out of consideration the philosophy of the Far

les origines de la philosophie grecque," in *Études de philosophie antique* (Paris: Presses universitaires de France, 1955), pp. 33–43.

East in an exposition of Western philosophy. The situation is far from being so clear: In the first place, the easy commercial relations which existed between the Greco-Roman world and the Far East from Alexander down to the Arab invasions made intellectual relations possible in the ancient world. We have some positive evidence; the Greeks, travelers or philosophers, wrote a great deal on India in this period. The remains of this literature, especially in the second and third centuries of our era, bear witness to at least a strong curiosity about Indian thought. On the other hand, in the high Middle Ages a philosophy developed in Moslem countries in which Greek thought, Aristotelian or Neo-Platonic, was certainly the essential part but which nevertheless seems to have felt at various times the influence of neighboring India. Now, it will be seen what place Arab philosophy had in Christendom, from the thirteenth to the sixteenth century. It is therefore very important to know the degrees and limits of this Indian influence, direct or indirect. But it is also very difficult to know: The influence of Greece on the Far East, which is today substantiated in matters of art, was no doubt very considerable in the intellectual realm and much greater than the reverse influence of India on Hellenism. Given the uncertainty of dates in Indian literature, the resemblances between Greek and Indian thought cannot prove from which of the two the influence came. Apparently it was only through Greek influence that the Hindus gave to the exposition of their ideas the systematic and ordered character which our intellectual habits, inherited from the Greeks, make us consider inseparable from the very notion of philosophy.

In spite of these difficulties, a history of philosophy does not have the right to ignore Far Eastern thought. So, in addition to the information we have given on oriental influences as they are manifested in the Occident, we asked a recognized specialist of Indian thought, who is at the same time a philosopher, P. Masson-Oursel,[6] to com-

---

[6] Paul Masson-Oursel, *Esquisse d'une histoire de la philosophie indienne* (Paris: P. Geuthner, 1923); see also his contribution in *L'Inde antique et la civilisation indienne* (Paris: La Renaissance du livre, 1933). Cf. Paul Oltramare, *L'Histoire des idées théosophiques dans l'Inde,* Vol. I (Paris: E. Leroux, 1907), Vol. II (Paris: P. Geuthner, 1923). See the first supplementary fascicle of this series, *La philosophie en Orient* by Paul Masson-Oursel (Paris: Presses universitaires de France, 1957).

plete this history with an account of the development of philosophy
in the Middle and Far East.

II

Our second problem is that of the degree of independence of the
history of philosophy as compared with the history of the other intellectual disciplines. But we refuse to raise it dogmatically, as if it
were a matter of deciding the question of the relations of philosophy,
taken as a thing in itself, to religion, science, or politics. We wish
to raise it and solve it historically; this is to say that it cannot have
a simple and uniform solution. If the history of philosophy is to
be accurate, it cannot be an abstract history of ideas and systems,
separated from the intentions of their authors and from the moral
and social atmosphere in which they are born. It is impossible to
deny that, in different periods, philosophy has occupied very different
places in what we can call the intellectual regime of the time. In
the course of history, we will encounter philosophers who were primarily scholars; others were primarily social reformers, like Auguste
Comte, or moralists, like the Stoic philosophers, and preachers, like
the Cynics. Among them there are solitary meditators, professionals
of speculative thought, like a Descartes or a Kant, along with men
who aim at an immediate practical influence, like Voltaire. Personal
meditation is sometimes simply reflection on one's self and sometimes borders upon ecstasy.

And it is not only because of their personal temperament that
they are so different, but because of what society, at each period,
requires of a philosopher. The noble Roman who sought a spiritual
guide, the popes of the thirteenth century who saw in the philosophical teaching of the University of Paris a means of strengthening
Christianity, the Encyclopedists who wanted to end the oppression
of the forces of the past, all demanded very different things of
philosophy; it became in turn missionary, critical, doctrinal.

It will be objected that these are accidents. It matters little what
society does with philosophy; the important thing is what philosophy

continues to be in the midst of the different intentions of those who use it. However philosophies may diverge, there is philosophy only where there is rational thought, in other words thought capable of criticizing itself and making an effort to justify itself with reasons. May we not think this aspiration toward a rational value to be a trait sufficiently characteristic and permanent to justify that abstract history of doctrines, that "history of pure reason," as Kant, who outlined the idea, called it?[7] Sufficient to distinguish philosophy from religious belief, this trait would distinguish it also from the positive sciences; for the history of the positive sciences is completely inseparable from the history of the techniques from which they have sprung and which they perfect. There is no scientific law which is not, in another aspect, a rule of action on material things; philosophy is pure speculation, pure effort to comprehend, without any other concern.

This solution would be highly acceptable, if its immediate consequence were not to eliminate from the history of philosophy all doctrines which ascribe a part to belief, to intuition, intellectual or not, to feeling; in other words, the dominant doctrines. It implies, therefore, a fixed opinion concerning philosophy, rather than an accurate view of its history. To isolate a doctrine from the movement of ideas which brought it about, from the feeling and the intentions which guide it, to consider it as a theorem to be proved, is to replace a living and significant thought by a dead thought. We can understand a philosophical notion only by its relation to the whole of which it is an aspect. How many different shades of meaning there are, for example, in the famous "Know thyself"! For Socrates, self-knowledge signifies dialectical examination and testing one's own opinions; for St. Augustine, it is a means of attaining knowledge of God by the image of the Trinity which we find in ourselves; for Descartes, it is a kind of apprenticeship in certainty; in the Upanishads of India, it is knowledge of the identity of the self and the universal principle. How, then, are we to grasp this notion and give it a meaning independently of the ends for which it is used?

[7] Immanuel Kant, *Critique of Pure Reason,* chap. iv.

One of the greatest difficulties standing in the way of the idea of an abstract history of systems is the fact which we may call the displacement in the level of doctrines. In order to give a salient example, let us think of the intense polemics, continued for centuries, about the limits of the realms of faith and reason. We can easily find doctrines presented at one time as revealed faith and at other times as doctrines of reason. The barrenness and poverty of philosophy as such in the Middle Ages were compensated by the wealth of the spiritual life which passed into the theological writings of Saint Ambrose and St. Augustine from pagan philosophy. The immateriality of the soul which in Descartes is rationally proved is for Locke a matter of faith. What could be more striking than Spinoza's transposition of the religious notion of eternal life, when he interpreted it through notions inspired by Cartesianism! From these facts, which we could easily multiply, it follows that one cannot characterize a philosophy sufficiently by indicating the doctrines it maintains. It is much more important to see the spirit inspiring them and the intellectual realm in which it is situated.

In other words, philosophy cannot be separated from the rest of the intellectual life, which also expresses itself through science, religion, art, and ethical or social life. The philosopher takes into consideration all spiritual and intellectual values of his time in order to sanction, criticize, or transform them. There is no philosophy where there is no effort to arrange values hierarchically.

The historian of philosophy, therefore, must constantly strive to remain in contact with general political history and the history of all intellectual disciplines, and avoid any temptation to isolate philosophy as a separate technique.

But these relations to other spiritual disciplines are not at all uniform and invariable but appear in a very different way according to the times and the thinkers. Philosophical speculation can sometimes be related to the religious life, sometimes to the positive sciences, sometimes to politics and to ethics, sometimes to art. There are times when the role of a particular discipline predominates, while others are almost obliterated. Thus, in the course of classical antiquity, we can observe a gradual decline in the role of the sciences, accompanied by an increase in the role of religion. Whereas in Plato's time the evolution of mathematics has a very special interest for the historian, in Plotinus' time it is the upsurge of the oriental religions of salvation that will call for consideration. It is at this juncture that we must raise the problem, still so difficult to solve, about the exact influence of Christianity on philosophy. The present time is witnessing in the realm of philosophy a bitter enough struggle for domination to indicate that this meditation on the past is not completely useless.

III

There is a third problem on which the historian of philosophy is obviously obliged to take a position. Does philosophy have a law of development, or is the succession of systems contingent and dependent upon the accident of individual temperaments? This question is of utmost importance. The history of philosophy has behind it a long past which weighs heavily upon it; it has, especially in the area under consideration here, traditions to which it rarely fails to make some kind of accommodation. It is these traditions which we wish to single out in order to appraise them properly.

The idea of considering the history of philosophy a single unified development is a relatively recent one. It is an aspect of those doctrines concerning the "progress of the human spirit" which appeared at the end of the eighteenth century. Both the positive philosophy of Auguste Comte and the philosophy of Hegel contain as a necessary element a history of the philosophical strivings of humanity. The human mind cannot be defined in isolation from its own history.

The history of philosophy at the dawn of the modern period was not at all like this. Our history of philosophy really came into existence at the time of the Renaissance, when the West discovered the compilers of late antiquity: Plutarch, whose writings include a treatise *On the Opinions of the Philosophers,* Sextus Empiricus, Stobaeus, the *Stromateis* of Clement of Alexandria, and especially the *Lives of Philosophers* by Diogenes Laertius who collected remains of all ancient works on the history of philosophy since the work of Aristotle's disciples. Perspectives which had entirely escaped medieval thought were opened by these authors concerning the diversity of the ancient sects and concerning the succession of the leaders of schools and the schools themselves. The first histories simply imitate these compilations; they were treatises like the one by Burleus on the *Lives of Philosophers* (1477).

It follows from this that history was limited at first to ancient philosophy or, more accurately, to the period which extends to the first century of our era, in other words to the period where the compilers we have mentioned generally stop. The history of later ancient philosophy was, it is true, introduced as a result of direct study of the great Neo-Platonic works; but antiquity was thus completely separated from the Middle Ages, and the idea that there might be a continuity from one to the other was completely overlooked. This separation was so pronounced that Jonsius, collecting sources for the history of philosophy in 1649, still limited himself to a short chapter on ancient writers who wrote on the history of philosophy (*De Scriptoribus historiae philosophicae,* Book IV [1649]). Yet, about this time the history of philosophy in the Middle Ages began to be studied for itself; Launoy wrote a history of the medieval schools.[8]

The history of philosophy, then, was mainly the history of sects at this time; Bacon conceives it this way in his outlines of the sciences.[9] For him the history of sects was one part, the last, of literary history. Literary history, as a whole, aims to show the origin, the progress, the regressions, and the rebirth of "doctrines and arts." "Let us add," said Bacon, "the sects and the most famous controversies which have occupied the learned; let us enumerate the authors, the books, the schools, the succession of the heads of schools,

---

[8] Jean de Launoy, *De Scholis celebrioribus seu a Carolo magno seu post Carolum per occidentem instauratis* (Lutetiae Parisiorum, Typis viduae Edmundi Martini, 1672).

[9] Françis Bacon, *De Dignitate et augmentis scientiarum,* Book II, chap. iv.

the academies, the societies, the colleges, the orders." This is the Baconian plan followed by Georg Horn, the author of the first general history of philosophy, which traces its development from the beginnings to the eighteenth century. The Preface refers to Bacon and the complete title of the work clearly indicates its character: *Historiae philosophicae libri septem, quibus de origine, successione, sectis et vita philosophorum ab orbe condito ad nostram aetatem agitur*.[10] He was less interested in analysis and precise knowledge of the content of doctrines than in their enumeration and their succession. He has the same relation to history of philosophy proper as church history has to the history of dogma; and a true history of philosophy did not exist at this time any more than a history of dogma did.

The fact is that the aim of Renaissance men was, not to inform themselves about the past, but rather to restore it and to enable human thought to return to its living sources. Hence they took a deep interest in the sect which they studied; they could not be historians of Platonism without at the same time being Platonists. There were thus Platonists and Stoics, Epicureans and Academicians, and even Pre-Socratics. History derives the greatest benefit from these encounters. Marsilio Ficino made Plato and Plotinus known. In the first half of the seventeenth century Justus Lipsius studied attentively and classified all the known texts on the Stoics. Bérigard, in his *Circulus Pisanus,* called attention to the first physicists of Greece. Gassendi tried to give an accurate account of Epicurus.[11]

It is in these works of the "sectaries" rather than in the works of pure erudition that we must seek the history of doctrine proper. One of these sects has, from our point of view, particular importance; this is the Academicians and Pyrrhonians. A traditional argument of skepticism is, in fact, the existence of different sects. And

[10] Georg Horn, *Historiae philosophicae libri septem* (Lugduni Batavorum, apud J. Elzevirium, 1645).

[11] Marsilio Ficino, *Theologia platonica* (1482); Bérigard, *Circulus pisanus, de vetere et peripatetica philosophia* (1643; 2d ed., 1661); Justus Lipsius, *Manuductio ad philosophiam stoicam, Physiologia Stoicorum* (1604); Pierre Gassendi, *Commentarius de vita, moribus et placitis Epicuri seu animadversiones in decimum librum Diogenis Laertii* (1649); *Syntagma philosophiae Epicuri* (1659). See also Jean Chrysostome Magnen, *Democritus reviviscens* (1648).

one of the historian's principal sources is the large treatise of Sextus Empiricus, *Against the Dogmatists,* edited and translated in part by Henry Estienne in 1562. In it Sextus expounds at length the varieties of opinion on one and the same subject. There were many Academicians at this time and there were none who did not employ the same procedure.[12]

So from all the learning of the Renaissance only one thing results, the fragmentation of philosophical thought into a host of sects. Either you choose one of these sects and become a sectary; or else you destroy them by one another and become a skeptic. The only way to escape this fatal result is to separate philosophy entirely from philology; this was the task of the great thinkers of the eighteenth century. As early as 1645, Horn remarked quite rightly that this century, with Descartes and Hobbes, was the century of philosophers, whereas the preceding one had been that of philologists. What is now attempted is no longer to restore a sect or to substitute a new sect for an old, but to find, beyond the opinions of the sects, the sources of true philosophy in the very nature of the human mind.

In these new conditions, the history of philosophy will either continue to be purely and simply the history of sects, in which case it will only enumerate errors or aberrations of the human mind and will be only an encumbering erudition; or else it will have to transform its perspectives and methods profoundly.

That the history of philosophy resembles a museum of eccentricities of the human mind, was the common theme of the rationalists of the seventeenth and eighteenth centuries. To explain this unfavorable judgment on the past, we must see how it was presented to them by the histories of philosophy. Even in the great work of Brücker, the *Historica critica philosophiae* (1741–44), which, to the end of the eighteenth century and especially for the Encyclopedists, was the most widely used work, we find a traditional scheme of philosophical development which comes from St. Augustine's *City*

---

[12] Cf., for example, Guy de Bruès, *Les dialogues contre les nouveaux académiciens* (Paris: Guillaume Cauellat, 1557), p. 65; in a dialogue between Baïf and Ronsard, the author sets forth the various opinions of the philosophers "who only cause confusion in our minds."

of God[13] and which persisted through the centuries. Philosophy starts with the beginning of the world; the Greeks lied in saying that they were the first philosophers. In reality, they borrowed their doctrines from Moses, from Egypt, and from Babylonia. The first period of philosophy was not, therefore, the Greek period, but the barbarian. Almost all historians, down to Brücker, began with a long series of chapters on "The Barbarian Philosophy": Philosophy which has a divine origin was transmitted to the Jewish patriarchs, and from these to the Babylonians, to the Chaldean Magi, to the Egyptians, to the Ethiopians, to the Indians, and even to the Germanic peoples. It was only later that the Greeks collected these traditions, which faded out gradually; these traditions degenerated among the Greeks into a host of sects. They ended, on the one hand, in the skepticism of the New Academy, which was the end of philosophy, and on the other, in Neo-Platonism, which tried to corrupt Christian philosophy.

In a word, the history of philosophy is the history of a gradual and continuous decadence of the human mind, and the proof of this decadence is the number of sects which have replaced the original unity. Greek thought in particular was neither a point of departure nor an advance; individual imagination, given free rein, has almost destroyed whatever truth was still preserved in the oriental traditions. In these old histories the Greeks do not, we see, have any of the importance and value which they assume later. This criticism of the Greeks originates with the Church Fathers. Almost all the philosophers of the eighteenth century, Voltaire in particular who never ceased deriding Plato, adhere fully to this old prejudice. But what is more, they show the same prejudice about modern philosophy; it is the basis of the *Traité de systèmes* of Condillac (1749). All philosophical systems are the fruit of the "imagination." "A philosopher dreams easily. How many systems have been created? How many more will be? If only one were found consistently

---

[13] St. Augustine, *The City of God,* Book VIII, chap. ix; cf. Clement of Alexandria, *Stromates,* beginning of Book I. Justus Lipsius uses these texts at the beginning of his *Manuductio ad physiologiam stoicam.*

acceptable to all its partisans! But how can one rely on systems that suffer a thousand changes, in the course of passing through a thousand different hands?"[14]

Such, in the eighteenth century, is the judgment of philosophy on its own past; it resulted from the conflict between a conception of history dating from the Renaissance and a new conception of philosophy. But simultaneously and from the seventeenth century on, through a reverse movement, the conception of history and the perspective from which history was seen were transformed. The new theme was the idea that the unity of the human mind remains visible through the diversity of the sects. As early as the beginning of the seventeenth century (1609), in his *Conciliator philosophicus,* Goclenius had tried to classify the contradictions of the sects on every subject; and he drew up this list of antinomies only to resolve them and to show that they were only apparent. This "syncretism," which affirms the agreement of philosophical thought with itself, is considered by Horn to be the true result of the history of philosophy.[15]

Bound up with this syncretism, which effaced the differences between the sects, was an eclecticism which was itself above all sects, but which, instead of uniting, selected and distinguished. "There is only one sect," Justus Lipsius was already saying, "to which we can subscribe with safety: it is the eclectic sect, the one which reads with diligence and chooses with judgment; foreign to every faction, it will readily become the partner of truth." This spirit of conciliation and eclecticism, which in Leibniz had an illustrious representative in the seventeenth century,[16] inspired the great *Historia critica philosophiae* of Brücker,[17] the source from

---

[14] Etienne de Condillac, *Oeuvres complètes* (Paris, 1803), III, 7, 27.

[15] Rudolph Goclenius, *Historia philosophica* (Leyden, 1645), p. 323.

[16] See also J. C. Sturm, *Philosophia eclectica* (1686) and *Physica eclectica* (1697–1722); Jean Baptiste du Hamel, *De consensu veteris et novae philosophiae* (1663); also the survey of the history of philosophy in Leibniz, *Die Philosophischen Schriften von Gottfried Wilhelm Leibniz,* ed. C. J. Gerhardt (Berlin: Weidmann, 1875–90), VII, 146–56.

[17] Johann Jakob Brücker, *Historia critica philosophiae a mundi incunabulis ad nostram aetatem perducta* (5 vols.; Leipzig: B. C. Breitkopf, 1742–44).

which all writers of the second half of the eighteenth century derived their knowledge of the history of philosophy. The proper use of history is to make known the characteristics which distinguish true philosophy from false. The history of philosophy "develops a sort of history of human intelligence"; it shows "what the power of human intelligence is, how it has been wrested from darkness and illumined by the light of truth, how it has attained, through so many perils and trials, the knowledge of truth and felicity, through what windings it went astray, how it has been led back to the royal path."[18] The history of the sects, then, is only a means of freeing us from sects. The eclecticism of Brücker is visible throughout the *Encyclopédie*. In the article "Eclecticism" Diderot praises the eclectic "who dares to think for himself, and, from all the systems which he has analyzed without fear or favor, creates for himself one that is individual and personal."

But syncretism and eclecticism are not the only way of interpreting the past and rising above the diversity of the sects. While maintaining this diversity, there is also a search for a link and a historical continuity. In a slightly earlier work than Brücker's, Deslandes protested against the very idea of a history of the sects.

To collect separately the different systems of ancient and modern philosophers, to enter into the details of their actions, to undertake accurate analyses of their works, to gather their maxims, apophthegms and even their witticisms, is precisely the least instructive content of the history of philosophy. The principal thing in my opinion is to go back to the source of the most important thoughts of men, to examine their infinite variety and at the same time the *imperceptible relationship, the delicate connections* between them; to show how these thoughts originated one after another and often one from the other; to recall the opinions of the ancient philosophers and to show that they actually could not say anything other than what they did say [emphasis added].[19]

These efforts to disentangle the history of philosophy from the

[18] *Ibid.*, pp. 10–21.
[19] André Deslandes, *Histoire critique de la philosophie* (Amsterdam, 1739), I, 3, 5, where he discusses its origin, progress, and the various revolutions which have occurred down to the present.

dusty remains of the sects find a natural support in the theorists of progress. For Condorcet the division of philosophy into sects is a necessary but passing state, from which philosophy frees itself little by little, tending "to only admit proven truths" and not opinions. Within this historical perspective, Greece has a special place because mankind must recognize in her the initiator "whose genius opened for her all the paths of truth." [20]

Hellenism is no longer considered as a decay but as a beginning. Thus an outline is drawn of the historical development of philosophy in which we see a purely occidental philosophy beginning with the Greek thinkers of Ionia and finding its type in Socrates who wanted "not so much to have men adopt a new system and to subject their imagination to his, as to teach them to make use of their own reason." It was this philosophy which, after the long eclipse of the Middle Ages, was fully realized by Descartes. We are finished with the medley of so-called barbarian and oriental philosophy and the accusations of plagiarism against the Greeks. On the other hand, we must certainly mention all that is left out of this outline of the progress of the human mind, so broad in its scope toward the end of the eighteenth century, and which remains, basically, the outline of our histories of philosophy: The whole of Christianity and the Orient is missing.

The thinkers of the eighteenth century, then, tried to introduce unity and continuity into the history of philosophy. Now the whole of the first half of the nineteenth century witnessed an effort to construct what had been only outlined. What is now sought is a principle of internal connection which will enable us to understand doctrines in themselves and to grasp their historical significance. We are strongly critical of the light manner in which ideas not our own are rejected as absurd, when they are necessary aspects of the human mind. What historians have most lacked is historical sense, the sensitive perception of the nuances of the past. This is what

[20] Condorcet, *Esquisse d'un tableau historique des progrès de l'esprit humain* (written in 1793); fourth and fifth epochs.

Reinhold points out very clearly in an article in 1791, "On the concept of the history of philosophy," where he said:

The reason why the history of philosophy appears in our manuals as a history of the follies rather than the wisdom of men, why the most famous and often the most meritorious men of antiquity were abused in the most unworthy manner, why their most profound insights into the sanctuary of truth were misinterpreted and conceived as the most commonplace of errors, was that their ideas were misunderstood, and had to be misunderstood because of an adherence, while judging them, to the later principles of one of the four principal metaphysical sects, or because of a bias against profound research on the part of the oracles of common sense, accustomed to the methods of popular philosophy.[21]

It was Reinhold's program that Tennemann followed in his history of philosophy.[22] According to him this history must not assume any philosophical ideas; it is only the description of the gradual formation of philosophy, the description of the efforts of reason to realize the idea of a science of the laws of nature and freedom.

But the principle of internal unity itself appears in two forms: on the one hand as a principle of classification of doctrines which attempts to reduce all possible sects to a handful of types inherent in the human mind; on the other, as a gradual development with each important doctrine forming an essential moment in the process. The first point of view is that of J.-M. de Gérando.[23] He states explicitly that he is abandoning, as both sterile and impossible, the old method of the history of the sects.

The philosophical opinions which came into being in different countries and in different periods are so varied, so numerous, that the most learned and faithful compilation will only introduce uncertainty and confusion into our ideas and overwhelm us under the weight of a barren erudition, unless skilful comparisons guide our attention.[24]

---

[21] Karl Reinhold, *Ueber den Begriff der Geschichte der Philosophie,* in Fulleborn, *Beiträge zur Geschichte der Philosophie* (1791), I, 33.

[22] Wilhelm Tennemann, *Geschichte der Philosophie* (11 vols.; Leipzig: J. A. Barth, 1798–1819).

[23] J.-M. de Gérando, *Histoire comparée des systèmes de philosophie, considérés relativement aux principes des connaissance humaines* (3 vols.; Paris, 1804).

[24] "Introduction," *Histoire comparée,* p. 23.

In place of "narrative history" we must substitute, in Bacon's words, "inductive and comparative history." This consists first in determining the very small number of primary questions which each system must answer; according to these answers, we can grasp the spirit of each one and group them into natural classes. This classification made, we can compare them, understand their points of difference, and, finally, considering each of them as experiments made in the course of the progress of the human mind, judge which is best. In fact the fundamental question which gives De Gérando the basis for his classification concerns the nature of human knowledge. The history of systems becomes "an essay in experimental philosophy" which tests the value of each solution given to the problem of the origin of knowledge.

The method of Victor Cousin does not add much to that of J.-M. de Gérando. It is a sort of mean between the method of the botanist, who classifies plants by family, and a psychological explanation which connects philosophies to the primitive facts of the human mind. At the beginning of his 1829 lectures he says: "What perplexes and discourages us at the beginning of the history of philosophy is the prodigious number of systems in every country and age." Then, "characteristics, different or similar, will appear as if by themselves, and will reduce this endless multitude of systems to a rather small number of principal systems which include all the others." After classification comes explanation. These great families of systems come from the human mind. That is why the human mind, as invariable as nature itself, reproduces them endlessly. The history of philosophy thus reduces in the end to psychology which, the starting point of all sound philosophy, "even furnishes history its most trustworthy light." [25] Thus we master history by repudiating it, since we replace the development of doctrines in time by their classification.

The second point of view which allows for some kind of unity in the history of philosophy is that of a dynamic connection between systems, in which each appears as a necessary moment of a single

[25] Victor Cousin, *Histoire générale de la philosophie* (4th ed.; Paris, 1867), p. 4.

history. Here the history of philosophy only reflects the general tendencies of the beginning of the nineteenth century, which gave rise to the moral and social sciences. It is no longer believed that general history is oriented toward the success of a particular religion or empire. It advances rather toward a collective civilization which concerns the whole of humanity. Likewise the history of philosophy is not oriented to the benefit of one sect; it has an immanent law which one can recognize by direct observation.

"No science can be understood without its own history, always inseparable from the general history of humanity."[26] No remark condenses the ideas of Auguste Comte on intellectual history more neatly than this. It is impossible to separate the present from the past, to consider the present stage of intelligence except as part of a dynamic development from whose past stages it has originated. It is impossible to separate the history of intellectual development from that of the whole of civilization. Positivism affirms "human continuity" which "Catholicism anathematizing antiquity, Protestantism condemning the Middle Ages and Deism denying all filiation" denied. Comte's thinking was connected with the general movement which we saw spring up in the eighteenth century against the idea of a history of philosophy as a mere enumeration of incoherent sects. "Dynamic continuity" (p. 27) prohibits us from believing that there were ever any "radical changes" in human judgments; they changed in virtue of the same impulse which still modifies them, the impulse toward a growing subordination of our judgments to the objective order. Each of these stages has its normal and necessary place. The "purely subjective logic" (p. 31) of the fetishist who animates phenomena "is, in the beginning, as normal as the best scientific methods are today."

This vision of a continuous progress which cannot be retrogressive led Comte to completely transform the value which the historians of the eighteenth century gave to each period of the past, especially to Greek and medieval thought. He formally protested

[26] Auguste Comte, *Système de politique positive* (4th ed.; Paris: Crès, 1921), III, 2.

against "the irrational hypotheses of certain scholars concerning a supposed anteriority of the positive state in relation to the theological state" (p. 73), doubtless an allusion to a possible objection based on the fact that Greek positive science preceded medieval thought. These hypotheses, he adds, "have been irrevocably destroyed according to superior scholarship." The union of theology and metaphysics which characterizes the Middle Ages, a union which, in the eyes of Protestant writers like Brücker and the Encyclopedists, is a scandal and a monstrous alliance, is precisely what constitutes the superiority of the Middle Ages over antiquity and which prepares for the advent of the modern age. Theology without metaphysics inevitably turns out to be polytheism; it "alone constitutes the true theological state, in which the imagination prevails freely. Monotheism results always from an essentially metaphysical theology, which restrains fiction through reasoning."

Philosophy as Comte understands it, then, is not so much the technical systems of specialists of philosophy as a mental state diffused through society which will manifest itself in legal institutions, literary works, or works of art at least as well as in the systems of philosophers. One philosophical system, singled out, may, it is true, illustrate with particular clarity this state of mind, because it concentrates traits scattered elsewhere and elucidates them fully;[27] but it will never be studied except as symbol and symptom. What interested historians inspired by the positivist spirit were "collective representations," and individual views received their attention only if they were the reflection of the collective whole. Hence a change in method: this manifests itself by the lack of concern shown for that part of philosophy that is somewhat technical. What was of interest were the fundamental theorems of philosophers, the contents of their opinion, and not their absolute truth. Each system of opinions was related to a period and drew from this relation the only justification to which it could lay claim.

[27] Cf. *ibid.*, p. 34, on the necessity of fixation of beliefs in instruction: "L'anarchie moderne a pu seule susciter le rêve subversif d'une foi sans organe."

Before Auguste Comte, Hegel was similarly concerned to defend the systems by showing that their diversity is not opposed to the unity of mind.

The history of philosophy [he says], makes clear, in the different philosophies which appeared, that there is only a single philosophy in different stages of development, and also, that the particular principles on which a system rests are only divisions of one and the same whole. The newest philosophy to evolve is the result of all the preceding philosophies and must contain the principles of all of them.[28]

This is neither a sectarianism which excommunicates nor a skepticism which takes advantage of the differences of systems to dismiss them all. Sectarianism and skepticism imply that there are several philosophies; history declares there is only one. "In order to justify contempt for philosophy, they grant that there are different philosophies, of which each is a philosophy and not the philosophy —as if there were cherries that are not also fruit." The history of philosophy is the development of a "single living mind" taking possession of itself; it merely sets forth in time what philosophy itself, "liberated from external historical circumstances, sets forth in a pure state in the element of thought."

Unity of the human mind and continuity in its development; these are the *a priori* certainties which, evident to the historian even before he has begun his research, put in his hands the thread which will enable him to find his way. What this thesis implies is the existence of a kind of historical *a priori,* an a priori which consists in the nature of mind and which cannot itself be known by historical methods. This history of philosophy is the history of the manifestations of Mind; as such, it is freed from contingencies and accidents. The historian is certain to find a dialectical connection between succeeding systems.[29]

With Hegel and Comte we are at the opposite extreme of the

---

[28] Georg W. F. Hegel, "Introduction," *Encyclopedia of the Philosophical Sciences,* Sections 13 and 14.

[29] In the same way, Comte ultimately bases his law of three stages, not on historical induction, but on the nature of the human mind (*Politique positive,* Vol. III).

situation in which the Renaissance had left the history of philosophy. The past is no longer opposed to the present; the past conditions it and, justified by it, the past merely unfolds the unity of a systematic and preconceived plan. The whole evolution of the history of philosophy down to our time rests upon a discussion of this postulate.

In reality the knowledge of the law immanent in this development is not the result of historical observation and induction. The unity of philosophy, in Hegel, is not a verified fact but clearly a postulate. It is a postulate which can only be accepted with the philosophy of which it is a part. Is this the way history appears to an uncommitted view? "Any man of ordinary judgment placed in the presence of the spectacle that the history of philosophy presents will immediately form a singularly different idea of it than the sophism of the Hegelian philosophy would have him do." Renouvier, who expressed this opinion,[30] goes back in fact, beyond French eclecticism, Hegel and Diderot, to that tradition of sectarianism, against which the eighteenth and nineteenth centuries had rebelled, because it did not satisfy the passionate desire for the unity of the human mind. According to Renouvier, the division of philosophers into opposed sects is not a historical accident resulting from temporary prejudices which enlightenment will dispel but a normal phenomenon, characteristic of the constitution of the human mind.

For twenty-five centuries, in the West, the greatest oppositions between philosophers have persisted. No doubt, the controversy and the progress of positive knowledge have been able to eliminate certain questions and to suppress certain differences, but most of the differences, and the most serious ones, have only been postponed or have been transposed to another area.

The human mind is antinomic by nature; the dominant controversy is the one which exists between the doctrine of freedom and that of determinism. According to Renouvier, all others reduce to

---

[30] Charles Renouvier, "Esquisse d'une classification systématique des doctrines philosophiques," *La Critique religieuse*, July, 1882, p. 184.

this controversy and we can systematically classify all systems by bringing them under one or the other of these two doctrines. Now, we cannot look forward to one side ever convincing the other by compelling reasons. Thus the existence of sects is explained and justified. The error of eclecticism and Hegelianism is only to have seen in the sects sometimes an arbitrary product of the imagination or, on occasion, a necessary but entirely ephemeral moment in the development of thought.

From the point of view of Renouvier, then, the history of philosophy hardens into a timeless dialogue between two contradictory and forever reviving theses. From one age to another there are no philosophically important differences; the "variations in terminology, the diversity of relations under which each problem may be considered" and which enable us "to give a form and new expressions to opinions which are in reality old," is the one subject left to history as such. On the other hand, it has permanent categories, the very ones which permit "the systematic classification of doctrines." But these categories come from the necessities of thought and not from historical facts. The one initiative still allowed to the human mind is not the construction of systems, which are in essentials predetermined (just as in De Gérando or Cousin), but the free adoption of one of the two possible directions. Originality does not consist, as was believed, in the intellectual invention of a system, but in the attitude of the will with regard to pre-existing systems.

Renouvier's point of view already marks the abandonment of the doctrine of an alleged historical necessity. His own age and still more ours give us the spectacle of a kind of disintegration of the great historical syntheses. Our time has a clear aversion to the great constructions, be they Hegelian or positivist. The outward signs of this state of mind are that the outstanding works in the history of philosophy are no longer the general histories but works limited to one period like the *Philosophy of the Greeks* by Edouard Zeller, or to one nation or one problem, like the *System of the World from Plato to Copernicus* by Duhem, or philological collections like the *Pre-Socratic Fragments* and the *Greek Doxographers* by H. Diels, or monographs like Hamelin's *System of Aristotle* or *System of Descartes*. The general histories of philosophy themselves have a method that is more analytic than synthetic, and aim more to collect the results of work presented in monographs than to discover an immanent law of development. The *Analytic Philosophy of History* by Renouvier is of this kind, as are Weber's *History of Philosophy,* the *History of Philosophy by Problems* by Janet and Séailles, and still more clearly the great *History of Philosophy* by Ueberweg, which aims only to inform the reader of recent original work on each question.

The causes of this situation, which is new, are of two kinds. The first is the enormous amount of philological work, which, since about 1850—thanks to critical editions, the discovery of texts, the collecting of fragments—has, while enriching our information and making it more accurate, rendered difficult or even impossible those general views on which the historians of former times prided themselves. This is inevitable if we consider the conditions of the philological method: from its point of view, as a matter of fact, periods of history are distinguished less by certain events which marked their beginning and end than by the nature and state of the sources which reveal them. To take just one rough example, how different is the state of our sources pertaining to ancient philosophy with its rare original works, and the state of the sources of medieval or modern philosophy, whose abundance startles the imagination. The work of criticism and textual interpretation must follow different methods in the two cases and even involves rather different mental habits, so different that one can hardly aspire to possess both at once. But the same would have to be said of very much shorter periods; Stoicism and Epicureanism, for example, known through fragments of texts, cannot be studied in the same way as the system of Aristotle, whose teaching is preserved in its entirety.

On the other hand, the conclusions of the philologist, when it is a matter of interpreting a thought and staying close to its meaning, are often provisional and at the mercy of a new discovery or a new comparison. The interpretations of ancient systems like Platonism, or even of modern doctrines, like those of Descartes or Kant, are innumerable; how can one find a solid point of support here for a synthetic construction?

To the exigencies of the philological method is added a second reason which is perhaps even more decisive in turning us away from an ambition to describe the whole philosophical past. Comte and Hegel, and even Renouvier, concerned themselves with philosophy and not with philosophers. Whether they considered the ideas of the universe they studied as eternal outlines imposed by the very nature of reason or as kinds of collective representations, evolving and changing with society, they made philosophy something impersonal,[31] or, at least, they made the personal expression which a philosopher gives of the thoughts of his time only an accident. The essential point is somewhere else, in that rational or social *dictamen,* a sort of deity, to which individual consciences naturally submit, —be they those of a Plato or of a Descartes.

Now the history of philosophy has evolved like history in general. The minute care given to the study of sources would be inexplicable without the historian's desire to reach what is individual, irreducible, and personal in the past. His research would be quite useless, if the problem were to determine types or laws as formerly. What use is a new specimen of a type that is already known, if the specimen is worthless in itself and in what distinguishes it?

This taste for what is individual, which is perhaps still the dominant trait of our literary criticism, makes us see the past in an entirely new perspective. There are no longer either "sects" as in the Renaissance, or "systems" as in Cousin, or "collective mentalities" which the historian aims to reach. There are individuals, in all the varied richness of their intelligence. Plato, Descartes, or Pascal are neither expressions of their environment nor of historic moments, but real creators. What strikes us at first sight is the discontinuity of

[31] As far as Renouvier is concerned, the choice between two opposed doctrines is certainly personal and free, but the doctrines between which the choice is made are altogether determined.

their efforts. Windelband remarks that there is no continuous progress, "since each of the great systems gives the problem a new form and solves it as if the others had not existed." [32]

We must add that these two reasons, the requirements of the philological method and the search for what is individual, although both are opposed to historical synthesis, do not lead the mind in the same direction. The philologist has a tendency to search for the relationship of thoughts and formulas. This tendency is at times excessive, if it is not tempered by the taste for and the sense of living thoughts; it is exaggerated to the point of making a new doctrine a mosaic of past doctrines and of confusing the inventor with the compiler. By a reverse turn of mind the critic wants only to look for the colorfulness of doctrines, and he portrays the history of ideas as an impressionist, having greater interest in the variety of minds than in the deep unity which it may conceal.

To the purely doctrinal differences of the ancient and medieval ages, the modern age adds another, the difference of national minds which gives its particular nuance to each of the philosophies, English, German, or French. We must also bear in mind the immense complexity of modern culture, which is dissolving, as Auguste Comte anticipated and feared, into a series of special and technical cultures each one absorbing the life and resources of a man. The philosopher, limiting himself to one of the aspects of this culture, is today a logician or an epistemologist, a philosopher of mathematics or a philosopher of religion, without any clear correspondence and, even less, any unity between one point of view and another. He oscillates between a general culture which is superficial and a deep culture which is narrow.

Are there not many doctrinal diversities irreducible to reason: diversities due to personality differences, national character, mode and degree of culture? How is the historian to compare doctrines with such different origins?

So we see the best historians of our time hesitating over the

[32] Wilhelm Windelband, *Geschichte der Philosophie* (Freiburg: J. C. B. Mohr, 1892).

method to be followed. Victor Delbos,[33] for example, while not renouncing the idea of a rational connection between the successive
aspects of philosophical thought, sees his desire for unity weighed
against a fear that he will not be accurate and that he will lose the
very substance of history. And, in fact, his vigorous mind left an
admirable series of monographs whose very title[34] indicates the difficulty, perhaps an insurmountable one, which he was to find in
writing a general history of philosophy.

We find the same hesitation, but more concealed, in Windelband.[35] The development of philosophy, as he views it in his Preface,
results from three factors, and we could even speak of three histories
in juxtaposition. First, pragmatic history: the internal evolution of
philosophy based on the disagreement between former solutions and
new ideas of reality. Second, history in its relation to the history of
culture: philosophy receives its problems from the ideas which
dominate the civilization of an epoch. Third and finally, the history
of persons. In the first aspect, history has a kind of law of development; but what exactly is the importance of this aspect in relation
to the two others which make the course of the intellectual life depend on many accidents? This is not clearly indicated by the author.

Is this the definitive state of the history of philosophy? Must it
abandon all hope of being itself philosophical, to become just a
chapter of philology and of literary criticism? Is it doomed to oscil-
late perpetually between the mosaic and the impressionistic method,
incapable of doing anything more than temper one method by the
other?

Whatever the appearances, something surely remains of the ideas
of Comte and Hegel. They have taught us to see in the systems of
philosophy of the past more than closed sects or individual fancies,
particular aspects of the human mind. They learned to take the
intellectual past in all seriousness, and they understood better than

[33] Victor Delbos, "La méthode en histoire de la philosophie," *Revue de métaphysique et de morale*, 1917, pp. 279–89.

[34] Victor Delbos, *Figures et doctrines de philosophes* (Paris, 1919), and *La Philosophie française* (Paris, 1921).

[35] Windelband, *op. cit.*, p. 9.

many others the intellectual solidarity of succeeding generations. However, we cannot claim to remedy the crisis which affects the history of philosophy by returning to one of those general formulas of development dear to the positivists and Hegelians. All that we have attempted recently in this direction has been either unsuccessful or at the very least premature.[36] Like the first two problems we raised, this third problem cannot be solved except in an approximate and provisional manner, with all the uncertainties that history entails.

It should be noted that, in the first place, that if philological erudition has overthrown the Comtist or Hegelian constructions, as we remarked earlier, it puts us on the track of a positive solution. As we advance in intimate and detailed knowledge of the past, we see more clearly new doctrines finding a place to insert themselves in earlier doctrines, and we establish continuities and transitions where at first we saw only radical originality and absolute opposition. General formulas such as those of Comte or Hegel, for whom development must proceed by an obvious and clear opposition, render a very poor account of the varied reality which history shows us. In return, this continuity of minds which historical criticism reveals cannot be expressed by a general law and must constitute the object of a thousand detailed studies. The idea of studying the systems of the world from Plato to Copernicus in their continuity and genesis could not have occurred to historians imbued with the idea of a radical opposition between antiquity and the Middle Ages. And it took the marvelous erudition of Duhem to recover the continuity of two or three themes of thought through this period. The revival of such justifiable interest which the history of the philosophy of the Middle Ages has met with is not based only on motives irrelevant to the interest of history but also on genuine discoveries which show its unity with modern philosophy. The abandonment of

[36] Among these attempts, one of the most interesting in our opinion is Paul Masson-Oursel's *Philosophie comparée* (Paris: F. Alcan, 1923), which tries to infer a law of development by comparing the general course of philosophical thought in Europe and the Far East. See also the ingenious interpretation of history by J. de Gaultier in *Mercure de France,* January 1, 1923, p. 11.

the a priori method, far from being prejudicial to the idea of the unity of philosophy and intelligence, has therefore enabled us to give it a more complete and concrete meaning, although more difficult to translate into formulas; for it is not the unity of a gradually realized plan but a series of original efforts and of many inventions.

In the second place, the abandonment of the idea of inevitable progress, which dominated the history of philosophy until about 1850, has been equally favorable to an accurate appreciation of philosophical development. The idea of a ceaseless and continuous progress is quite contrary to historical reality. Bacon had observed more accurately than his disciples of the eighteenth century when he perceived, along with periods of progress, periods of retrogression and oblivion, followed by revivals. The truth is that the course of intellectual life is, so to speak, extremely tortuous, and only detailed studies can give an idea of its windings. Nevertheless they can give an idea of it, and here the work of philological criticism is no longer destructive. It merely points out several possible schemes of development, where historical a priorism saw only one. Sometimes there is progress of thought toward a greater disagreement, toward dissipation into a spray of sects which are opposed to one another, as in Greece in the period following the death of Socrates. Sometimes, on the contrary, there is a progress toward unity of thought, toward almost complete agreement, as in the second half of the eighteenth century when English empiricism dominated. Sometimes philosophical thought becomes shifting, suggestive, transforming itself into a method of spiritual life, into a tendency of mind, as in Socrates or Plato. Sometimes it takes the form of a positive doctrine which has a ready answer to all questions and attempts to impose it by an irrefutable dialectic, as in the time of the scholastics. There are times when the intellectual life, almost exhausted, surrenders all claims to affirm its own worth and yields to doctrines which attempt to reach reality through intuition, feeling, or revelation. For example the intellectualism of the eighteenth century, with its reliance on reason, is followed closely by the romantic orgy, a very instructive alternation and one which, perhaps, is a general law of the history of philosophy.[37] We see by these examples how criticism by itself, without being the least a priori, will enable us to classify systems and to order them.

History will even allow us to judge them up to a point. In reality the value of a system is not independent of the spiritual impulse which it has created. Philosophical doctrines are not things but thoughts, subjects of meditation which offer themselves to the future and whose fecundity is never exhausted except in appearance, tendencies of mind which may always be recovered. The ideas from which they are formed are not inert materials of a mental edifice which could be demolished and whose materials could be used again just as they are in other constructions. They are germs which will develop; they claim to be a "good capable of being communicated." [38] Now, historical research must enable us to understand the original impulse and the way in which it develops, ends, and sometimes begins again. History is not finished; this is what the historian of thought must never forget. Plato or Aristotle, Descartes or Spinoza, have not ceased to be alive. One of the greatest services history can render is doubtless to show how a doctrine is transformed, in quite different ways according to cases. It happens sometimes that in becoming permanent a doctrine hardens into dogma which becomes generally accepted. Thus, after three centuries of existence, Stoicism, in Epictetus, became a law which no longer needed to be demonstrated. It also happens that a philosophical theme, seeking to establish itself as a doctrine and to become a dogma, ends by exhausting itself in a sort of complexity and mannerism, calling to mind the brilliant decadence of artistic schools whose formulas are spent. For example, Ionian philosophy in the time of Plato was reduced to the stammerings of the last Heracliteans, who, for fear of fixing the moving stream of things, no

---

[37] Louis Cazamian, *L'Évolution psychologique de la littérature en Angleterre* (Paris: F. Alcan, 1920), p. 4 ff. Cf. also some remarks on regular variations of style in philosophy, in my book *La Philosophie et son passé* (Paris: F. Alcan, 1940), p. 8. On this notion of style, see the remarkable book by Karl Joël, *Wandlungen der Weltanschauung* (Tübingen: J. C. B. Mohr, 1928).

[38] Baruch Spinoza, *De emendatione intellectus.*

longer wished to make use of language. Or again, the description of intelligible things, in the last Neo-Platonists like Proclus and Damascius, ends in such minute precision that one is forced to feel all the artifice of a professional technician and to see in it a lack of sincerity. We can say the same of the final forms of the systems of Fichte or Schelling. So we see emerging as historical, moving, modifiable categories, some general themes of thought which should replace the massive categories which the eclectic or Hegelian historians used in the past.

These very brief indications exclude the possibility of ending this introduction with the formulation of anything like a law of development of philosophical thought; it is not a matter of constructing, but only of describing. What may no longer be done is to write history as a prophet after the event, as if desiring to give the impression that philosophical thought arose gradually and was realized progressively. We can no longer accept, like Aristotle, the father of the history of philosophy, the idea that history is oriented toward a doctrine which it contains potentially. The history of philosophy teaches us that philosophical thought is not one of those stable realities which, once discovered, continues to exist like a technical invention. Philosophical thought is constantly in question, constantly in danger of being lost in formulas which, by fixing it, betray it. The spiritual life exists only in the undertaking, and not in the possession of a supposed acquired truth.[39]

The present work strives to give as clear and as living an outline as possible of this undertaking. It has been inspired by the desire to serve as a guide in the immense past of philosophy, which detailed historical research reveals each day to be more complex and

[39] On questions of method in the history of philosophy, I refer to my work, *La philosophie et son passé*, pp. 1–78. Cf. also George Boas, "L'Histoire de la philosophie," in *L'Activité philosophique contemporaine en France et aux Etats-Unis,* ed. Marvin Farber (Paris: Presses universitaires de France, 1950), I, 30–49, and my article "L'Esprit de l'histoire de la philosophie en France," in *ibid.,* II, 64–75. See also the Preface by Ortega Y. Gasset (in Spanish) to the Spanish translation of my *History of Philosophy* (Buenos Aires, 1944); Rodolfo Mondolfo, *Problemas y métodos de la investigación en historia de la filosofía* (Tucumán: Universidad Nacional de Tucumán, 1949); V. de Magalhães-Vilhena, *Panorama de pensamento filosofico,* I (Lisbon, 1959).

subtle. Hence it has been judged indispensable to give the reader the means of judging the fidelity of this outline and of making it more specific. This is why each chapter is accompanied by references to the most important texts and followed by a bibliographical summary, indicating, with editions, the books and articles which have seemed essential.

GENERAL BIBLIOGRAPHY

General Works

UEBERWEG. *Grundriss der Geschichte der Philosophie.* 4 vols. Vol. I, *Das Altertum,* by Praechter. 12th edition, 1926. Vol. II, *Die patrische und scholastische Zeit,* by Baumgartner. 11th edition, 1928. Vol. III, *Die Neuzeit bis zum Ende des achtzehnten Jahrhunderts,* by Frischeisen-Koehler and Moog. 12th edition, 1924. Vol. IV, *Die deutsche Philosophie im 19. Jahrhundert und die Gegenwart.* 12th edition, 1924. Vol. V, *Die Philosophie des Auslandes im 19. Jahrhundert und die Gegenwart.* 12th edition, 1928.

WEBER. *Histoire de la philosophie occidentale.* New edition, Paris, 1925. Vol. II, corrected by D. Huisman, 1957.

RENOUVIER. *Philosophie analytique de l'histoire.* 4 vols. 1896–97.

DELBOS. *Figures et doctrines de philosophes.* 1918.

BBUNSCHVIGG. *Les étapes de la philosophie mathématique.* 1912.—*L'Expérience humaine et la causalité physique.* 1922.—*Le progrès de la conscience dans la philosophie occidentale.* 1927.

FREDERICK COPLESTON. A History of Philosophy. 7 vols. 1946–63.

FRANCK. *Dictionnaire des sciences philosophiques.* 1885.

F. ENRIQUEZ and G. DE SANTILLANA. *Storia del Pensiero scientifico.* Vol. I, *Il mondo antico.* Milan, 1932.

P. DUHEM. *Le système du monde de Platon à Copernic.* 10 vols. Paris, 1915–59.

R. TATON. *Histoire générale des sciences.* 3 vols. Paris, 1957 and following.

M. DAUMAS. *Histoire de la science* (Encyclopédie de la Pléiade). Paris, 1957.

W. and M. KNEALE. *The Development of Logic.* Oxford, 1962.

JOURNALS.—*Revue philosophique* (from 1876), *de métaphysique et de morale* (from 1893), *des sciences philosophiques et théologiques* (from 1911), *de philosophie* (from 1900); *Archiv für die Geschichte der Philosophie* (from 1886); *Archives de philosophie* (from 1923); *Mind* (from 1876); *Revue d'Histoire de la philosophie* (1927–29).

Ancient

RITTER and PRELLER. *Historia philosophiae graecae.* 9th edition by Wellmann, 1913.

ZELLER. *Die Philosophie der Griechen.* Part I, *Die vorsokratische Philosophie.* 6th edition, by Lortzing and Nestle, 1919–20 (4th edition translation by Boutroux, 2 vols., 1877–82). Part II, Section 1, *Sokrates-Plato.* 5th edition, 1922 (1st part translated by Belot, 1884). Section 2, *Aristoteles.* 4th edition, 1921. Part III, *Die nacharistotelische Philosophie.* Section 1, 4th edition, 1909, and Section 2, 5th edition, 1923.

W. K. C. GUTHRIE. *A History of Greek Philosophy.* Vol. I. Cambridge, 1962.

GOMPERZ. *Les penseurs de la Grèce.* Translated from the German by Reymond. 3 vols. 1908–9 (down to the first Peripatetics).

BURNET. *Greek Philosophy.* Part I, *Thales to Plato.* 1914.

ROBIN. *La pensée grecque et les origines de l'esprit scientifique.* 1923. 4th edition, 1948.

A. and M. CROISET. *Histoire de la littérature grecque.*

ARNOLD REYMOND. *Histoire des sciences exactes et naturelles dans l'antiquité gréco-romaine.* Paris, 1955.

C. J. DE VOGEL. *Greek Philosophy: A Collection of Texts.* 3 vols. Leiden, 1950–59.

P. ROSSI. *Antologia della critiqua filosofica,* I, *L'eta antica.* Bari, 1961.

E. BRÉHIER. *Études de philosophie antique.* Paris, 1955.

H. -J. MARROU. *Histoire de l'Éducation dans l'Antiquité.* Paris, 1948.

R. MONDOLFO. *Il pensiero antico, Storia della filosofia greco-romana esposta con testi scelti dalle fonti.* Florence, 1950.

Middle Ages

BAEUMKER and HERTLING. *Beitrage zur Geschichte der Philosophie des Mittelalters.* From 1891.

HAURÉAU. *Histoire de la philosophie scolastique.* 3 vols. 1872–80.

DE WULF. *Histoire de la philosophie médiévale.* 4th edition, 1912. 5th edition, Vol. I, 1924.

GILSON. *La philosophie au moyen âge.* 2 vols. 1922.

E. BRÉHIER. *La philosophie du moyen âge.* 1937.

P. VIGNAUX. *La pensée au moyen âge.* 1938.

A. C. CROMBIE. *Histoire des sciences de saint Augustin à Galilée* (400–1650). Paris, 1959.

A. FOREST, F. VAN STEENBERGHEN, and M. DE GANDILLAC. *Le mouvement doctrinal du XIe au XIVe s.* Paris, 1951. Vol. XIII of *L'Histoire de l'Église,* by A. Fliche, V. Martin, and E. Jarry.

Modern

HOEFFDING. *Histoire de la philosophie moderne.* Translated by Bordier. 2 vols. 1906. *Les Philosophes contemporains.* Translated by Tremesaygues. 1908.

KUNO FISCHER. *Geschichte der neueren Philosophie.* 10 vols. 3d to 5th editions, 1904–21.

DELBOS. *La philosophie française.* 1919.

SORLEY. *A History of English Philosophy.* 1920.

ZELLER. *Geschichte der deutschen Philosophie.* 2d edition, 1873.

E. BRÉHIER. *Histoire de la philosophie allemande.* 1921. 3d edition completed by P. Ricoeur, 1954.

E. LEROUX and A. LEROY. *La philosophie anglaise classique.* Paris, 1951.

THE PRE-SOCRATICS

IN THE first period, the Hellenic, which closed with the death of Alexander (323), philosophy developed successively in different centers of the Greek world. This succession corresponded to changing political fortunes. Philosophy began in the sixth century in Ionia, in the very rich and commercial maritime cities. After 546, Ionia was subjugated by the Persians and the great city of Miletus was destroyed in 494. The center of intellectual life shifted and philosophy was carried to southern Italy and Sicily. Finally, after the Median wars in the time of Pericles (d. 429), Athens became the intellectual capital of Greece and of the new maritime empire which was to last until the Peloponnesian War. In this development the Ionians played the principal role: the first philosophers of Magna Graecia were Ionian emigrants; the first to propagate philosophy in Athens were likewise Ionians. However, in each of these centers philosophic thought took on a different character.

1 *Milesian Physics*

It is hard to pin down the precise meaning and the wider significance of the movement of ideas that took place at Miletus in the sixth century B.C. Of the three Milesian philosophers following one after the other in the most powerful and prosperous city in Greek Asia Minor, the first,[1] Thales (640–562), wrote nothing; he is

[1] Aristotle *Metaphysics* A. 3. 983b 20.

36

known through a tradition which does not go back further than Aristotle. The two others, Anaximander (born about 610 and still living in 546) and Anaximenes (end of the sixth century), who each wrote a prose work later given the title *On Nature,* are scarcely known to us except through what Aristotle and the writers of his school said about them.

Now, what Aristotle looked for above all in their teaching was an answer to this question: What is the matter of which things are composed? It was Aristotle who put the question and he put it in the language of his own doctrine. We have no proof that the Milesians themselves were concerned with the problem for which a solution was sought in their writings. So when we are told that, according to Thales, the principle of all things is water; or that, according to Anaximander, it is the infinite, and according to Anaximenes, air, we must beware of seeing in these formulas an answer to the problem of matter.[2]

In order to get at the meaning of these formulas we must, if possible, look to see what problems they actually discussed. These were, it seems, of two kinds. First, they were problems of scientific technique; thus, Anaximander was reputed to have invented the gnomon and to have drawn the lines of the solstices and of the equinox. He probably also drew the first geographic map and discovered the obliquity of the zodiac. But they were primarily problems of a second kind; problems about the nature and cause of meteors or astronomical phenomena, earthquakes, winds, rains, lightning, and eclipses, and also general geographical questions about the shape of the earth and the origins of terrestrial life.

As far as these scientific techniques are concerned, our Milesians doubtless only made known to the Greeks what had been handed on to them by the Mesopotamian and Egyptian civilizations. The Babylonians had been observers of the heavens, and for their land surveys they drew up plans of cities and canals and even tried to construct the map of the world.[3] As for the mechanical arts, they

[2] *Ibid.* A. 3. 983b 6–11; 984a 2–7.
[3] Delaporte, *La Mésopotamie* (1923), pp. 260–61, concerning mathematical knowledge; cf., among others, Thureau-Dangin, *Revue d'Assyriologie* (1940).

show a very rich and diversified development in all Hellenic countries between the seventh and the fifth centuries,[4] which the Ionian philosophers doubtless witnessed rather than originated. They were very sympathetic witnesses, seeing the superiority of man in his technical activity, and their outlook found its most striking expression in an Ionian of the fifth century, Anaxagoras. According to him, man is the most intelligent of the animals because he has hands, the hand being the tool par excellence and the model for all tools.[5]

The originality of the Milesians appears to have consisted in the choice of the images by which they represented the heavens and meteors. These images retain nothing of the fantastic nature of myth; they are borrowed either from the arts or from direct observation. All the analogies which make up their science show, along with a great imaginative precision which unlike myth admits no mysterious background, a great desire to understand inaccessible phenomena by relating them to the most familiar facts.

One of these familiar facts observed by the Milesians, preoccupied as they were with navigation, was that of thunderstorms and tempests. They saw, in calm weather, thick black clouds forming, suddenly rent by a flash of lightning, a harbinger of the windstorm which was to follow. Anaximander, seeking an explanation, taught that the wind, inclosed in the cloud, tore it asunder by its violence and that lightning and thunder accompanied this sudden bursting.[6] Now, it was by analogy with the thunderstorm that he conceived the nature and formation of the stars: to arrive at Anaximander's conception of the heavens, one need only replace the cover of thick clouds by an opaque cover (sheath) of condensed air ("air" just meaning vapors for him), the internal wind by fire, the rents in the cover by some sort of air holes (vents) or bellow tubes, through which fire erupts. If we suppose that these covers are circular in form and arranged around the earth like the rims of cart wheels around their hubs, the stars will be nothing but that part of the

[4] Espinas, *Les origines de la technologie* (1897), pp. 75 ff.
[5] Aristotle *On the Parts of Animals* iv. 10. 687a 7.
[6] Aetius *Placita* iii. 6. 1.

inner fire which issues through these vents (air holes). Eclipses and the phases of the moon will be explained as temporary closings of these vents. Anaximander conceived three of these circular covers, impelled in a rotatory motion. Farthest from the earth were those of the sun and of the moon, which have only one opening; nearest was that of the fixed stars (doubtless the Milky Way) which has a great number of openings.[7]

Comparisons of this sort make it possible to state the cosmogonic problem in a new way. The formation of the heavens is not fundamentally different from that of a thunderstorm. The question is to know how fire, which originally encircled the earth as the bark does a tree, is broken up and distributed in the interior of the three circular rings. Now, the cause seemed to Anaximander to be the same as the one at work in rains, thunderstorms, and winds, where the vapors, generated from the sea by evaporation, burst the sphere of fire and envelop it in rings.[8]

The fundamental phenomenon in Milesian physics is in fact the evaporation of sea water due to the effect of heat. The products of this evaporation (vapors, winds, clouds, etc.) were traditionally thought of by the Greeks as having vital properties.[9] So Anaximander was only following a very old view when he asserted that life originates in warm moisture evaporated by the sun. He also insisted on the priority of the forms of marine life, of fishes, of creatures inclosed in a spiny shell, which had had to modify their kind of life when, their shells bursting, they were cast up on land.[10]

These views of Anaximander may enable us to state precisely the meaning of the assertions about primitive substance which Aristotle considered the heart of Milesian teaching. These assertions seem to bear, not on the material composition of beings, but on the thing from which the world arose. Thales, in teaching that it was water, only repeated an extremely widespread cosmogonic theme. But

[7] *Ibid.* ii. 13. 7; 15. 6; 20. 1; Hippolytus *Refutations of All Heresies* i. 6. 4–6.

[8] Aetius iii. 6: i (origin of wind), compared to Aristotle *Meteorologica* ii. 1. 353b 5. Cf. Burnet, *Early Greek Philosophy* (trans. Reymond [1919], p. 67).

[9] Plutarch *Weakness of Oracles* 18; Aristotle *On the Soul* A. 5. 410b 27.

[10] Aetius v. 19. 1.

judging from the development of Milesian thought, we surely have to understand by water something like the ocean span, with all the life that emerges from it. Thales taught, moreover, that the earth is like a flat disk borne upon the primeval water like a vessel upon the sea. What led Anaximander to replace the water of Thales by what he called the Infinite? There is little agreement on the meaning of this expression. Is it a Milesian form of the Hesiodic myth of Chaos, before the gods, the earth, and the heavens—just as the thesis of Thales referred to an old cosmogony? The Infinite would then be the qualitatively indeterminate thing from which determinate things like fire, water, etc., arise, or at the very least the mixture where all the things are merged which later separate out to form the world. It appears that the Infinite of Anaximander is rather the unlimited in size, that which is without bounds, in contrast to the world, which is contained within the bounds of the heavens, since the Infinite contains worlds.[11]

This interpretation agrees with the thesis of the plurality of worlds, one of the theses of Anaximander which was taken up again by Anaximenes. He asserted, in fact, the simultaneous existence of several worlds which arise and perish in the bosom of the eternal and ageless Infinite. From this Infinite, worlds are born, he tells us, by an "eternal motion," that is to say by an unceasingly repeated generating motion, having as its effect the separation of opposites, such as the hot and the cold; these opposites acting on one another produce, as we have seen, all cosmic phenomena.[12]

Anaximenes, in taking air as the principle ("principle" meaning "first beginning") was not disagreeing with Anaximander. The word *air* serves only to specify the nature of the Infinite; his principle is an infinite air (without limit), out of which all things arise; like the Infinite of Anaximander, it is animated by an eternal motion. It seems that Anaximenes did not believe this motion would solve the problem of the origin of things; a shaking motion, like the motion

[11] Theophrastus, as cited by Simplicius (Diels, *Doxographi Graeci* [1879], pp. 376, ll. 3–6). See also Burnet, *Early Greek Philosophy*, pp. 61–66.

[12] Hippolytus i. 6. 1–2, compared to Aristotle *Physics* iii. 4. 203b 25 (as cited by Burnet, *op. cit.* p. 66, n. 1).

one gives to a sieve, may well separate mixed things, but it will not produce them. In addition to this eternal motion, therefore, Anaximenes gave another explanation of the origin of things. Air through its rarefaction gives rise to fire, and, through its successive condensations, to winds, clouds, water, and finally to earth and stones. In the last kind of transmutation, he was doubtless thinking of very concrete and easily observed phenomena—winds rising in the still and invisible air, then the formation of clouds which become rain, giving rise in turn to rivers which deposit alluvia. The inverse process, that of rarefaction, is the one giving rise to fire; that is to say, doubtlessly, the one giving rise to all igneous meteors and to the stars.[13]

Milesian physics, then, is a physics of geographers and meteorologists, but their general picture of the universe in no way heralds the progress of astronomy the following century was to see. For Thales and Anaximenes the earth is a flat disk, which Thales has floating on water and Anaximenes on air. For Anaximander the earth is a cylindrical column, whose diameter at the base is equal to a third of its height, and whose upper part, which we inhabit, bulges out slightly. It is held in equilibrium because it is equidistant from the boundaries of the universe. Anaximenes returned, even, to a quite ancient mythical picture, if it is true that he believed the sun after its setting does not pass under the earth but skirts the horizon, where it is hidden from view by high mountains, to rise again in the east. In Anaximenes' determination of the distances of the celestial rings from the earth, one can just barely sense a foreshadowing of what mathematical astronomy will be like.[14]

Moreover, onto this physics, where everything is pictured in concrete and familiar terms, a mode of explanation of a quite different kind is superimposed. The rise and destruction of worlds are regulated according to a certain order of justice: "It is into the things from which beings take their rise that they dissolve according to

[13] Hippolytus i. 4. 1–3.
[14] Thales, according to Aristotle *Metaphysics* A. 3. 983b 21; Anaximenes, in Hippolytus i. 7. 4, and 6; Anaximander, in *ibid*. i. 6. 3, and in Plutarch *Stromata* (Diels, p. 579, l. 11).

necessity; they pay to each other the chastisement and punishment of their injustice, according to the order of time." Here emerges the idea of a natural order of succession which is also an order of justice: a social image of a world order that was very widespread in oriental civilizations and will play a role of first importance in Greek philosophy. This notion of justice is unquestionably connected with the divine character the Milesians give both to the world and to the primordial substance which Anaximenes calls immortal and imperishable.[15]

II *Mythical Cosmogonies*

This Ionian sagacity, these clear-cut images, were opposed by efforts undoubtedly made about this time to revive interest in the ancient mythical cosmogonies. Onomacritus, who lived in Athens around the time of Pisistratus (d. 547) is thought (though probably incorrectly) to have collected these ancient legends. It is doubtless the remains of his compilation or of similar compilations which we find in our oldest sources; these sources do not go back further than Plato, Aristotle, and Aristotle's disciple, Eudemos. Each of these cosmogonies, as in Hesiod, presents a series of mythical figures issuing from one another; but their fantastic character goes beyond Hesiod. Here we encounter real decadence; it is no longer a matter of introducing an order but of impressing the imagination. In Plato we see Heaven and Earth uniting to engender Oceanus and Thetis, who gave birth to Cronus and Rhea, who in turn brought forth Zeus, Hera, and their brothers.[16] In Aristotle, the theologians are said to take darkness as a principle.[17] Through Eudemos, Aristotle's disciple, we have a prize collection of analogous cosmogonies which, for that matter, may be relatively late imitations:[18] less cautious than his masters, Eudemos shows better how coarse the imaginations of

---

[15] Theophrastus, in Simplicius (Diels, p. 476, ll. 8–11). Cf. Cornford, *From Religion to Philosophy*, pp. 174, 176.

[16] *Timaeus* 40e.

[17] *Metaphysics* 1071b 25.

[18] In Damascius *The Principles*, Chapter 312.

these theologians were. According to Hellanicos, for example, the first couple, Water and Earth, engendered Cronus or Heracles, a tricephalic winged dragon with a god's head between the heads of a bull and a lion; he united with Ananke or Adrastus to engender in Ether, Erebus, and Chaos an egg from which the world was to come. Among these lucubrations, the one Eudemos attributed especially to the religious association of the Orphics (the Orphic Rhapsodies), showing Cronus, the supreme being, engendering Ether and Chaos who produce the world-egg and the winged god Phanes, has nothing to distinguish it from the others.

But, taken as a whole, the theogonies in Eudemos do exhibit one remarkable feature—the place they give to mythical figures such as Cronus, Time, or Adrastus; in other words, to those half-abstract figures which stand for a law or a principle: it is these we have seen appear in the Ionian cosmogonies under the name of Justice. On the other hand, it seems that these cosmogonies gradually established themselves among Orphic religious groups and merged with their body of beliefs about the origin and destiny of souls. Plato gives us the earliest and the only reliable detailed account of these beliefs. The soul, imprisoned in the body as in a tomb, will take its place after death at a banquet where it will revel eternally.[19] Perhaps the golden tablets discovered in second-century tombs at Thurii and Petelia in Magna Graecia and at Eleutherne in Crete, on which are engraved advice about the itinerary the soul ought to follow after death and the formulas it ought to pronounce, as in an Egyptian book of the dead, did not belong to the Orphic sect. In any case, the old story of uncertain age about the divine origin of man that Plato alludes to is connected with the Orphic myth cycle and the Dionysian cycle.[20] The Titans, enemies of Zeus, are driven by Hera to put to death Zeus's son Dionysus. Dionysus is torn apart by them, and they eat his bleeding limbs, except the heart, which is swallowed by Zeus and from which a new Dionysus will be reborn. Zeus then strikes the Titans dead with lightning and from

---

[19] *Republic* 363c; *Phaedo* 62b, 69c.
[20] Cf. Rohde, *Psyche*, II, 116.

their ashes the human race is born, in which good, which comes from Zeus, is mixed with evil, the Titanic element. The poet Pindar (fl. 478) gives evidence of the wide currency which analogous beliefs enjoyed at a quite early time. In everyone, "the body yields to all-powerful death, but while still living, it remains an image of our being; for it alone comes from the gods." [21] We will encounter these beliefs later in the philosophers; but this will be far from Ionia.

III *The Pythagoreans*

Starting in 494 (the date of the destruction of Miletus), the Milesian school and along with it all traces of Ionian physics disappeared for a time. Although intellectual life had already been carried to the flourishing colonies of Magna Graecia and Sicily, some of the men who made themselves known there came from Ionia. Pythagoras was born in Samos and Zenophanes in Colophon. And these two men gave rise in the Italian colonies to two important movements of ideas—the philosophy of number and Eleaticism—which between them were to dominate the whole subsequent development of ideas.

Pythagoreanism was not only an intellectual movement but a religious, moral, and political movement resulting in the formation of a brotherhood that sought to carry on propaganda and secure influence in the cities of Magna Graecia. It is difficult to get an accurate idea of this very complex movement. The life of Pythagoras itself is known only through legends that took shape as early as the first generations of the brotherhood.[22] Moreover, the history of Pythagoreanism consists in two very distinct periods, the first lasting from the foundation of the school at Croton (about 530) until about the time of Plato's death (348–347), and the second, Neo-Pythagoreanism, beginning about the first century of our era. Now, even granting we can distinguish the doctrines of the first period from those of the second (which is difficult to do since we often have to

[21] *Threnes,* Frag. 2 (Puech ed., IV, 196).
[22] Isidore Lévy, *Recherches sur les sources de la légende de Pythagore* (1926).

use texts dating from the new Pythagoreanism in order to know the old), the doctrines collectively labeled as earlier Pythagorean contain so many flagrant contradictions that it is quite impossible to attribute them to Pythagoras alone. We must be satisfied to classify them without being able to determine either their relationships or their authors.

Pythagoras, born in 570, founded a religious society at Croton around 530. There was nothing unusual about it. Societies of this kind, the Orphics for instance, existed in Greece. The mission these societies devoted themselves to was that of teaching methods of purification which were revealed only to the initiated. The Pythagorean society was like this; it had secrets that were not to be revealed to the impure.[23] Quite ancient traditions attribute to the teaching of Pythagoras promises of a blessed life after death for the initiated. The society, open to women and to foreigners, went beyond the bounds of a civic religion. The famous prohibitions contained in the Pythagorean catechism (do not eat beans, do not speak obscurely, do not wear a ring with the effigy of a god, do not sacrifice a white rooster, etc.)[24] were taboos of the most common sort.[25] It is not necessary to see any moral symbolism in them, as was commonly done later, but only marks intended to serve as a way of distinguishing the members of the sect from other men.

The doctrine of the transmigration of souls through the bodies of men and animals, a doctrine which a very ancient source[26] attributes to Pythagoras, can no longer pass as the result of philosophical reflection. It is a belief frequently held by primitive peoples who see in birth only a reincarnation[27] and is connected with the tales, so frequent in folklore, in which the soul comes out of the body and goes to live in an animal or an inanimate object;[28] by no means can

---

[23] Cf. Iamblichus *Life of Pythagoras* 75–78 (letter of Lysis to Hipparchus on the Pythagorean secret).

[24] *Ibid.* 83–84: Cf. Larguier De Bancels, "Sur les origines de la notion de l'âme, à propos d'une interdiction de Pythagore," *Archives de psychologie*, Vol. XVII (1918).

[25] Frazer, *The Golden Bough*.

[26] Xenophanes Frag. 7.

[27] Lévy-Bruhl, *Fonctions mentales dans les sociétés inférieures*, p. 398.

[28] Frazer, *The Golden Bough*, Vol. I.

it be linked to a particular historical origin. Finally, the precept of abstinence from meat, if it really formed a part of the primitive catechism of the school, doubtless came from the same faith in the unity of all living creatures which gave rise to the doctrine of transmigration.

What, then, is there to distinguish the Pythagorean from the Orphic sects, so incapable of progress and so fixed in their ritual and their fantastic myths? Herodotus relates that the Thracian Zamolxis, having been the slave of Pythagoras at Samos, learned from him "the Ionian way of life." [29] It seems clear also that Pythagoras brought Milesian cosmology into Magna Graecia; like Anaximenes, he taught that the world was immersed in the depths of an infinite atmosphere; by a sort of respiration it absorbed the nearest parts of this atmosphere; these parts, entering into it, separated and isolated things from each other; the infinite atmosphere, also called obscurity, night, or vapor, thus produced multiplicity and number in things.[30] Like the Milesians, Petrus, a Pythagorean of the oldest period, is credited with having accepted the plurality of worlds,[31] a limited plurality, it is true, and with worlds arranged in a geometrical order. But between Pythagoras' Milesian physics and the practical rules of the order it is impossible to discern the slightest relationship.

Nor is there any obvious connection between this cosmology and the famous doctrine traditionally attributed to Pythagoras that all things are numbers. This doctrine comes to us in three different aspects, with no apparent connection between them. In the first place it refers to a certain relation between numbers and geometrical forms. Pythagoras represented number not by the usual letter symbolism but something like the way they are represented on our dominoes, each number being a group comprising as many dots as it has units, and these dots being arranged according to a geometrical order; hence the notion of triangular numbers, that is

---

[29] Frazer, *The Golden Bough,* IV, 95.
[30] Aristotle *Metaphysics* M. 3. 1091a 17.
[31] Phanias of Eresus, in Plutarch *Weakness of Oracles* xxii, xxiii.

to say, numbers represented by dots laid out in a triangle, like 3, 6, 10, etc., squares, represented by dots laid out in a square, like 4, 9, etc., and oblongs represented by dots laid out in a rectangle, like 6, 12 etc.[32]

A second aspect of the doctrine has to do with number and musical harmonies. The three musical chords, the Fourth, the Fifth, and the Octave, are represented by simple numerical relations; namely 2/1, 3/2, 4/3. Moreover, one can define a certain proportion, the so-called harmonic proportion, which contains all three of them; to wit: the proportion 12:8:6, in which the mean is less than one extreme by a third of this extreme, and greater than the other extreme, again by a third of that extreme: $8 = 12 - 12/3 = 6 + 6/3$.

Finally, the third aspect is a primitive symbolism in which numbers represent the essences of things: 7 is opportunity, 4 justice, and 3 marriage, according to the most arbitrary analogies. If we leave aside this last aspect which gave rise to the fantastic arithmology men were to play with for centuries, we can see how Pythagoras was led to bring to light and study certain numerical series and also certain privileged numerical relations. If he first studied them less for themselves than for the things they represented (attributing for example a singular value to the triangular number 10, the famous tetractys, the sum of the first four numbers, by which the members of the sect swore), he was nonetheless led to recognize all sorts of new arithmetical properties.[33] On the other hand, the discovery of the so-called Pythagorean theorem led him to see that between certain lines, in this case the side of a square and its diagonal, there is a relation which cannot be numerically expressed. Pythagorean science thus found its limits as soon as it began.

Religious organization, Ionian cosmology, physical mathematics—these three aspects should be completed by adding a fourth, the political activity of the order. We are completely ignorant of the conditions under which the order seized power at Crotona and what

---

[32] Cf. Burnet, *Early Greek Philosophy,* pp. 102–3.

[33] Harmony, according to Iamblichus 115; symbolism, according to Aristotle *Metaphysics* M. 4. 1078b 21; Pythagorean Oath, Iamblichus 150.

the political tendencies of the Pythagoreans were. Only the fact is certain; what is equally certain is that one of the noblest and richest men of the city, Cylon by name, led a successful revolt against the new masters. The house where the principal Pythagoreans of Crotona were assembled was surrounded and set on fire; only two were able to escape, Archippus and Lysis, afterward the teacher of Epaminondas at Thebes. It was doubtless after this catastrophe, which took place toward the middle of the fifth century, that the Pythagoreans emigrated to continental Greece where we will later find them.[34]

IV *Heraclitus of Ephesus*

The first two thinkers whose writings survive to any great extent are Heraclitus, called the obscure, and Zenophanes: they both take us back to the cities of Ionia. Heraclitus was a citizen of Ephesus where he flourished toward the end of the sixth century. Since 546 the whole of Ionia had been under Persian domination and we may suppose that Heraclitus witnessed the revolt of the Ionian cities which, with the exception of Ephesus, united to fight the Persians in 498 and were most ruthlessly punished by Darius. Heraclitus lived in the midst of these civil catastrophes and it may have been their impression that gave his thought its pessimistic tendency with its characteristically aloof and proud air, expressing itself in a succinct and brilliant style, epigrammatic and full of sumptuous and familiar comparisons. His work, *On the Universe,* written in prose, is the first in which we clearly see a genuine philosophy, that is to say, a conception of the meaning of human life grafted onto a considered theory of the universe. It was perhaps he who divided his work into the three parts which became traditional: physics, theology, and politics.[35] And it is under these three heads that we are able to classify the one-hundred-and-thirty short fragments which have come down to us.

In many respects, the cosmology of Heraclitus is Milesian in

---

[34] Account of Aristoxenus, contemporary of Aristotle, in Iamblichus 248–51.

[35] Diogenes Laertius *Life of the Philosophers* ix. 5.

origin. In it we encounter two principal Milesian themes: the explanation of the stars (gleaming fires) by a kind of dry evaporation emanating from the earth, and of clouds or winds by vapors rising from the sea; and the explanation of the transmutation of fire into water and water into earth, and the reverse transmutations by condensation and rarefaction as in Anaximenes.[36] We also find in it, clearly developed, the idea of the autonomy of the world, implied in all Milesian doctrine, the idea of a world which none of the gods or men has made.[37] But he added some new features, new at least for us; first, a disdain for minute and exact research, for the polymathy which characterized both the erudition of a Hesiod and of a Hecate collecting all the traditions in order to write a poem or a history, and the nascent science of a Pythagoras.[38] From his taste for immediate intuition ("the eyes being better witnesses than the ears")[39] came the images of his cosmology which do not go much beyond myth. The stars are produced by the accumulation of dry evaporations in some kind of celestial boats, whose openings are turned toward us. Eclipses take place when these boats turn around. The brightness and the heat of the sun are explained by the proximity of the solar boat to the earth, although it is beyond the misty region in which the moon loses light and heat. The daily creation of a new sun, and possibly the denial of the existence of a southern hemisphere, indicate, rather than any progress, a peculiar contempt for rational research and a retrogression toward primitive forms of thought.[40]

The personal thought of Heraclitus developed around four distinct themes whose unity is not easy to grasp. First, strife (Polemos) is the father of all things; the birth and the conservation of beings are due to a conflict of opposites which oppose and maintain each other. To wish, with Homer, to see "discord die out between the

---

[36] Aetius ii. 17. 4; Theophrastus (Diels, p. 475, l. 15 ff.); Diogenes Laertius ix. 9.
[37] Frag. 20 (according to the order of Bywater).
[38] Frags. 16–17
[39] Frag. 15
[40] Diogenes Laertius ix. 9; Aetius ii. 22. 2; 29. 3; frag. 32; Burnet, *Early Greek Philosophy*, p. 151, n. 4.

gods and men" is to ask for the destruction of the universe. This fruitful conflict is at the same time harmony, not in the Pythagorean sense of a simple numerical relation but in the sense of an adjustment of forces acting in opposite directions, like those which keep a bowstring drawn: thus harmony and discord, day and night, winter and summer, life and death limit and unite one another. Every excess of an opposite, which goes beyond the assigned measure, is punished by death and corruption. If the sun goes beyond its limits and does not set at the hour appointed by destiny, its heat will burn up everything. The theme of opposites applies both to simultaneous opposites which are limited in space and to successive opposites, whose succession is regulated by excess and want, satiety and famine, which are limited in time. Their mutual harmony is maintained by Dikē, Justice, in whose service are the avenging Furies; so, in Hesiod and Pindar, the Horae, daughters of Themis, were goddesses of order, justice, and peace (Eunomia, Justice, Eirene).[41]

The second Heraclitean theme is the unity of all things; it is the pre-eminent truth which the common people, unable to pay attention to the things around them, do not notice; the gold that is found only after much digging of the ground and which nature likes to hide, in the way the Delphic Apollo reveals the future but conceals it in enigmatic words. It is the wisdom which is not the vain erudition of a Hesiod or of a Pythagoras collecting every legend, but one thing, standing alone, confiding in the eyes rather than the ears, in intuition more than tradition; this is a wisdom that consists in recognizing the one thought which governs all things. What then is this unity? Is it the Milesian unity of a primordial substance? Yes, in one sense: the primordial substance is fire, in which all things may be exchanged, as all merchandise is exchanged for gold; everything arises and progresses just as fire, eternally living, in turn bursts into flame or dies down. But fire is no longer one of those great

[41] See, successively, frags. 44, 43, 45, 36, 59, 29, and H. Gomperz, *Reihenfolge einiger Bruchstücke des Heraklits* (Hermes, 1923), pp. 20–56. On justice, frags. 60–62.

physical environments like the expanse of the sea or the tempestuous atmosphere, which obsessed the imaginations of the Milesians. Rather it is a constantly active force, an "ever living" fire. The choice which Heraclitus made, then, calls attention less to the substance of things than to the order, the thought, the Logos, which determines the exact measures of its transformations.[42]

The third Heraclitean theme is the perpetual flux of all things. "You cannot step twice into the same river; for fresh waters forever flow in upon you." Being is inseparable from this continual movement; beer becomes decomposed if it is not stirred; rest is nothing but change; time displaces things, like a child playing at checkers; the young become old; life gives way to death, vigil to sleep. Cold things become warm; what is moist becomes dry.[43]

The fourth theme is a kind of ironic vision of contrasts, a reversal which reveals in things the opposite of what we first saw in them. For hogs, mire is worth more than clear water, and for asses, straw is superior to gold; the wisest man in relation to God is only an ape; sea water is both the purest and the most impure, for it is beneficial to fish and fatal to man.[44]

These themes are most certainly related: opposites can be maintained only by virtue of the unity which envelops and limits them, the one by the other. All the intuitions of Heraclitus tend toward a single doctrine of remarkable depth. All its contrasts are met with again in a single contrast: the permanent, or One, and the changeable are not exclusive of each other. On the contrary, the One and the permanent are found in change itself, in discord, but in a measured change and in a regulated discord.[45] Heraclitus had the intuition that wisdom consists in discovering the general formula, the Logos, of this change. Among these regularities, one of the principal ones concerns the periodic changes of time, which bring back, always after such a cycle, the days, the months, the years. In drawing inspiration from very ancient traditions which date from the Baby-

---

[42] Cf. successively, frags. 1, 5–11, 16–19, 22, 20, 21.

[43] Frags. 41, 84, 83, 79, 78, 39.

[44] Frags. 53, 51, 97, 99, 52.

[45] Frag. 59.

Ionian civilization, Heraclitus attempted to determine a great year which would be, in the life of the world, what a generation is in human life.[46] The end of this great year was to be marked, if we can believe later sources, by a universal conflagration or re-absorption of all things into fire, after which the world would be born again from fire; but this may have been an erroneous interpretation of Heraclitus by the Stoics. It is doubtless true that, for him, all is transformed into fire, but simultaneously this transformation is balanced by an inverse transmutation of fire into other things; "the upward path," the conflagration, is identical with the "downward path" or the extinction of fire in air; at one and the same time "it scatters and it gathers; it advances and retires." [47]

The wisdom of Heraclitus has only contempt for the vulgar: contempt above all for popular religion, for the veneration of images and especially for mysterious cults, Orphic or Dionysian, with their ignoble purifications through blood, for the traffickers in mysteries who foster man's ignorance of the hereafter. This is the contempt, too, of a member of the nobility, born of a family where the title of king was hereditary, for the political incapacity of the multitude, who drove the best men out of the city. Unquestionably his God was the very nature of the world, "which does not wish and yet does wish to be called by the name of Zeus," which is day and night, winter and summer, and assumes a variety of forms. The unity of God, at the beginning of Greek thought, is like a reflection of the unity of the world.[48]

Of the outcome of Heracliteanism during the fifth century and at the beginning of the fourth, two echoes remain. First, the treatise On Government, preserved in the collection of works attributed to Hippocrates; and second, the lifelike group portrait of contemporary philosophers of change that Plato creates in the Cratylus and

[46] Aetius ii. 32. 3.

[47] Cf. the discussion of Burnet, Early Greek Philosophy, pp. 136, 138; frags. 40 and 69.

[48] Frags. 124–30, 60, 110–15; Diogenes Laertius ix. 6; on the "kings" of Ephesus, see Strabo Geography xiv. 1. Certain interpreters, like Tannery (Pour l'histoire de la science hellène pp. 182 ff.), believe they see Orphic beliefs in frag. 38 and in some others.

the *Theatetus*. The medical treatise applies the cosmological doctrine of Heraclitus to the theory of health. Health is the harmony of the whole; that is to say, an adjustment between the two opposed forces, energizing fire and nourishing water. We shall see later, in fact, that there was not a single cosmological doctrine which was not at the same time medical; the idea of man as a microcosm was, during this period, one of the most common and widespread. Our Heraclitean physician accumulated, not without virtuosity of style, all the paradoxes of the master: "Everything is similar being dissimilar; everything is identical, being different; everything exists in relation and without relation; everything is intelligent and is without intelligence." [49] As for those Plato tells us about, namely his own teacher Cratylus and Cratylus' disciples, they were radical Heracliteans who, pushing to the extreme the principle of universal motion, denied there is anything stable and refused all discussion and even all speech on the pretext that discussion and speech imply the continued existence of the things discussed. Heracliteanism, in its later phases, was thus hostile to the dialectic philosophy which we shall see develop in the course of the fifth century. [50]

v *Xenophanes and The Eleatics*

It was no doubt the misfortunes of Ionia following the Persian conquest (546) which forced Xenophanes of Colophon to leave his own country. It was then that Ionians, fleeing their country, founded several colonies around the Tyrrhenian Sea, among them Elea on the Lucanian coast. Xenophanes was one of those emigrants, whom he describes in a poem as meeting in a distant land and asking one another: "From what country are you . . . and how old were you when the Medes arrived?" [51] Enough lines are left of his elegies and satires to enable us to form an idea of his interests. Xenophanes preserves to some extent the spirit of the Milesians, explaining the

[49] The Heraclitean origin is especially evident in Book i, chaps. iii–xxiv; cf. Bernays, *Gesammelte Abhandlungen*, I, p. 1 ff.

[50] Plato *Theaetetus* 179d 180.

[51] Frag. 22 (Diels' numbering, *Die Vorsokratiker*).

stars and the sun as emanations or clouds arising from the evaporation of the sea, seeing in the land a kind of alluvial deposit of the sea and using the existence of fossils as a proof, and asserting the existence of innumerable worlds. But he did not have the same scientific inclinations as his predecessors. He cared little about knowing the shape of the universe and of the earth; he held the view that today's sun will continue its course indefinitely in a straight line and will be replaced tomorrow by another and that the earth extends indefinitely beneath our feet.[52]

His main interest is elsewhere. He gives definite form to an idea already explicit in Heraclitus; the idea of the incompatibility of human reason (matured through Milesian science and experience) with traditional mythology. The gods of Homer and Hesiod, begotten like men and guilty of all their offenses, with dress, voice, and form like men, these gods are the inventions of men. An Ethiopian imagines them black; a Thracian gives them blue eyes; oxen or horses, if they had any, would give them the form of their kind.[53] In contrast to Pindar, Xenophanes not only had great contempt for the myths, he also had nothing but disdain for the delight his contemporaries took in the Olympic games.[54] But he adds to his negations, in a cautious manner to be sure and without claiming certainty, a positive theory of the one God who is not like men, since "he sees and thinks everything at once and, being everything at once, he understands," and, being completely motionless, governs all things through the intelligent power of his thought.[55] It seems indeed that this God who is one, intelligent, and motionless is a deification of nature. With Xenophanes and Heraclitus we are at the point where Ionian physics gives birth to a theology entirely opposed to mythical conceptions, in which God takes on something of the impersonality, immobility, and intelligibility of a natural law.

The work of Parmenides took a very different direction. He was a citizen of Elea, an Ionian colony founded in Italy, on the Tyr-

[52] Frags. 28–30; Aetius ii. 20. 3; Hippolytus i. 14. 5.
[53] Frags. 10–16.
[54] Frag. 2.
[55] Frags. 35, 23–26.

rhenian Sea, about 540; he flourished in this city about 475 and wrote some of its laws. We know the names of two Pythagoreans, Ameinias and Diochaetas, whose disciple he was.[56] This was an intellectual center quite different from Ionia. Even the literary form was new. Parmenides was the first to write a philosophical work in verse; we have the beginning of it, which is as solemn as the account of a religious initiation. The poet sees himself borne in a chariot by the daughters of the Sun, to the gates of the day, which are guarded by avenging Justice. Justice, implored by his guides, opens the gates to him, and he enters and receives the words of truth from the goddess.[57] This is an account probably adapted from some Orphic book of the dead and, with its fanciful machinery, quite removed from the simplicity of Ionian prose and also from the realistic images of Heraclitus. The little that we know of his cosmology also reveals an altogether new spirit. If it is true that he taught that the earth is a sphere and that the evening and morning stars are the same,[58] this proves that he had a precise geometrical image of the world, very remote from the heavens which the Ionians conceived on the model of meteors.

Indeed, it was the fundamental theses of Ionian cosmology, especially in the form given to it by Heraclitus, that were completely ruined, never to recover, by the doctrine of Parmenides. The birth and becoming of things, their alternating separation and reunion, their oppositions, divisions, changes, everything that Heraclitus had claimed to derive from direct experience, Parmenides denied in the name of reason.

For the way of belief, which, guided by the senses and linguistic habits, leads to Ionian cosmology, he substitutes the way of truth, which leads to a quite different conception of reality. The novelty of Parmenides' thought lies in his rational and critical method which is the point of departure of all philosophical dialectic in Greece. When we think of the real, we have to say it exists; we

[56] Diogenes Laertius ix. 23. 21.
[57] Frag. 1 (according to the order of Diels, *Die Vorsokratiker*).
[58] Diogenes Laertius, *ibid*.

cannot say it does not exist, for we can neither know nor talk about what does not exist. Now, that is what the Ionians do, when they assert the existence of a primordial substance which at the same time is and is not that which is derived from it, the same as its products without being the same. That is what they do in asserting the birth of things, φύσις, which causes beings to grow; for from non-existence no existence can come. It is impossible for things to be dissipated and divided; for that which is does not have any degree and cannot be less in one place than in another; we cannot conceive things in motion, since there is neither birth nor corruption. Finally, the infinite substance of the Ionians is an absurdity, since being infinite it lacks completion.[59]

In place of the Ionian world, Parmenides substitutes the only reality which thought can conceive; a perfect and finite sphere, equally heavy from the center in all directions, the only thing satisfying the conditions of what is. It is uncreated, indestructible, continuous, immovable, and complete. Existence is not an abstract notion for Parmenides, neither is it a sensible image: it is, one could say, a geometrical image, arising from contact with Pythagorean science. On the other hand, the sphere of Parmenides takes on the divine character which the order of the world had for Heraclitus: Parmenides invokes the half-abstract deities, Justice, Necessity, Destiny, which for the Ionians directed the regular course of things, in order to guarantee the complete immobility of his sphere.[60]

Such is the way of truth. Does this mean that we must not follow the way of belief? Not at all, as long as we realize clearly that it is only belief. Parmenides superimposed a cosmology on his philosophy, but this cosmology seems to be little more than a collection of traditional opinions about the birth and destruction of things. In that way it is different in spirit from Ionian cosmology, for it admits theogonic myths like those of Hesiod and the Orphics. For example, love is considered the first of the gods.[61] Moreover, it does

[59] Frags. 5, 6, 8.
[60] Frag. 8.
[61] Plato *Symposium* 195c; Frag. 13.

not admit a primordial substance as a principle, but rather a pair of opposites, Day and Night, or Light and Darkness.[62] These terms recall Hesiodic fancy more than Ionian positivism; the pair of opposites is a thoroughly Pythagorean feature. Finally, a new mark of religious and traditional thought, the heavens, for Parmenides, as they are in certain Platonic myths, are the thoroughfare of souls, where Necessity, Ananke, resides and distributes their lots among them.[63] It must be added, of course, that in his explanations of details Parmenides is indebted to the Ionians. The structure of his heavens, composed of concentric bands with the earth at their center, recalls the rings of Anaximander; there is a band of pure fire or light, which is the most distant and touches the extremities of the universe; the other, intermediate, bands are mixed with darkness and light; the stars are their luminous parts.[64]

With Parmenides, we see the formation of two opposing currents in Greek thought: on the one hand, Ionian positivism which is intuitive and experimental, ignorant of mathematical physics, the declared enemy of myths, religious traditions, and the new initiation cults, and for this reason neither very popular nor apt to be so; on the other hand, the rationalism of Parmenides and Pythagoras, seeking to construct reality through thought, tending toward dialectic, not very sympathetic toward direct experience, and, for this reason, receptive to myths when dealing with sensible things, inclined to give considerable attention to the problem of destiny, naturally popular and having a taste for propaganda. The close solidarity of rationalism and mythical imagination against positivism seems to be the salient trait of this period.

Parmenides' disciple Zeno of Elea, who flourished around the middle of the fifth century, developed the analytical side of Parmenides' thought. Aristotle made him the founder of dialectic,[65] that is to say of the art of refuting a speaker by starting from principles

[62] Frags. 8, 9.
[63] Aetius ii. 7. 1 (Diels, *Doxographi*, p. 335, l. 15) provided one accepts the reading of the manuscripts κληροῦχον.
[64] *Ibid.*
[65] According to Diogenes viii. 57.

admitted by him. If he did not himself write any dialogues, he was on the way to this new literary form. Plato tells us that he proved the thesis of Parmenides, the existence of the immovable One, by showing the absurdities which resulted from the opposite thesis.[66] It is to be noted that by the opposite thesis, Zeno did not mean the Ionian cosmological doctrines alluded to by Parmenides, but rather the Pythagorean thesis that things are numbers, that is, made of discrete units, such as points. The contrast in Zeno is between two accounts both aiming at rationality, between the continuity of the Parmenidean sphere and the discontinuity of the Pythagorean world. This discontinuity is absurd; to compose the multiple from units without magnitude or points is to compose it of nothing. But to give each unit a magnitude is to say that it is not a unit, since it is then a composite. Besides, if a point added to an extension does not make it greater, how could it be a component of this magnitude? Finally, assuming a magnitude made of points, there will be between two of these points a magnitude which must be made of other points, and so on to infinity.[67] Let us add the famous arguments by which Zeno demonstrates the impossibility of motion, on the hypothesis that extension is made up of points. The argument of the runner: it is impossible for the runner to reach the end of the race course since he has to traverse an infinite number of points. Achilles and the tortoise: Achilles pursuing the tortoise does not overtake it, since he must first reach the place from which the tortoise has started, then to set out again from it in order to reach the place where the tortoise then is, and so on to infinity, if it is true that the distance between him and the tortoise will always be composed of an infinite number of points. The argument of the arrow: at each moment of time, the arrow in flight occupies a space equal to itself; at each instant, therefore, it is motionless, if we assume that time is made up of indivisible moments. The argument of the race course: if two runners move with equal speed in opposite directions and meet in passing before an immobile object, they will each move

[66] *Parmenides* 128ab.
[67] Frags. 1–3 (in Diels, *Die Vorsokratiker*).

twice as fast in relation to the other as in relation to the object. On the assumption that bodies are composed of points and that the interval between one point and another may be traversed in one indivisible instant, it follows that for one runner the instant required to pass from one point of the immobile object to the following point will be half of the instant required to pass from a point of the other runner to the following point.[68] In sum, it is the continuous sphere of Parmenides that Zeno defended against the Pythagoreans, by showing them that their very principle, which is to compose things of units or points, destroys their own thesis.

Melissus of Samos, however, a disciple of Parmenides and some ten years younger than Zeno, brought the conflict with Ionian physics to the foreground again. Considering his origin (Melissus was the Samian general who defeated the fleet of Pericles in 440),[69] he must have come to know the Eleatic doctrine only after he knew Ionian philosophy. This would explain the fact that while he gives reality the properties of the Parmenidean sphere—unity, eternity, continuity, and plenitude—he retains something of Ionianism by making the sphere infinite in magnitude. Besides, he insisted with a great deal of force on the insufficiency of sense knowledge; if we affirm truthfully that a thing is warm, we shall have to consider erroneous the sensation showing us a warm thing becoming cold, and this applies to all the observations on which the notion of change in Ionian physics is founded.[70]

VI *Empedocles of Agrigentum*

In spite of the hostile attitude of Parmenides, physical speculation began again with vigor in the middle of the fifth century. It was the age of Empedocles of Agrigentum who was born about 494 and died after 444, of Anaxagoras of Clazomenae (500–428), of some

---

[68] Aristotle *Physics* vi. 9. 239b 8 ff.

[69] Plutarch *Life of Pericles* 26.

[70] Infinity, frags. 3–6 (order of Diels, *Die Vorsokratiker*); against sense knowledge, frag. 8.

young Pythagoreans, and, at the close of the century, of the great Democritus of Abdera (born about 460).

But an entirely new trait is common to all these doctrines: there is no transformation, no real birth,[71] for nothing comes from nothing. There are only various combinations of an infinite number of very small corpuscles, each of which is immutable and endowed with properties that are quite permanent. There were as many ways of conceiving these corpuscles and the modes of their union and separation as there were different cosmologies.

In a poem filled with images, Empedocles expounds the doctrine of the four elements, or rather "roots" of things: fire, air, water, and earth. They are to the world what colors are to the painter or what water and flour are in the making of dough. Everything arises from their union, their separation, their different proportionings; but none among them is first; equally eternal, they do not originate from each other.[72] This doctrine recognizes for the first time the existence and the independence of atmospheric air. Empedocles proves this existence by the experiment with a clepsydra which one immerses in water while closing up the upper orifice with the finger. The air contained in the apparatus resists the entry of water through the lower orifice.[73] Every change takes place either through combination or dissociation of the elements. Therefore, there are two active powers: one which unites them when they are separated, Love, and another which separates them when they are reunited, Hate. Love and Hate alternately acquire preponderance over each other. If we start with the state in which everything is united through Love, from the *sphaeros* (analogous to the sphere of Parmenides), Hate gains admittance little by little and gradually drives out Love until things are in the state of complete separation in which Love has completely disappeared. Then, by a reverse movement, Love, re-entering the world, gradually drives out Hate and restores the original *sphaeros*. There are, therefore, two opposite courses in the

[71] Empedocles frag. 8 (order of Diels, *Die Vorsokratiker*).
[72] Frags. 6, 8, 9, 25, 33, 34, 17.
[73] Frag. 100.

world which are eternally alternating: one which proceeds from mixture to dispersion, and one which proceeds from dispersion to mixture, an inescapable order, because Hate and Love are bound by an oath to yield the preponderance alternately.[74] Our present world[75] is the one in which Hate is making headway. From the *sphaeros* were separated out, first, the air which surrounds it like an atmosphere, then fire, which rose to the highest altitude, then the earth, and from the earth water gushed forth. In one of the celestial hemispheres fire is preponderant, and it produces the light of day; in the nocturnal hemisphere, there are only traces of fire in the middle of a mass of dark air.[76] Moreover, the sun and the moon are not fiery masses. Empedocles knew that the moon only reflects the sun's light and he recognized the true cause of eclipses and the nature of night, which is only the shadow of the earth. The moon, which is a mass of condensed air, reflects light like the glass mirrors which were beginning to be common in Greece in the fifth century.[77] Empedocles, in a way that is obscure in other respects, applied this mirror theory to the sun; the sun is a reflection of the fiery hemisphere onto the sky.[78] The present procreation of animals by sexual union, which followed a primitive androgynous state, is further evidence of the progress of Hate.[79] In contrast to this picture of our world, Empedocles vaguely sketches a world in which Love makes headway, and new creatures are engendered through union. In connection with this phase we find descriptions of those solitary wandering members who seek to be united, heads without necks and arms without shoulders, whose union gives birth to the strangest monsters, oxen with faces of men or men with heads of oxen.[80]

Empedocles' physics is rich in physiological explanations of details. The doctrine of the four elements gave birth to a medical school

[74] Frags. 16, 17, 26; concerning the sphere, frags. 27, 28.
[75] As Burnet shows, *Early Greek Philosophy,* p. 267.
[76] Aetius 11. 6. 3; Plutarch *Stromata* (Diels, *Doxographi,* p. 582).
[77] Frags. 45–48; cf. Kafka, "Zur Physik des Empedokles," *Philologus,* LXXVIII, 283.
[78] Plutarch *ibid.*
[79] Aetius v. 19. 5; Bignone, *Empedocle,* p. 570.
[80] Frags. 35, 61.

known by the name of Philistion. The properties of these elements—the warmth of fire, the coldness of air, the moisture of water, the dryness of earth—are considered as the active forces whose combinations in the organism produce health, degree of intelligence, and the different temperament or characters.[81] An important theory, not clearly related to the rest, is that of external perception. Effluvia emanate from things and make their way to pores located in the sense organs; if there is proper correspondence, the effluvium penetrates and perception is produced. Vision (an idea which Plato will take up in the *Timaeus*) is produced by the encounter of the effluvium coming from external light with the fiery ray emanating from the fire contained in the eye.[82]

Empedocles was not only a physicist; he presented himself to the inhabitants of Agrigentum as an inspired seer who, a fillet on his brow, knew how to cure them and taught them about the origin and destiny of the soul and the necessary purifications. Empedocles was of the lineage of the Orphics and the Pythagoreans. He believed in the transmigration of souls into the bodies of animals and based the precept of abstinence from flesh on this belief. He knew that the soul is a daemonic spirit and that the sequel to its mortal life is an expiation, bound to continue thirty thousand years, for any crime, murder, or perjury which it has committed. Earth is the cavern, the land without joy in which death and wrath exist.[83] The relation of this religious teaching to his cosmology is not very clear; but should we not note the relation between Empedocles' pessimism and his belief that the present phase of the history of the world is dominated by Hate?

VII *Anaxagoras of Clazomenae*

With Anaxagoras of Clazomenae we leave Magna Gracia again, with its prophets and its initiates, to return to the positivist inspira-

[81] Galen *Works* (Kuhn ed., X, 5), frags. of Philistion, in Wellmann, *Fragment-sammlung der griechischen Aerzte,* Vol. I (1901).

[82] Theophrastus *De sensibus* § 12 (Diels, *op. cit.,* p. 502).

[83] Frags. 112–48 which are attributed to a poem different from the first and entitled "Purifications."

tion of the Ionians. An event of capital importance: this Ionian came from a land where the Milesian traditions were preserved, we do not know how, to reside in Athens, the prosperous Athens after the Median wars, the capital of the new maritime empire. He lived there thirty years and was the friend of Pericles,[84] the leading man of the time. In spite of this support, the old Athenian spirit, so well represented by the *Clouds* of Aristophanes, did not agree with that of the Ionians, who denied the divinity of the celestial bodies and taught that the sun was an incandescent stone and the moon an earth. He was accused of impiety and driven out of Athens.[85] But his influence remained alive as Plato shows.

Anaxagoras gave a new solution to the conflict between Parmenides and the Ionians. He remained attached to the now dominant principle that there is neither generation nor corruption; "nothing originates or is destroyed, but there is mixture and separation of the things that are."[86] But the problem was to explain change, and how one thing can arise from another. Anaxagoras, like all Ionians, was very keenly aware of the infinite variety of things; there are many things and things of all sorts: bone, flesh, etc., each having irreducible properties. His point of view was at least implicitly opposed to that of Empedocles; the latter explained things by the combination and the proportioning of four elementary qualities. Anaxagoras believed, on the contrary, that bone, flesh, hair are, as such, indestructible qualities. Yet we see things arising from one another; hair from what is not hair, flesh from what is not flesh. How is this possible if there is really no birth? It is because the product already existed in the producer. Production is therefore only separation. From a state in which things are mixed and in which, because of this mixture, we cannot distinguish them from one another, they pass to a state in which they are separated. Nature would be more nearly comparable to the art of the metallurgist who extracts iron from ore than to the art of the painter who combines.

[84] Plato *Phaedrus* 270a.
[85] Plato *Apology* 26d; Diogenes Laertius ii. 12. 14; cf. *Clouds* 364–80, in which the theory of Anaxagoras is put in the mouth of Socrates.
[86] Frag. 17 (order of Diels, *Die Vorsokratiker*).

But the transformations of things are infinite, and all things unceasingly give rise to other things; each thing must then contain within itself, mixed and not discernible because of their mixture, the seeds of all things; "things are not cut off from each other with a hatchet, neither the hot from the cold, nor the cold from the hot." [87] Each thing is named after the quality which predominates in it, but the infinitude of other qualities is present in it, although indistinct; therefore separation, which is in process of taking place, is never completed and is always, in fact, just as far from completion as it ever was; it is a movement that is without end. It is these seeds of all things, each containing an infinity, which Aristotle, using a name which has become traditional, called the homeomeries or homogeneous parts.[88] But it must be clearly noted that they are not component parts of things, limited in number. Anaxagoras can only assert the infinity of the movement of division because he asserts correlatively infinite divisibility and, with it, an infinity of homeomeries within a limited body which makes possible indefinitely the process of separation.[89]

From then on one can translate the old Milesian cosmogonies into new terms. The infinite of Anaximander becomes the infinitely great mixture in which "all things are together and cannot be distinguised because of their smallness." [90] Cosmogony will be the history of the continuous process of separation, through which the parts of the world are separated from one another; on the one hand, the dense and the damp, the cold and the dark which gather together toward the center, while on the other the rare and the warm move toward the outer region.[91] But Anaxagoras posed other questions. First, what could the source of motion be, in this completely homogeneous infinite? It can only be in a reality external and superior to the mixture, just as, in Empedocles, it is external to the elements.

---

[87] Frag. 8; cf. frags. 10, 11.
[88] Aristotle *On Generation* i. 1. 314a 18.
[89] Frags. 3, 7.
[90] Frag. 1.
[91] Frag. 15.

This cause without mixture, simple, existing in itself, which is the principle of the ordering of the world is Intelligence (Nous). Through what mechanism does Nous act? Anaxagoras, impressed by the changes produced by the celestial revolutions, asserts that the first cause which separates things from each other is a circular motion or vortex. He therefore imagined Nous first animating itself with a circular motion, then producing a small vortex in a limited space extended little by little from its center, diffusing itself through infinite space. The separation of things is brought about, in a way difficult to understand, by the mechanical action of this vortex. Stars for example result from the ether tearing away stones from the earth and setting them on fire by the rapidity of its motion. The same process, moreover, may be produced in innumerable points in boundless space, and we must accept, following Milesian teaching, an infinity of worlds.[92]

The biology of Anaxagoras does not have any obvious connection with his cosmology; he maintained no doubt that all living beings, plants included, had in them a fragment of universal intelligence.[93] He taught that sensation takes place through opposites; the pupil, perfectly dark, is the place where a luminous image can appear. We are warmed or chilled by something warmer or colder than ourselves; therefore every sensation involves pain, because pain is contact with the dissimilar.[94]

VIII *The Physicians of the Fifth Century*

After Anaxagoras, in the course of the fifth century, Ionian ideas gained ground, but without having any distinguished representatives. The physicians are ridiculed by the writers of comedy, Hippon by Cratinus,[95] Diogenes of Apollonia by Aristophanes. Plato in the *Cratylus* (409) speaks of the Anaxagorians. One sees a revival of all the old Milesian theses. Hippo takes water as the principle of

[92] Frags. 12–16; frag. 4; cf. Burnet, *Early Greek Philosophy*, p. 310.
[93] Frag. 11; Aristotle *De plantis* i. 1.
[94] Theophrastus *De sensibus* 27 (Diels, *Doxographi*, p. 507).
[95] Scholium to *Clouds* 94.

things; Diogenes of Apollonia takes air; Archelaus of Athens, with Anaxagoras, takes Nous and the primordial mixture. But these authors are generally less concerned with cosmology than with physiology and medicine.[96]

We are in possession of a series of forty-one medical treatises under the name of Hippocrates, born at Cos in 450, which show the immense importance medicine had in the intellectual life of the Greeks toward the end of the fifth century. All the authors of these treatises were free from the old superstitions, and we all know the magnificent beginning of the treatise on *Epilepsy:* "I believe that epilepsy, also called the sacred disease, has nothing more divine nor is it more sacred than the others; men first gave it a divine origin and divine causes through ignorance." Yet there arose among these authors an important conflict about method, concerning the relations of medicine to philosophical cosmology. Some, like the author of the treatise *On Ancient Medicine,* feared most of all the effects of the dogmatism and uncertainty of physics on their art. It is wrong to appeal to fruitless hypotheses, like that of the cold and the hot, the dry and the moist, as causes of disease and health. Assumptions like these are fitting when we are dealing with celestial motions, about which nothing certain can be said. Genuine medicine is autonomous and it has discovered through observations, without the help of these hypotheses, an infinity of things of which it is sure. This empirical method was opposed by the physiologist physicians whose point of view Plato has so perfectly defined in a passage of the *Phaedrus* (270c). It is not possible, Plato thought, to understand the nature of the soul apart from that of the universe, and, if Hippocrates is to be believed, one cannot even talk about the body apart from this method. We must examine with respect to every being whether it is simple or compound, and, if it is compound, we must enumerate its parts and examine with respect to each of them the actions and passions which belong to it.

---

[96] Hippo, in Hippolytus i. 16. 1; Diogenes of Apollonia, according to Theophrastus (Diels, *Doxographi,* p. 477, l. 5); Archelaus, according to Hippolytus i. 9.

IX *The Pythagoreans of the Fifth Century*

The Pythagoreans of this period were also divided: the acousmatics were a purely religious order where observance and belief continued to be the essential thing, whereas the mathematicians[97] sought only the scientific development of mathematics, astronomy, music, those sciences which were later to be considered by Plato as the point of departure for philosophy. These formed the little known group whose head appears to have been Philolaus, and which included Cebes and Simmias, portrayed by Plato in the *Phaedo* conversing with Socrates, Archytas of Tarentum, the political head of his country, a friend of Plato and the kind of philosopher king he approved of, and Timaeus of Locri, in whose name Plato expounded his own physics. It is impossible to construct an accurate history of this intellectual milieu in which the dogmas of Platonism were foreshadowed. Our only certain source, apart from the fragments of Philolaus whose authenticity is contested,[98] consists of the texts in which Aristotle expounds the doctrines of the Pythagoreans without going into much detail. One of their characteristics that must be kept in mind is their almost complete emancipation from Ionian cosmogony. To say, as they do, that things are made of numbers cannot have the same meaning as to say that they are made of fire or of air. In whatever way we conceive these numbers, as series of points or as extensions,[99] they are not like fire or air, substances capable of transformation into others; they imply a fixed and permanent order. Hence the character of their cosmology which does not permit a cosmogony in the Ionian manner but, contenting itself with describing an order, a cosmos, tends to become, instead of a physics, a pure mathematical astronomy. In their system of the world, the center is occupied by a fire; around this gravitate a primary planet

---

[97] Iamblichus 81, implies that this division took place after Pythagoras.
[98] Burnet, *Early Greek Philosophy*, p. 324.
[99] Compare Aristotle *Metaphysics* M. 6. 1080b 18 and 1083b 8.

called the counter-earth, then the earth which belongs to the planets, then the sun, the five planets, and the fixed stars. Nothing indicates that they sought for the origin of this system. Furthermore, the place they assigned to the earth completely excludes the ideas of the Ionians who, being more or less obsessed by the assimilation of celestial phenomena to meteorological phenomena, insisted unshakably that the earth rests motionless beneath the cloudy vault. Of these imagined astronomical realities inaccessible to observation, the counter-earth and the central fire which illuminates the terrestrial hemisphere we do not inhabit, one, the central fire, has no cosmogonic character but is meant to provide an explanation of solar light already encountered in Empedocles; the other, the counter-earth, is meant to explain eclipses by the interposition of this opaque body between the central fire and the moon or the sun.[100] This new Pythagoreanism, then, appears to be, in a sense, a real liberation from the dynamic and qualitative physics of the Ionians, which showed signs of exhaustion with the last Anaxagoreans and Heracliteans. There must have been an abundance of hypotheses, around this time, about the order and motions of the celestial bodies, but only traces of these have remained. One of them, perhaps, is the idea of the Pythagorean Hicetas, who explains diurnal motion by the rotation of the earth on its axis. We are acquainted with him through a passage in Cicero which many centuries later attracted the attention of Copernicus.[101]

x Leucippus and Democritus

At the same time, however, Ionian thought underwent a remarkable envigoration, but in a completely different direction. Leucippus of Miletus, who received instruction from Zeno at Elea, was the initiator of the movement which Democritus of Abdera continued. Democritus was born about 460 and founded his school at Abdera

[100] Aristotle On the Heavens ii. 13; Aetius ii. 20. 12.
[101] Theophrastus, in Cicero Academica Priora § 39; add the considerations on the harmony of the spheres, that is to say the sounds produced by the stars in their courses; see Aristotle On the Heavens ii. 9.

about 420. With Democritus, who was ten or twelve years younger than Socrates and who died advanced in years, a type of encyclopedic natural science developed, characterized by very extensive collections of zoölogical and botanical observations. "Nobody," he said of himself, "has traveled more than I, seen more countries and climates, listened to more discourses by learned men." The titles of some fifty treatises on the most diverse subjects have been preserved: they are on ethics, cosmology, psychology, medicine, botany, zoölogy, mathematics, music, technology; nothing escaped him. Of his work, which is immense in range like Aristotle's and, in its striving for universality, manifests the character of the age of the Sophists to which it belongs, there remain but a few fragments.[102]

In its general design, the cosmogony of Leucippus, which cannot be distinguished from the one expounded by Democritus in his two Diacosmoi or Systems of the World, is faithful to the Milesian conception: an infinite mass from which the material of innumerable worlds—produced successively or simultaneously—is drawn. For a world to be formed, it suffices that a fragment break away from this mass and that it be animated by a whirling motion. The differentiation and arrangement of the parts of the world are, as in Anaxagoras, the necessary effects of this whirling motion.[103] Certain details of Democritus' world have an openly archaic character, archaic even for the end of the fifth century. Like Anaximander, he gives the earth the shape of a tambourine or a disk.[104]

But he introduced an important innovation into this archaic mold: the doctrine of atoms. Democritean physics is the first thoroughgoing corpuscular physics. The infinite mass in which the seeds of all the worlds are mixed is made of an infinity of small corpuscles, invisible because of their smallness, indivisible (atoms), absolutely solid, eternal, each retaining the same shape but presenting an infinity of different shapes, to which he gave the name *ideas,* the very one Plato will give later to equally eternal essences. There are

[102] Diogenes Laertius ix. 47.
[103] *Ibid.* ix. 31–33.
[104] Aetius iii. 10. 4–5.

no differences between atoms except in size and shape or, should they have the same size and shape, in position. Between many combinations of the same atoms there is no difference except in the relative order of the atoms.[105] The origin of a world, namely, the detaching of a portion from the infinite mass, implies a void into which this portion will fall. Without void there is no motion, and void has to be understood as space entirely deprived of solidity, that which is not, as opposed to that which is. To assert the void, then, is to assert the necessity of the existence of that which is not; it is to contradict the great principle of Parmenides.[106] The mass of atoms, we said, is animated by a whirling motion whose origin, it must be added, is obscure. The effect of this motion is to produce multiple shocks among atoms of all weights. As in a vortex of wind or water, the lightest atoms are driven back toward the outside void while the dense atoms collect in the center where they form an initial spherical grouping. This sphere gradually separates into a spherical covering, which grows thinner and thinner, and a central core, which partly incorporates the atoms carried away from the membrane. In the membrane the celestial bodies are formed at the expense of outside atoms, which touch the vortex and are incorporated in it.[107]

Thus, for the first time in Greek cosmology, no appeal is made to qualitative powers such as cold and heat; nor is there any appeal to moving causes external to the elementary realities, such as Intelligence, Love, or Hate. There is nothing but a corpuscular mechanism in which only the properties of form, impenetrability, motion, and position, play a role. True reality belongs to the atom and the void; the other properties that we give to things, such as taste, heat, or color, belong to them merely by convention.[108] They are only affections of sensation, which arise from the change of the organ by the object, as in the doctrine which Plato ascribes to the Sophist Protagoras of Abdera, according to which the quality per-

---

[105] Aristotle *Metaphysics* A. 4. 985b 15.

[106] Theophrastus 1–3 (Diels, *Doxographi,* p. 484).

[107] Diogenes Laertius ix. 31.

[108] Sextus Empiricus *Against the Mathematicians* vii. 135.

ceived is the result of the concourse of two motions; this is how Democritus conceived vision. Air situated in the interval between the eye and the object seen contracts under the double influence of effluvia emanating from both of them; the air is thus fitted to receive the impression which it transmits to the pupil where the reflection of the object is located.[109]

Thus, along with a mechanistic physics, skepticism naturally appears in regard to the senses; the knowledge they give us is a "spurious knowledge"; "legitimate knowledge" comes from reason.

Mobility, then, does not depend on any qualitative power but on the shape or dimensions of atoms. That is why corpuscular physics contains a theory of the soul. The soul, being mobile and the cause of motion, is made of spherical atoms like those of fire or like the specks of dust we see dancing in a ray of sunlight; its atoms, which are equal in number to those of the body and which are juxtaposed to those of the body by alternating with them one by one, are continually restored by respiration.[110]

It is very hard for us to perceive the principles of Democritus' work. Judging from the whole of his treatises and from ancient testimonies, however, we must consider him not so much a theorist as an observer. Aristotle, not without critical intent, lets it be known that Democritus was content to gather facts as they occurred and to note their constancy when they occurred without trying to determine further their principle. He collected and classified natural facts with the same curiosity and in the same spirit as the Ionian historians of the fifth century, Hecate of Miletus or Herodotus, gathered the facts of history.[111]

To this science, so positivistic in spirit, Democritus added an ethics which, completely foreign to the tragic sense of life and of destiny manifested in the philosophical poets of Magna Graecia, has as its principal theme the calm of a soul exempt from fear and

---

[109] Plato *Theaetetus* 52, compared with Theophrastus *De sensibus* § 63 (Rivaud, *Le Problème du devenir* [1905], p. 160).

[110] Aristotle *On the Soul* i. 2. 404–5; Lucretius *On Nature* i. 370.

[111] Aristotle *Physics* viii. 1.

superstition. Democritus admitted the existence of the gods; but, for the same reason as men, they are transitory combinations of atoms and subject to universal necessity.[112]

XI The Sophists

The last philosophers we have talked about lived in the midst of the extraordinary spiritual ferment which marked the end of the Median wars (449). Greece escaped the barbarian peril; the Athenian maritime empire included some of the islands of the Aegean Sea and the ancient land of civilization that was Ionia. Pericles (d. 429) introduced the democratic constitution to Athens. There was a very profound moral agitation which was expressed in the theater: while Aeschylus (d. 546) had represented on the stage the dangers of excess and crimes consisting in overstepping the limits marked by divine justice, Euripides (d. 411) constantly noted the human, provisional, conventional character of the rules of justice. On the other hand Attic comedy, defending the old traditions, derided, because it feared, the new ideas introduced by Ionian science and also by the teaching of the Sophists.

Sophistry, which characterized the second half of the fifth century, does not designate a doctrine but a way of teaching. The Sophists were professors who went from town to town seeking an audience and, for a stipulated fee, taught their students, either in formal lessons or in a series of courses, methods for successfully proving any kind of thesis. In place of the pursuit and proclamation of truth, they substituted the pursuit of success, based on the art of convincing, persuading, and seducing. This was the period when intellectual life, whose center moved to continental Greece, took the form of a competition or game, the agonistic form, so familiar to Greek life. It was all a matter of theses defended or contested by competitors to whom a sovereign judge, which was often the public, awarded the prize. This is the kind of discussion Aristophanes shows us arising between the just proposition and the unjust proposition.

[112] Diogenes Laertius ix. 45; Cicero *On the Nature of Gods* i. 28; very contested fragments from the moral works in Stobaeus, *Florilegium*.

"Who are you?" asks the just.—"A proposition."—"Yes, but inferior to mine."—"You claim to be superior to me and I have won."—"What skill do you have then?"—"I invent new reasons." Such is the debate on the goal of life which Euripides depicts in the *Antiope* between the soul of the Muses and the politician. Plato shows us, in contrast, Socrates avoiding these competitions: in the *Protagoras,* Hippias tries in vain to start a debate of this kind between Socrates and Protagoras; in the *Gorgias,* Callicles, having delivered a speech in favor of natural justice, complains that Socrates violates the rules of the game by not replying to him with another speech.[113] There is an interest here on the part of the audience which we scarcely knew before. The philosopher no longer reveals truth; he proposes it and submits in advance to the verdict of the listener. This is a characteristic which became permanent. After the age of the Sophists, men attempted to define the philosopher in terms of the orator, the politician, or the Sophist; that is, of all those who address themselves to a public.[114]

Under these conditions the principal intellectual values are erudition, which puts man in possession of all knowledge useful for his purpose, and virtuosity, which enables him to choose his topics expediently and to present them in a captivating manner. Hence we find the two essential characteristics of the Sophists: on the one hand, they were technicians who boasted of knowing and teaching all the arts useful to man; on the other hand, they were masters of rhetoric, who taught how to win the good will of the listener.

With respect to the first, sophistry can be considered an assertion of the superiority of social life based on techniques ranging from the humblest crafts to the highest art, political virtue, which the Sophists prided themselves on teaching.[115] That is the trait common to four great Sophists familiar to us mainly through the descriptions Plato gave of them in the next generation: Protagoras of Abdera, who

[113] Aristophanes *Clouds* (in the year 423) v. 887 ff.; Euripides frag. 189 (Nauck ed.); Diogenes Laertius (ix. 52) attributes to Protagoras the institution of the contests of orations; Plato *Protagoras* 338a; *Gorgias* 497bc.
[114] For example in Aristotle *Problems* 30. 9, 11.
[115] Compare Plato *Hippias* ii. 368bd and *Protagoras* 318d, 319a.

flourished about 444 and who scandalized the Athenians by his indifference in matters of religion; Gorgias of Leontium, who was ambassador from his city to Athens in 427 and died almost a centenarian about 380 and whose Athenian students were not philosophers but writers like Isocrates and Thucydides; and finally, Prodicus of Ceos and Hippias of Elis.

This humanism, which expects everything of art and culture, is attested by the famous opening of the treatise of Protagoras: "Man is the measure of all things, of what is, that it is, and of what is not, that it is not." Moreover, men should only concern themselves with human things. "As to the gods, I can neither know that they exist nor that they do not exist; there are too many obstacles standing in the way, the obscurity of the subject and the shortness of life." [116] Here there is a whole program which aspires to a humane and rational culture; man in general is the object of study. Thus Hippias, according to Plato, considered all men as "parents, relatives, fellow-citizens according to nature, if not according to law." [117] Thus Protagoras, in a celebrated myth, told how Zeus saved mankind, which was about to perish for lack of natural means of defense, by giving to all men justice and shame, two natural and innate virtues, enabling them to establish cities and to perpetuate their race by helping one another—a magnificent panegyric of social life.[118] The Sophist was always prepared to defend the arts; in Plato, Hippias attributes his independence to the arts, since he even knows how to make the clothes he wears. In precisely the same vein we have the anonymous *Defense of Medicine* in the collection of the works of Hippocrates. It points out, against their detractors, the usefulness of doctors. And it opens with these words, so characteristic of the spirit of progress of the period: "Indeed, some people try to discredit the arts. . . . But the true end of a good mind is either to discover new things or to perfect those which are already invented." [119]

---

[116] Diogenes Laertius ix. 51.

[117] *Protagoras* 337c.

[118] Ibid. 320c–323a; cf. the article by Nestle, in *Philologus*, LXX, 26–28.

[119] Cf. Gomperz, *Die Apologie der Heilkunst* (1910).

In this environment, ethical questions had to be raised: Prodicus of Ceos, in particular, appears to be the moralist of the group. Xenophon expounded in his name the famous apologue of Hercules, choosing between vice and virtue; the wits of the time set in contrast, in order to defend it, Paris' preference of the goddess Aphrodite over Athena and Hera. These ethical themes, like the pessimistic theme of the transitory character of the blessings of human life, were to be the subject of real preaching which had a continuing history.[120]

But it was in politics that the Sophists especially asserted the power and autonomy of man. Law is a human invention and, to a certain extent, is artificial and arbitrary. This view is illustrated by the actual work of legislators of the time who, both in Athens and the colonies, continually revised the foundations of the constitution. Protagoras gave laws to Thurium as Parmenides had done for Elea. Law is thus opposed, as an artificial work, to nature. There are, it is true, unwritten laws, traditional customs which have a religious value. But they carry no weight compared with the deliberate work of the legislator. This was the point of view of Antiphon, the Sophist, whose fragments have been discovered recently. He did not deny the conflict between the artificial justice of laws and natural justice. For example, the law, when it obligates us to testify truthfully before a court, often obligates us to injure someone who has not injured us; in other words, to contradict the first rule of justice. Yet Antiphon apparently saw a superiority in this conventional character of laws.[121]

This intellectual movement, obviously a very important one, had a rather unhappy ending; at the beginning of the fourth century it culminated in political cynicism on the one hand, and in mere

---

[120] Compare Xenophon *Memorabilia* ii. 1. 21 ff.; and Isocrates *Eulogy of Helena* xx, in which the superiority of Theseus, the Athenian hero, over Hercules is also sustained. Gomperz (*Greek Thinkers*, I, 453) attributes to him the paternity of the pessimistic discourses of the pseudo-Plato, Axiochus.

[121] On the unwritten law, see Sophocles *Antigone* v. 450–55; frag. of Antiphon in *Oxyrinchus Papyri* xi and xv. See A. Croiset, *Revue des Études grecques*, 1917.

virtuosity on the other. On the one hand there is the political cynicism of the Athenian aristocrats Critias and Alcibiades, so often
expressed in the *History of the Peloponnesian War* of Thucydides[122]
and immortalized by Plato in the character Callicles in the *Gorgias*:
the instruction in rhetoric by Gorgias is bound to lead to the political
and moral depravity of a Callicles, for whom power was only a
means of satisfying his appetites. On the other hand there is mere
virtuosity, of the kind already found in the treatise by Gorgias on
non-being in which, using the dialectical techniques of Eleaticism,
he demonstrates that there is nothing or, if something exists, it is
unknowable or, if it is knowable, it is impossible to communicate
it to others.[123] This virtuosity is expressed in the importance attributed to good speaking, as in the rhetorical instruction of Gorgias,
the works on general grammar by Protagoras, or the researches of
Prodicus on synonyms. This virtuosity found resources for argumen-
tation in such little works as the *Twofold Discourses* which sum up
schematically the twofold contrary themes which one may have to
maintain on moral questions; a virtuosity which finally made its
last appearance in the art of disputation or eristic, which Plato so
mercilessly mocked in the *Euthydemus*. Eristic has some very facile
ways of overcoming an opponent by two or three very simple principles such as: error is impossible, and refutation is impossible.[124]

These were the results, in spite of the superior talents of the
Sophists, of a conception of the intellectual life guided solely by success. Yet, nothing in this movement that was positive was lost, any
more than from those that preceded it. Ionian naturalism, the rationalism of Magna Graecia, the religious spirit of Empedocles and
of the Pythagoreans, the humanism of the Sophists—we will see all
these come together in the most famous of the Greek philosophers,
in Plato.

[122] In particular iii. 83. 1; cf. *Gorgias* 482c ff. and the citations of an anonymous
Sophist in Iamblichus *Protrepticus* xx.

[123] On the treatise of Gorgias, see Pseudo-Aristotle *On Gorgias, Xenophanes and
Melissus* (end); on Protagoras, see Aristotle *Rhetoric* iii. 5; on Prodicus, see Plato
Protagoras 337bc.

[124] Cf. On the relations between the Sophistic and the Eristic, see Isocrates *Eulogy
of Helena*, "Introduction."

Bibliography

Texts

H. Diels. *Die Fragmente der Vorsokratiker: Griechisch und deutsch.* Berlin, 1903. 7th edition by W. Kranz. 3 vols., 1954.
————. *Doxographi graeci.* Berlin, 1879. See the editions of the fragments of Xenophanes, of Parmenides, and of the Sophists contained in the *Biblioteca di Studi Superiori* by M. Untersteiner, and those of the Pythagoreans due to Mme. Timpanaro-Cardini.
C. J. de Vogel. *Greek Philosophy.* Vol. I. Leiden, 1950.
G. S. Kirk and J. E. Raven. *The Presocratic Philosophers.* Cambridge, 1957.
R. Walzer. *Eraclito* (an edition of fragments). Florence, 1939. See also *Les fragments d'Héraclite d'Ephèse.* Translated by K. Axelos. Paris, 1958.

Comprehensive Studies

J. Burnet. *Early Greek Philosophy.* London, 1892. 3d edition, 1920; 4th edition, 1930.
A. Rey. *La jeunesse de la science grecque.* 1933.
R. Mondolfo. Italian translation of E. Zeller, *La filosofia dei Greci.* Vol. I, *Origini e periodi della filosofia greca.* 1932; Vol. II, *Ionici e Pitagorici.* Florence, 1938. The translator has added extended notes.
F. M. Cornford. *From Religion to Philosophy: A Study in the Origins of Western Speculation.* London, 1912.
A. Diès. *Le cycle mystique: la divinité, origine et fin des existences individuelles dans la philosophie antésocratique.* Paris, 1909.
A. Rivaud. *Le problème du devenir et la notion de la matière dans la philosophie grecque depuis les origines jusqu'à Théophraste.* Paris, 1905.
P.-M. Schuhl. *Essai sur la formation de la pensée grecque.* 1934. 2d edition, 1949.
P. Tannery. *Pour l'histoire de la science hellène: De Thalès à Empédocle.* Paris, 1887. 2d edition, 1930.
W. J. Stace. *A Critical History of Greek Philosophy.* Macmillan, 1920.
H. Cherniss. *Aristotle's Criticism of Presocratic Philosophy.* Baltimore, Md., 1935.
E. R. Dodds. *The Greeks and the Irrational.* Berkeley, Calif., 1956.
R. Schaerer. *L'homme antique et la structure du monde intérieur d'Homère à Socrate.* Paris, 1958.
W. Jaeger. *The Theology of the Early Greek Philosophers.* Oxford, 1947.
H. Frankel. *Dichtung und Philosophie des frühen Griechentums.* New York, 1951; *Wege und Formen früh-griechischen Denkens.* 2d edition; Munich, 1961.

R. B. Onians. *The Origins of European Thought about the Body, the Mind, the Soul, the World, Time and Fate.* Cambridge, 1951.

J.-P. Vernant. *Les origines de la pensée grecque.* Paris, 1962.

Special Studies

Articles of Doerfler on Thales, in *Archiv für Geschichte der Philosophie,* XXV (1912), 305; of Tannery and of Diels on Anaximander, in *ibid.,* VIII (1895), 443; X (1897), 228.

Charles H. Kahn. *Anaximander and the Origins of Greek Cosmology.* New York, 1960.

W. Guthrie. *Orpheus and Greek Religion: A Study of the Orphic Movement.* Cambridge, 1935.

O. Kern. *Orphica.* 1922.

J. Harrison. *Prolegomena to the Study of Greek Religion.* Cambridge, 1903.

H. Jeanmaire. *Dionysos: Histoire du culte de Bacchus.* Paris, 1951.

C. Ramnoux. *La Nuit et les enfants de la Nuit dans la tradition grecque.* Paris, 1959.

A. Delatte. *Études sur la littérature pythagoricienne* (Bibliothèque de l'École des Hautes Études, sciences historiques). Paris, 1915.—*The Life of Pythagoras by Diogenes Laertius.* Critical edition. Brussels, 1922.—*La politique pythagoricienne* (Bibliothèque de la faculté de philosophie et lettres de l'université de Liége). Liége-Paris, 1922.

G. Méautis. *Recherches sur le pythagorisme* (Collection of works of the Faculty of Letters of Neuchâtel). 1922.

A. Olivieri. *Civiltà Greca nell'Italia Meridionale.* Naples, 1931.

P. Kucharski. *Étude sur la doctrine pythagoricienne de la Tétrade.* Paris, 1952.

J. E. Raven. *Pythagoreans and Eleatics.* Cambridge, 1948.

M. Détienne. *Homère, Hésiode et Pythagor.* Brussels, 1962.

Max Wundt. "Die Philosophie des Heraklits," *Archiv für Geschichte der Philosophie,* XXIX, 431.

V. Macchioro. *Eraclito.* Bari, 1922.

G. S. Kirk. *Heraclitus: The Cosmic Fragments.* Cambridge, 1954.—"Logos, harmonie . . . dans Héraclite," *Revue philosophique,* 1957, pp. 289–99.

C. Ramnoux. *Vocabulaire et structures de pensée archaïque chez Héraclite.* (*Héraclite ou l'homme entre les choses et les mots*), Paris, 1959.—"Études présocratiques," *Revue philosophique,* 1961, pp. 93–107, and 1962, pp. 76–89.

A. Jeannière. *La pensée d'Héraclite d'Ephèse.* Paris, 1950.

R. Mondolfo and E. Zeller. *La filosofia dei Greci,* I, 4. 1961.

M. Levi. *Senofane e la sua filosofia.* Turin, 1904.

H. Diels. *Parmenides Lehrgedicht, griechisch und deutsch.* Berlin, 1897.

V. BROCHARD. "Sur Zénon d'Elée," in *Études de philosophie ancienne et moderne.* 1912. Pp. 3–22.—and W. J. VERDENIUS. *Parmenides.* Groningen, 1942.

A. KOYRÉ. "Remarque sur les paradoxes de Zénon," *Études d'histoire de la pensée philosophique.* Paris, 1961. Pp. 9–32.

CHIAPELLI. *Sui fragmenti e sulle dottrine di Melisso di Samo* (Rendiconti della Academia degli Lincei). 1890.

G. CALOGERO. *Studi sull'Eleatismo.* Rome, 1932.

R. MONDOLFO. *L'infinità dell' Essere in Melisso.* Sofia, 1933.

J. H. M. LOENEN. *Parmenides, Melissus, Gorgias.* Assen, 1959.

J. BIDEZ. *La biographie d'Empédocle.* Gand, 1894.

E. BIGNONE. *Empedocle, Studio critico.* Turin, 1916.

M. DÉTIENNE. "La 'démonologie' d'Empédocle," *Revue des Études grecques,* LXXII (1959), 1–17.

J. BOLLACK. *Empédocle* (to be published).

J. GEFFCKEN. "Die Asebeia von Anaxagoras," *Hermes,* XLII, No. 1.

F. M. CLEVE. *The Philosophy of Anaxagoras.* 1949.

Œuvres d'Hippocrate. Text and translation by Littré. 10 vols. Paris, 1839–61.

DIÈS. "Les Œuvres d'Hippocrate," *Revue de philosophie,* XXI (1912), 56 and 663.

P.-M. SCHUHL. "Les premières étapes de la philosophie biologique," *Revue d'Histoire des Sciences,* 1952, pp. 197–221.—"Les débuts de la psycho-pharmacologie dans l'antiquité grecque," *Annales Moreau de Tours,* Vol. I, pp. 4–8. Paris, 1953.

L. BOURGEY. *Observation et expérience chez les médecins de la collection hippocratique.* Paris, 1953.

E. FRANCK. *Plato und die sogenannten Pythagoreer.* Halle, 1923.

A. DYROFF. *Demokritstudien.* Munich, 1899.

H. GOMPERZ. *Sophistik und Rhetorik.* Leipzig, 1912.

W. NESTLE. "Die Schrift des Gorgias über die Natur," *Hermes,* LVII (1922), 51.

BODRERO. "Protagoras," *Rivista di filologia,* XXXI, 558.

F. DUPRÉEL. *Les Sophistes.* Neuchâtel, 1948.

M. UNTERSTEINER. *I sofisti.* Turin, 1949.

A. CAPIZZI. *Protagora.* Florence, 1955.

J. ROLLAND DE RENÉVILLE. *Essai sur le problème de l'Un-multiple et de l'attribution chez Platon et les Sophistes.* Paris, 1962.

W. VOLLGRAFF. *L'oraison funèbre de Gorgias.* Leiden, 1952.

SOCRATES

THE CENTURY which preceded the death of Alexander (323) was the great century of Greek philosophy; at the same time it was pre-eminently the Age of Athens. With Socrates and Plato, with Democritus and Aristotle, we reach a climactic moment when philosophy, sure of itself and its methods, claims to base its right to be a universal guide of men on reason itself. It was the time of the founding of the first philosophical institutes, the Academy and the Lyceum. But during the same century the mathematical sciences and astronomy also had an extraordinary growth. Finally, the brilliant development of the systems of Plato and Aristotle must not blind us to the existence of schools issuing from Socrates that were foreign or hostile to the Platonic-Aristotelian development. They provided the doctrines which were to prevail after the death of Alexander and which were to cause Plato and Aristotle to be neglected for a long time.

In the month of February in the year 399, Socrates died at the age of 71, condemned by his fellow citizens. He had been accused before the democratic court of being an impious man who did not honor the gods of the city but introduced new divinities and who corrupted the youth by his teaching.[1] This extraordinary man, unlike the sages we have discussed so far, was not the head of a school. The schools which later invoked the name of Socrates were numerous

[1] On the date of the trial, article by Praechter, 1904, p. 473; concerning the leaders of the accusation, Plato *Apology* 24bc; *Euthyphro* 2d, 3b; Xenophon *Memorabilia* i. 1.

and were opposed to one another on many points; they had no common doctrinal tradition. We can therefore neither reach Socrates directly, since he wrote nothing, nor through a single tradition, but only through many traditions, each giving us a different portrait of him. Let us add that these portraits were by no means meant to be faithful; the earliest one, in the *Clouds* by Aristophanes (written in 423 when Socrates was forty-seven years old) where Socrates is represented on the stage, is a satire. Then, after his death, came the whole literature of the Socratic discourses, dialogues where his disciples give the principal role to their master. These dialogues constitute a literary genre which does not pride itself on accuracy. Foremost among these are the Socratic works of Plato; first, the apologetic dialogues written in the outburst of indignation following the death of his master (*Apology* and *Crito*); then the idealized portraits (*Phaedo, Symposium, Theaetetus, Parmenides*); finally the works where Socrates is only the spokesman for the doctrine of the Academy. Second in rank is the *Memorabilia* of Xenophon, written rather belatedly (about 370), a sort of apology in which the author, who is anything but a philosopher, gives a rather dull imitation of the earlier Socratic discourses under pretense of reproducing the conversations of the master. Among the works on Socrates that have appeared, the one by E. Wolff, who contests the historical accuracy of Plato's *Apology*, and especially the one by O. Gigon, are very skeptical about the possibility of reconstructing Socrates' doctrine. One must add also the titles and very sparse fragments remaining of the dialogues of Phaedo and Aeschines and a few data from Aristotle. Finally there is a tradition hostile to Socrates which persisted to the end of antiquity, in Porphyry (third century) and in the rhetorician Libanius (fourth century), which appeared among the Epicureans and goes back to the pamphlet written by Polycrates in 390;[2] we see, for example, the Epicurean Philodemus of Gadara censuring Socratic irony as a form of pride.[3]

[2] On Polycrates, see Diogenes Laertius *Life of the Philosophers* ii, 38; *Enmity* in Epicurus (Cicero *Brutus* 85), Porphyry *History of the Philosophers*, frags. 8 and 9 (ed. Nauck).

[3] In the *De Vitiis*, col. x, 23, ed. Jansen, and col. xxi, 36–col. xxiii, 37. Cf. on

All agree, certainly, on the strangeness and originality of this sage;
the son of a stonecutter and the midwife Phaenarete, who, clad in a
common cloak and wandering through the streets barefoot, abstaining from wine and delicate fare, extraordinarily robust in temperament, coarse in outer appearance, snub-nosed and with the face of a
Silenus,[4] scarcely resembled the richly attired Sophists who attracted
the Athenians or the sages of former times who were usually important men in their cities: a new type, one which will later become
the lasting model of a thoroughly personal wisdom owing nothing
to circumstances. He was not a political man but simply an excellent
citizen always ready to obey the laws, whether by occupying his
post in the battle of Potidaea or by struggling in the magistracy to
which fate called him against the illegal whims of the tyrant Critias,
or finally by refusing, out of respect for the laws of his country, the
flight Crito proposed to him to escape death after his condemnation.[5]

Neither Sophist nor politician, he had in fact no doctrine and no
legislation to propose in the spontaneous conversations he held in the
market place[6] and in the stadium as well as in the homes of the
rich. Above all else he clearly intended to free his instruction from
the agonistic form. He had no theses to be judged; he merely claimed
that he would have each man become his own judge. In the
dialogues of Plato, Socrates is almost always the troublemaker who
does not want to conform to the rules of the game and who brings
it to an end. Callias advises Socrates and Protagoras, who refuse to
continue the discussion, to "choose an arbiter, an epistate, a Pry-
tanis"; Socrates answers humorously that "it would be improper to
choose an arbiter, since that would be doing Protagoras an injustice" (338b). But the truth is that his aim was to examine theses;

the different forms of irony, Aristotle *Nicomachean Ethics* iv. 7. Montaigne, to the
contrary: "Socrates faict mouvoir son âme d'un mouvement naturel et commun;
. . . d'un pas mol et ordinaire, il traicte les plus utiles discours" (Essais, Lv. III, chap.
xii).

[4] Diogenes Laertius *op. cit.* ii, 18; the comic Ameipsias in *Diogenes* ii, 28; Aristotle
Clouds 410–17; Plato *Symposium* 215 ff., *Crito*.

[5] Plato *Apology* 281; 32c; Diogenes *op. cit.* ii. 24.

[6] A Socratic dialogue of Phaedo bears the name of the shoemaker Simon (Diogenes
op. cit. ii. 105).

to test them out and not to make them win. The scenario of the third part of the *Gorgias* is typical in this respect. The discourse of Callicles against philosophy is a kind of fragment from a competitive contest. Plato indicates this rather clearly by referring several times to Euripides' *Antiope,* a play in which two brothers, in one of those jousts that are routine in tragedy, uphold in turn the superiority of the practical life and the superiority of the life consecrated to the Muses. Like the second of the two brothers, Socrates should have given a defense of philosophy in reply to Callicles. But nothing of the kind; he expresses no opinion himself but by his questions forces Callicles to examine himself. In short, philosophy (and perhaps this is what made it suspicious or at least strange in the eyes of a fifth-century Athenian) is something that cannot take the agonistic form and, consequently, is something that escapes the judgment of the crowd.

He must have educated himself before instructing others; we know nothing about this personal development. The Socrates of the *Clouds* (423) is a man of mature age, and he was over sixty years old when Plato knew him. One valuable document, at least, shows Socrates to be a man of violent passion; it is the testimony of his contemporary Spintharus, whose recollections of Socrates were edited by his son, Aristoxenus: "No one was more persuasive, thanks to his eloquence, the character expressed in his face, and, in a word, the special force of his personality; but only as long as he was not angry. When this passion consumed him, his unseemliness was frightening; there was then no word or act from which he refrained." His self-control was therefore a continual victory over himself.[7]

This inner drive he held in check was no doubt the reason for the power of fascination he had over all ardent natures, that of an Alcibiades[8] as well as that of Plato. The temperament of Socrates was too rich for him to be content with a mere internal reform and not to aspire to spread his wisdom around him. He did not want to live in solitude but with men and for men, to whom he wanted to com-

[7] According to Porphyry *History of the Philosophers* iii. 9 (ed. Nauck).
[8] Cf. *Symposium* 215.

municate the most precious thing he had acquired, mastery of self. Socrates felt this inner force which impelled him toward others as a divine mission. We must insist on this religious characteristic. Was not the answer of the Delphic pythoness to his enthusiastic friend Chaerephon, who was told that no one was wiser than Socrates, the point of departure of his activity at Athens? It was Appollo "who assigned him the task of living as a philosopher, by scrutinizing himself and others." [9] Moreover, there was nothing exceptional at this time in the interpretation Socrates gave to his own special bent. There were other men, like the Euthyphro Plato speaks of, who considered themselves to be in a special relation with the divine.[10] And Socrates in particular seems to have experienced the divine presence within himself through the famous daemon, or rather his daemonic sign, his inner voice, which revealed to him the acts one must avoid in situations where human wisdom is powerless to foresee the future.[11] Yet, we have to be quite clear about this religious aspect of the thought of Socrates: religion gave him faith and confidence in himself, but he inferred no theory about human destiny from it, and there is no reason to believe that he had been an adherent of Orphism.

What did he teach? If Xenophon and Aristotle are to be believed, Socrates was primarily the inventor of moral science and the initiator of the philosophy of concepts. "Socrates," says Aristotle, "dealt with the ethical virtues, and in connection with them, sought universal definitions . . . ; he sought for the what of things. He tried to make syllogisms, and the starting point of syllogisms is the what of a thing. . . . What we may rightly ascribe to Socrates is both inductive arguments and universal definitions, which together constitute the first step in science. But for Socrates the universals and the definitions are not separate existences; it is the Platonists who separate them and they give them the name of ideas." [12]

[9] Plato *Apology* 21a; 28e.

[10] Plato *Euthyphro* 3bc.

[11] Plato *Euthyphro* 3b; *Alcibiades,* 103–5e; Xenophon *Memorabilia* i, 1, 2–4 (the demon as a divinatory sign).

[12] *Metaphysics* M. 4. 1078 b 17; cf. Xenophon *Memorabilia* iv. 6.

Thus, according to Aristotle, Socrates understood that the conditions of moral science lay in the methodical establishment by the inductive method of universal concepts such as justice or courage. This interpretation of Aristotle, whose only purpose was to attribute to Socrates the beginning of the theory of ideas which, through Plato, continued down to his day, is obviously inaccurate. If his purpose had been to define the virtues, we would have to admit that in the dialogues where Plato shows Socrates trying unsuccessfully to define courage (*Laches*), piety (*Euthyphro*), or temperance (*Charmides*), he intended to underline the failure of his master's method. Was it really a theorist of concepts who said of himself that he was "attached to the Athenians through the will of the gods, in order to arouse them as a gadfly would arouse a horse," and that he never ceased to exhort and chide them, besetting them everywhere from morning to night? [13] Socratic teaching really consisted in examining and testing, not concepts, but men themselves, and in inducing them to give an account of themselves and of what they were. Charmides, for example, was universally thought to be the model of a reserved adolescent; but he was ignorant of what modesty or temperance is, and Socrates cross-examined him in a way which showed Charmides his ignorance of himself. Likewise Laches and Nicias were two brave men who were ignorant of what courage is. The holy and pious Euthyphro, questioned in every way, was unable to succeed in saying what piety is. Thus the whole method of Socrates consisted in making men know themselves. His irony consisted in pointing out to them that the task is difficult and that they are wrong in believing that they know themselves. Finally, his doctrine, if he has one, is that this task is necessary, for no one is voluntarily wicked and all evil derives from an ignorance of self which is taken for knowledge. The only knowledge that Socrates claimed to have is that he knew that he knew nothing.[14]

Such a conversation transforms the listener; the contact of Socrates is like that of the electric eel; it paralyzes and disconcerts; it induces

[13] Plato *Apology* 30e.
[14] Plato *Apology* 21b, 23b.

one to consider one's self, to pay attention to an unwonted course.[15] Men of passion, like Alcibiades, well know that they will find in him all the good of which they are capable, but they flee him because they fear this powerful influence which leads them to rebuke themselves. It was especially young men, almost children, that he tried to influence. It is possible that if corruption of the youth was the chief accusation brought against him, it was because he disturbed the prejudices young men had received in their family training. Socrates intervened only to assist them to educate themselves, to draw out all their power. The result of the examination which Socrates impelled his listener to undertake was, in fact, to make him lose his false tranquillity, to put him in disharmony with himself, and to suggest to him as a good the personal effort of recovering this harmony. Socrates, then, possessed no other art but maieutics, his mother Phaenarete's art of delivering; he drew out from souls what they have in them, without any pretension of introducing into them a good whose germ they would not bear.[16]

We cannot form any idea whatever of the extent of the subjects of his conversations. There is no reason to think that Socrates was not a man of culture interested in the sciences and arts. The truth is that everything suited him for testing men, from aesthetic discussions on expression in the arts to the choice of magistrates by lot, where he demonstrated the absurdity of the democratic regime of Athens.[17] Yet, we must note that, in contrast to the criticisms of the Sophists, the criticism of Socrates is focused neither on laws nor on religious practices but only on men and on human qualities. He was as conservative in his political ideas as he was liberal with regard to the men he wanted to reform and whose ignorance he pointed out. It was doubtless this extreme freedom which ruined him. The tyrannical government of Critias had already forbidden him to speak; it was the democracy which took his life.

[15] Plato *Meno* 79 ff.
[16] Plato *Theaetetus* 148 ff.
[17] Xenophon *Memorabilia* iii. 10.

Bibliography

A. Taylor. *Varia Socratica*. Oxford, 1911.—*Socrates*. 1932.

H. Maier. *Sokrates: Sein Werk und seine geschichtliche Stellung*. Tübingen, 1913.

L. Robin. "Les Mémorables de Xénophon et notre connaissance de la philosophie de Socrate," in *La Pensée hellénique des origines à Epicure*. 1942. Pp. 81–137.

E. Horneffer. *Der junge Platon*. 1922.

L. Robin. "Sur une hypothèse récente relative à Socrate," *Revue des Études grecques*, XXIX (1916), 129 (*La Pensée hellénique*. 1942. Pp. 138–76).

A. Diès. *Autour de Platon*. Vol. I, Book 2, Socrate: *La question socratique*. Paris, 1927.

E. Wolff. *Platos Apologie*. 1929.

E. Derenne. *Les Procès d'impiété intentés aux philosophes à Athènes aux Ve et IVe siècles*. Paris, 1930.

F. M. Cornford. *Before and After Socrates*. Cambridge, 1932.

H. Kuhn. *Sokrates*. Berlin, 1934.

O. Gigon. *Sokrates: Sein Bild in Dichtung und Geschichte*. Bern, 1947. (Cf. J. Patočka. "Remarques sur le problème de Socrate," *Revue philosophique*, 1949, p. 186.)

G. Bastide. *Le moment historique de Socrate*. Paris, 1939.

V. de Magalhães-Vilhena. *Le problème de Socrate.—Socrate et la légende platonicienne*. Paris, 1952.

C. Picard. "Nouvelles remarques sur l'apologue dit de Prodicos," *Revue archéologique*, July 1953, pp. 10–41.

Jean Humbert. *Socrate et les petits socratiques*. 1963.

PLATO AND THE ACADEMY

PLATO WAS born in Athens in 427 of an aristocratic family which included various notables in the city, among others his mother's cousin, Critias, who was one of the Thirty Tyrants. His youth was spent in the midst of the most serious political disturbances. In 404 the Peloponnesian War ended in the defeat of Athens, whose maritime empire was destroyed forever. Within the city there was a seesaw game between democracy and oligarchical tyranny. Democracy was overthrown in March, 411, by the oligarchy of the Four Hundred, which lasted only a few months. In 404, the Spartans forced the Athenians to adopt the oligarchical government of the Thirty Tyrants. These tyrants, whose chief was Critias, were thoroughly hostile to seafaring and to Athenian commerce. They fell in September, 403, and were replaced by the democratic government which eventually condemned Socrates. The work of Plato bears the mark of these events. Political instability of governments and the threat of an imperialism based on maritime commerce are the recurrent themes of his political works. As hostile to the tyranny of a Critias as to the democracy of Pericles, he had to search elsewhere than in Athenian surroundings for the possibility of a political renewal. The death of Socrates must have been a definitive reason for the political pessimism which appeared in the *Gorgias* (515c).

It was nine years after Socrates' death that Plato undertook his first great voyage (390–388), which led him first to Egypt, whose venerable antiquity and thorough political stability he never ceased to admire, then to Cyrene, where he made the acquaintance of Theodore, the geometer, finally to Magna Graecia where he met the Pythagoreans and to Sicily where he visited for the first time the tyrant Dionysius of Syracuse and became intimate with his nephew Dion. On his return he founded his school. Near the village of Colonus he bought a piece of land called the Academy, on which he erected a sanctuary of the Muses. This land became the collective property of the school or religious society which annually celebrated the festival of the Muses; it kept the land until the time of Justinian (529 A.D.). What did Plato teach? That is very hard for us to know because most of his works, intended for a large public, are not necessarily a true reflection of his teaching with the exception, however, of the kind of logical exercise which constitutes the second part of the *Parmenides* and the beginnings of the *Theaetetus* and *Sophist*. If we consider that these exercises were intended to test the logical power of the student, that furthermore Plato considered the influence of living speech to be much superior to writing (*Phaedrus*), and finally that speech as understood by a Socratic is less a continuous exposition than a discussion, we may certainly conclude that didactic procedures did not have the importance for him that they had for Aristotle.

Plato made a second trip to Sicily in 366, at the urging of Dion. Dion hoped that he might win over to his ideas Dionysius the Younger who had just succeeded Dionysius the Elder. But on Plato's arrival he found that Dion was in disfavor and exiled, and for a year Plato was the prisoner rather than the guest of the tyrant. In 361, at the urging of Dionysius, he made another trip to Syracuse which was as unfruitful as the first two. Received magnificently and entertained as a friend by the Pythagorean Archytas, tyrant of Tarentum, Plato was unable to reconcile Dion with his cousin. The last ten years of his life were saddened by the conspiracy of Dion against Dionysius (357); the attempt failed and Plato's friend perished tragically, victim of a plot (353).

We derive some information about Plato's trips to Sicily from his letters. We have no similar documents concerning his relations with the Athenian political advisers of his time, notably with Isocrates, who also aspired to be a philosopher. In his *Busiris,* Isocrates opposed the pamphlet by Polycrates against Socrates, but he rather violently criticized certain Socratics, like the cynic Antisthenes. Plato, in the *Phaedrus* (278e–279b) publicly showed his sympathy for this rhetorician who, like himself, had been a companion of Socrates; he thought that there was a philosopher in him. Isocrates, a prudent spirit, a friend of moderate democracy, and an enemy of political utopia, had in the main the same objective as Plato; the defense of Hellenism against the barbarian peril.[1] Plato died in 348 during the war that Philip had undertaken against the Athenians and which was to end in the final political downfall of the Greek city.

During his long career Plato published a large number of dialogues, all preserved, whose chronology may be reconstructed as follows:

1. Dialogues preceding or immediately following the death of Socrates: *Protagoras, Ion, Apology of Socrates, Crito, Euthyphro, Charmides, Laches, Lysis, Republic,* Book I (or *Thrasymachus*), *Hippias Major* (whose authenticity is at present contested), *Hippias Minor,* and *Alcibiades* I.

2. Dialogue preceding the founding of the Academy: *Gorgias.*

3. Dialogue syllabi following close after the founding of the school: *Meno, Menexenus, Euthydemus,* and *Republic,* Books II–X.

4. Dialogues containing the idealized portrait of Socrates: *Phaedo, Symposium,* and *Phaedrus.*

5. Dialogues introducing a new conception of knowledge and dialectic: *Cratylus, Theaetetus, Parmenides, Sophist,* and *Politicus* (the *Sophist* and the *Politicus* were to be followed by the *Philosopher,* which was never written).

6. Last dialogues: *Timaeus, Critias* (not completed), which were to be followed by the *Hermocrates, Laws* (an incomplete work published after the death of Plato which in many places gives the appearance of a collection of notes), and *Epinomis.*

[1] G. Mathieu, *Les idées politiques d'Isocrate* (Paris, 1925), pp. 177–81.

We must add the names of the dialogues which modern criticism rejects: *Alcibiades II, Rivals, Theages, Clitophon, Minos,* and *Hipparchus.*

Finally, the thirteen *Letters* preserved under the name of Plato—whose authenticity has been contested to the point that they have been considered fragments of exercises of Athenian rhetoricians—are today acknowledged to be authentic for the most part, notably the long letter vii, addressed to the friends of Dion and filled with details about the relations between Dionysius and Plato.

1 *Plato and Platonism*

Since the time immediately after Plato's death, there has been disagreement about the meaning of his dialogues. From antiquity to our own day we see divergent doctrines ascribed to him. In the time of Cicero, for example, some ascribed to Plato a dogmatism similar to that of the Stoics. Others saw in him an advocate of doubt and of suspension of judgment. A little later, beginning in the first century, the mystics and the restorers of Pythagoreanism seized upon the name and writings of Plato and Platonism became synonymous with a doctrine which raises the soul above Thought and Being and unites it with a Good which is beloved and delighted in rather than known. On the other hand, we see the emergence in the nineteenth century of a tendency, still very strong, to make Plato a pure rationalist who identified true reality with the object of intelligence and taught how to ascertain this object by a reasoned discussion whose model is borrowed from mathematics.[2]

Such a variety of interpretations is to be explained not only by the exceptional richness of his thought, all of whose aspects it is perhaps impossible and in any event very difficult to grasp at one time, but also by the literary form in which it is clothed. Let us dwell first on the second point. The Platonic dialogue is not at all like a didactic treatise, whose model had already been provided by the

[2] Cicero *Academica Posteriora* i. 15–18; Apuleius, *On the God of Socrates;* Natorp, *Platos Ideenlehre* (1903).

Ionian philosophers and the physicians of the Hippocratic collection. Only in the works of Plato's old age do we see something like that. All the physiological considerations at the end of the *Timaeus* and a good part of the *Laws* are simple exposition. But they are the works which Plato did not, except in certain parts, put into final form. Save for these exceptions, the works of Plato have an aspect which sets them quite apart; for, if dialogues were written in the Socratic schools nearly contemporary with Plato, this form of exposition was soon almost completely abandoned in spite of some occasional examples one could offer, such as the dialogues of Cicero or Plutarch. It is especially significant that the Neo-Platonists at the end of antiquity never imitated the literary methods of the master and tried in every possible way to find dogmatic substance in a dialogue. It is all the more important to seek to appreciate the literary form of Platonic thought, since it enters into the interpretation of his philosophy.

II *The Literary Form*

The Platonic dialogue has three aspects combined in varying degrees: it is a drama; it is nearly always a discussion; and it sometimes contains a continuous exposition.

First, a drama: sometimes the place, time, and circumstances are precisely indicated, as in the *Protagoras* (309a–310a); the dialogue is itself often inserted in a narrative, as in the *Symposium* (172–174); at other times, on the contrary, and this is more frequent as Plato progresses, the dialogue opens abruptly.[3] There are dialogues whose dramatic aspect is especially evident by the life of the characters and by the reversals which hold the reader breathless. There are others where drama has nearly disappeared, although there are none, even the most arid, the *Philebus* or the *Sophist,* for example, which do not contain some traces of humor and satire.[4] As to characters, Socrates comes first, then those with whom Socrates had been in

---

[3] In *Theaetetus* (143b), he even criticizes the first procedure.
[4] *Philebus* 15 ff.; *Sophist* 241d.

close association: Sophists or foreign philosophers, young men of noble Athenian families, political men in the city. In every case, as in the comedies of Aristophanes, the characters were known by everybody, several were still living, and many had family ties with Plato. Only the dialogues of his old age introduce fictitious characters, as the stranger in the *Sophist* and the *Laws* or the *Philebus*.

We know the partiality with which he described Socrates, the Socrates of the *Protagoras,* still young and without authority in the midst of rich and famous Sophists, the Socrates fully aware of his moral and social mission in the *Apology,* the man who disturbs the conscience of Alcibiades (*Symposium*) and who, disclosing to Meno his ignorance, benumbs him as a torpedo-fish would do, the "midwife of minds" of the *Theaetetus,* finally the advocate of the philosophic life in the *Gorgias* and the *Meno.* After that Socrates disappears, and with him the dramatic life of the dialogue. It is most unlikely that the young Socrates, who in the *Phaedo* (97c ff.) had instructed himself by reading Anaxagoras or, in the *Parmenides* (128e ff.), had submitted the theory of ideas to the old philosopher of Elea could be other than Plato himself.

Around Socrates is a whole populace of Sophists, rhetoricians, exegetes, poets, and prophets, whose wisdom is put to the test by the master. Plato parodies them fairly mercilessly: Hippias, who boasted of teaching and practicing all the arts; Protagoras, who could not end a discussion on the possibility of teaching justice without recounting a myth; Gorgias the rhetorician, who intended his instruction to be purely technical and who did not concern himself with the justice of his case; Ion, the interpreter of Homer, who followed only his inspiration, as the poet himself did; Euthyphro, the self-styled saint, who tried to avoid religious defilement rather than injustice.

Next come the young men: from Charmides, of noble birth, cousin of Plato's mother, typifying that reserve, that decency in attitude and speech called "*sophrosyne,*" to the Callicles of the *Gorgias,* the ambitious man of low birth, intelligent and cultured and full of an intense desire to impose himself on the Athenians.

Finally, the citizens and politicians of Athens: Critias the tyrant, a relative of Plato who shows himself to be violent and without respect for Socrates in the *Charmides;* Laches and Nicias, excellent soldiers, completely involved in discussions of strategy when asked what a young man ought to learn; the disturbing figure of Anytus in the *Meno,* the conservative citizen who fears Socrates' intellectual freedom and who will accuse him before the judges.

Several dialogues have a dramatic progression and contain crises, as plays do. Sometimes the scenario is borrowed from everyday life, as in the *Symposium,* where after drinking each guest speaks in praise of love; at other times it is borrowed from the dramatic events of the trial and death of Socrates. But occasionally the development arises from the very personalities of the characters; thus it often happens that dialogue is interrupted by the impatience of a listener, who refuses to submit any longer to the examination of Socrates: when Socrates has to deal with a hotheaded character, like Callicles in the *Gorgias,* the dialogue threatens to end at any moment.[5] It is the *Gorgias* which, as a whole, gives us the finest example of a dramatic progression. There are three perfectly connected episodes: Socrates' three conversations with Gorgias, Polus, and Callicles. Gorgias, seeing only the technical side of the orators' training, is incapable of giving his art any moral purpose. Polus will not use rhetoric for an evil end but only because he is timid and respects prejudices. But let a violent person like Callicles come along: he will find in the school of Gorgias not a restraint, but an instrument for the expression of his violence. In this fashion all consequences of the intellectual attitude of Gorgias are developed in a living and dramatic manner.

In view of this intense vitality, many have wondered whether Plato may not have intended to describe living persons, disguised as interlocutors of Socrates who were for the most part long since dead. It is certain that Plato was not careful about chronology in the way one would expect if he did really intend to describe persons of the time of Socrates' youth or maturity. Moreover, some of these

[5] For example, *Gorgias* 479b, 505cd, 506d.

persons, even in the dialogues of the first or second periods, are unknown to us: Callicles, for example, or the Sophists, Euthydemus and Dionysodorus, whom Plato gives principal roles in the dialogue *Euthydemus*. Nevertheless, one has no right whatever to equate any of these figures, known or not, with contemporaries of Plato. The truth seems to be that most of Plato's portraits are stylized; though pulsating with life, they assume a universal quality, and Plato is thus able to introduce naturally with these persons his own concerns and the concerns of his time.

Whether or not a dialogue has dramatic interest, the permanent and substantial part, with certain exceptions, is the *discussion*. To a question (for example: What is justice? or, Can virtue be taught?), the respondent answers with a formula. This is subjected to scrutiny in accordance with the single rule indicated in the *Meno* (75d): "On the part of the respondent, the discussion [or dialectic] consists not only in giving true answers, but answers which are derived from the conspectus of his knowledge." The discussion, therefore, implies a whole series of accepted postulates or hypotheses with which the definition to be discussed is confronted, in order to see whether or not it is in accord with them. The first definition refuted, the respondent proposes a second, then a third, and so on, often without ending in any definite result. Thus Charmides, in the dialogue bearing his name, when questioned by Socrates about the nature of *sophrosyne* answers that it consists "in acting with order and deliberation" (159b). But since Charmides acknowledges, on the other hand, that *sophrosyne* is among the finest things and that it is finer to act rapidly than deliberately, it follows that there is a discord between his formula and what he himself acknowledges to be true. He must, therefore, abandon it and propose another.

Discussion or dialectic, then, is not at all a confronting of two opposed opinions, each maintained by one speaker as in the contests of the Sophists; the respondent alone expresses positive opinions. Socrates "knows nothing, except that he knows nothing"; his only role is to examine the respondent or to put him to the test by showing him whether or not he is in agreement with himself.

In principle, Platonic dialectic will always remain what it first was in the Socratic dialogues. The *Theaetetus* examines successively the different opinions of Theaetetus on knowledge, as the *Hippias Major* refutes the successive opinions of Hippias on beauty. Nevertheless, the outward plan and the meaning do seem to change gradually. The Socratic dialogues are, in fact, at least as much an examination of persons as an examination of their opinions; the interest actually lies rather in the first than in the second. The concepts of temperance, courage, and piety are not objects of study in and for themselves. The main thing is to find out whether those who possess or think they possess these virtues know them; in a word, whether they really know themselves. The benefit of the discussion will be "self-knowledge."

It does seem that as Plato receded from the Socratic influence his center of interest shifted and turned from persons to the realities themselves. Consequently he attached more value to the conclusions he reached. Compare, for example, the *Protagoras* with the *Meno*. They deal with the same subject: Can virtue be taught? But in the first of these dialogues, Socrates is content to show that Protagoras is in disagreement with himself, since he first answers yes and then no; it is the claim of Protagoras rather than the subject itself that is examined. In the *Meno,* on the other hand, Plato, having certainly become the head of the Academy by this time, indicates positive methods of research and of teaching.[6] Even more, the Socratic method is entirely forgotten in the later dialogues. In the *Philebus* (11b), for instance, dialectic no longer consists in the examination of the respondent by Socrates; it includes two opposed theses which confront each other, one of which is maintained by Socrates himself.

Thus, in the course of Plato's literary career, dialectic gradually lost in dramatic and human interest and tended to be transformed into an impersonal method which deals with a problem for its own sake.

The third aspect we distinguished in Plato's works was continuous exposition. In the works of the first and second periods continuous

[6] Compare *Protagoras* 361ad and *Meno* 86c, 87b.

exposition appears in two forms, which have a great affinity for one another: the *speech* which defends a thesis is generally put in the mouth of the interlocutors of Socrates, and very often it has the character of a parody. The Sophists expounded their opinion in formal lectures and Plato enjoys imitating the style of Protagoras, Prodicus, or Gorgias.[7] Sometimes there are speeches which, although not strictly speaking lectures of Sophists, are very similar to them: such are the eulogies of love in the *Symposium,* where Plato parodies in turn the styles of the rhetoricians Lysias (in the speech of Phaedrus), Prodicus (Pausanias), Hippias (Eryximachus), and Gorgias (the speech of Agathon).[8] Such also is the speech of Callicles in the Gorgias; or the speech of Lysias in the *Phaedrus* which is intended to give a concrete example of defects in the techniques of the orators. But in every case these continuous speeches serve in some way as a contrast with the really scientific method of research, which is dialectic. Socrates "does not possess the art of long speeches" (*Protagoras,* 336b), and if these interlocutors, following their natural bent, try to evade discussion by delivering a speech (like Protagoras), if they are always ready, like Callicles, to give up the struggle when Socrates does not allow them to speak, then Socrates, on his part, complains that Protagoras does not want to distinguish between "a discussion among men who are gathered together and a speech addressed to the people" (*ibid.*). In a speech one is concerned only with persuading the listener by flattering his prejudices but not with searching for truth and self-consistency.

Yet, Plato did not maintain this hostile attitude toward the art of speaking throughout his career, and he seems to have given it an increasing place. Methods of persuasion retain their importance and value, when it is a matter of imposing views which do not admit rigorous demonstration. Let us compare in this respect the *Laws,* a work of his old age, and the *Republic.* In the *Laws* there is no longer any discussion; rather there are long prologues for each cate-

---

[7] *Protagoras* 320c–323a, 337bc; *Hippias* i. 291d; *Gorgias* 48c.

[8] Phaedrus, Pausanias, Eryximachus, Agathon were students of each of these orators or Sophists.

gory of law, designed to produce conviction rather than to prove. Such is the famous prologue to the laws concerning religion in Book X.[9] This procedure of Plato has had an immense influence and we have in it, in more than outline form, the moral preaching which will later become almost the whole of philosophy. As early as the *Phaedrus* (269c ff.), moreover, Plato pointed out how a reform of eloquence was possible and how by associating it with dialectic one could give order and consistency to speech. In the same dialogue he gave an example of stately and oratorical style (245c ff.) which contrasts with the malicious liveliness of the first dialogues.

As for myth, we first see it as an ornament in a speech; as such it belongs to the Sophists or the orators whom Plato parodied—the myth of Prometheus in Protagoras, for example,[10] or that of the birth of love in the speeches of the *Symposium*. But very early, as early as the *Gorgias,* Plato put myths into the mouth of Socrates. These myths have certain precise characteristics which contrast strongly with the kind of myth that is purely an oratorical ornament. In the first place, they are not parts of a more extensive speech but treatises in themselves. Such are the myths at the end of the *Gorgias* (523a) and the *Republic* (x. 614b). In both cases, the discussion is exhausted and the concept of justice is clarified when the myth begins; they are added to the discussion without forming a part of it. In the second place, these myths never concern the genealogy of the gods but only the destiny of the soul or, more generally, human history. Myths concerning the future life had naturally been linked since the *Odyssey* with a fantastic geography describing the land of ghosts. This kind of geography assumes a more and more important place in the Platonic myth. Whereas the *Gorgias* scarcely goes beyond Homeric notions, the *Phaedo* speculates about the reliefs of the terrestrial surface. The *Republic* (616c–617b) and the *Phaedrus* (247c) in particular closely connect the history of the soul with an astronomical system; the whole world is like a stage on which the souls of men and of the gods evolve. One might almost say that

[9] On the importance of persuasion, the *Laws* 903ab.
[10] *Protagoras* 320c–323a.

astronomical speculations were never introduced in Plato except in the interests of the myth of the soul. The mechanism of things is such (*Laws* x. 904b) that the soul is naturally attracted to the places where it has to submit to its punishment or enjoy its reward. The truth of the matter is that the world itself is a great living and animated being. The *Timaeus*, which takes the form of a narrative or myth, tells how the soul of the world was formed and formed a body for itself. This religious astronomy later had a considerable influence.

At times, although rarely, myth is also oriented toward legend in the form of a historic narrative, as in an incomplete dialogue of Plato's old age, the *Critias*, where prehistoric Athens and Atlantis are described.

Finally, we must add that in the *Timaeus* (61c to the end) the continuous exposition of the myth is connected without suture to another form of continuous exposition, the physiological or medical treatise. At the end of the dialogue the experimental sciences, as the Ionians or the physicians conceived them, make a fugitive and late appearance, and naturally are not expressed in any of the literary forms we have mentioned.

In judging the philosophy of Plato, it is impossible to disregard this extraordinary complexity of forms: tragedy and comedy, dialectic, continuous speeches, and myths—forms which are mixed in different proportions and which in addition undergo their own changes corresponding to the different periods.

III *The Goal of Philosophy*

The thing that gives unity to all these forms, the thing that in some way necessitates them, is the desire to establish the place of the philosopher in the city-state and his moral and social mission. In the Greece of that time, the philosopher was not defined by relation to other kinds of investigators, scientific or religious, but rather by his relation to, and his differences from, the orator, Sophist, and politician. Philosophy was the discovery of a new form of intellectual life, which, moreover, could not be separated from social life. The dialogues describe this life for us, and, with it, all the tragedies and comedies issuing from it. In certain respects philosophy went counter to customs that were firmly implanted in Greece at this time, and it inevitably produced conflicts whose tragic consequence was the death of Socrates.

What is the philosopher? There are many portraits of him in Plato. In the *Phaedo* (64e ff.), he is the man who has purified himself from the defilements of the body, no longer lives except in the soul, and does not fear death, since after this life his soul is separated from the body. In the *Theaetetus* (172c–177c), he is the man who is inept and awkward in his relations with others, who will never be at ease in human society, and who will remain uninfluential in the city. In the *Republic,* he is the leader of the city, and in the *Laws* (x. 909a), he has actually become a kind of inquisitor who, desiring "the salvation of the soul" of the citizens, prescribes for the inhabitants of the town belief in the gods of the city under threat of life imprisonment. Finally, he is the enthusiast and inspired man of the *Phaedrus* (244a ff.) and the *Symposium* (210a). In these successive portraits there are two outstanding traits which seem to contradict one another. On the one hand the philosopher has "to flee from here," [11] to purify himself, to live in contact with realities of which the Sophist and the politician are ignorant. On the other hand he has to build the just city which reflects in its social relations the exact and rigorous relations studied by science. On the one hand, the philosopher is the scholar withdrawn from the world; on the other hand, he is the wise and just man, the true politician who gives laws to the city. Was not Plato himself at one and the same time the founder of the Academy, the friend of mathematicians and of astronomers, but also the counselor of Dion and of Dionysius the tyrant? Besides, if as philosopher he was the discoverer or advocate of a rigorous logic, he was also the man of inspiration whose mind would remain barren without the impulse of Eros and who can only

[11] *Theaetetus* 176a.

beget in the beautiful.[12] To rational discussion is added a dialectic of love, expressed by lyrical effusions and mystical contemplations.[13] Scholar and mystic, philosopher and politician, these are characteristics which ordinarily occur separately and which we will not find together in the course of this history with the exception of several great reformers of the nineteenth century. That is why it is important to understand clearly what connected them.

IV *Socratic Dialectic and Mathematics*

First of all, what is Platonic science? It is characterized by intimate union between the object of knowledge and the method by which it is reached. Here is a point of prime importance which we cannot stress too much. We see Plato starting from what is ordinarily called the Socratic concept, but which he himself already called the "idea" (*eidos*)—courage, virtue, or piety—which, as he says in the *Euthyphro* (6d), is "the single character by which every pious act is pious" and which is used "as of a term of comparison to declare that everything that is similar is pious." The idea, then, is a characteristic which resides in things themselves but which can only be separated by Socratic examination. We are not certain, in fact, that the formula reached by the respondent really expresses the idea until it has withstood this examination and passed the test successfully. Neither revelation nor immediate intuition can dispense with this. Moreover, method is here much more important than the object. Socrates himself never arrived at the idea; but he disciplined the mind and removed its illusions.

Socratic inquiry confined itself to moral matters. Following the testimony of Aristotle,[14] we can grant that Plato only extended the method to ideas which were not in the sphere of action and that he "separated" these ideas, that is to say conferred a distinct reality on

[12] *Symposium* 203c ff., 206c.
[13] *Ibid*. 210e.
[14] *Metaphysics* M. 4. 1078b 17.

them. But in what way did this transformation take place? Did it have the purely arbitrary character which Aristotle gave it? It does not seem so: the *separation* of ideas, which makes them realities superior to sensible things, appears to coincide with the place that Plato gave to mathematics.

By using a rigorous method, mathematics can reach positive conclusions, Socrates notwithstanding. How and why? It is due to a process which Plato calls hypothesis and which he very clearly defines in the *Meno* (87a):

When one asks a geometer about a surface, for example whether a certain triangle can be inscribed in a certain circle, he will reply: "I do not know yet if this surface lends itself to it; but I believe it proper, in order to find out, to reason by hypothesis in the following manner. If this surface is such that the parallelogram of the same surface applied to a given line falls short of such surface, the result will be this; otherwise it will be that."

This method is an analysis which consists in proceeding from the conditioned to the condition, aiming above all to establish a relation of logical implication between two propositions while leaving aside temporarily the question whether the condition itself is realized. The condition can be the object of an analogous investigation and can itself be related to a condition which is assumed to hold.

Mathematical analysis is thus substituted for Socratic discussion in the *Meno*. Now, the existence and the *separation* of ideas are presented to us in the *Phaedo* with perfect clarity as resulting from the application of the method of analysis to the problem of the explanation of things as it was posed by physics. Plato tells how, having observed that the natural philosophers could not arrive at the explanation of the simplest facts, Socrates was won over by a book of Anaxagoras, where he read that "intelligence was the orderer and cause of all things" (87c). But in proceeding with his reading of Anaxagoras, he perceived that in the explanation of details of phenomena—of the shape of the earth or the movements of the stars, for example—intelligence does not intervene at all and that Anaxagoras has recourse to air, ether, water. He would explain that Socrates was seated in prison, not because he refused to escape, but because his physical organism had such or such a property. It was then that in order to solve physical problems Socrates decided to leave entirely out of account the realities given by sight or the other sensations and to attempt, in a "second reading," to use the method already indicated in the *Meno;* namely "to posit hypothetically the definition that I would judge to be the most sound, then to posit as true that which agrees with this definition, as untrue that which does not agree with it." In the problem of the explanation of things, this definition is the one which affirms the existence of ideas: "We will assume that there exists a beauty in itself, a good in itself, a greatness in itself, and so for the rest," and if a thing is beautiful without being beauty in itself, it will be explained by saying that it "participates" in beauty in itself. Plato's meaning becomes very clear when he compares his mode of explanation with that of the natural philosophers. In explaining, say, how two things form a pair, the natural philosopher tells us either that two things originally at some distance from each other have come close together or else that one and the same thing was divided into two. He thus gives us two contradictory explanations of the same fact, or rather he does not explain it. No physical operation can explain the genesis of the dyad; for the dyad exists in itself, independently of all physical operations, like an object of mathematics: it is by participation in this dyad in itself that every pair of two things arises.[15]

We see how the theory of ideas is tied to the analytic method or method of hypothesis. The method is in fact more extensive and broader than the theory of ideas, which is only one particular application of it. That is the whole spirit of Platonism to which the dogmatisms that are to follow will be so plainly opposed. For Plato, as for Socrates, the impulse of thought remains more important than its outcome.

[15] *Phaedo* 99c–100d; cf. 101e.

v *Platonic Dialectic*

But the analytic method poses a grave problem, foreseen in the *Phaedo* and treated at length in the *Republic*. According to this method, after a hypothesis has been used in a demonstration, it must itself be derived from a further hypothesis; but in this regression to conditions one has to stop at a terminal point which is "enough in itself" (*Phaedo* 101d) and which is not itself merely assumed (*Republic* 511b). Now here mathematics abandons us completely. In order to solve its problems it assumes straight lines or curves, even or uneven numbers; but these assumptions remain assumptions which can only be justified by a higher science, by a dialectic which arrives at the unconditioned. When Plato refers to this terminal point by the expressions "Good" or "idea of the Good" (508e), his meaning is tolerably clear: he means that the only definitive explanation one can give of a thing is that it is good or that it participates in the Good. According to the later dialogues, one can assume that, starting from the time he wrote the *Republic,* he reasoned in the same way as in the *Timaeus*. In the *Timaeus* (29e–30a), the mathematical relations or geometrical forms which are *assumed* by the astronomer to explain the motions of the stars are themselves only *explained* by the fact that they realize a plan of the Demiurge, a plan deriving from his goodness; goodness is what everything presupposes, without presupposing anything at all. What Aristotle will call the final cause is the true and absolute cause, which gives the last explanation. Like the virtues themselves, justice and beauty are worth nothing if one does not know "by what they are good" (506a). The Good is like a sun in whose light other things are known in their reason for being and by whose warmth they exist. "The Good is not then a being; it is beyond being in dignity and in power" (506b).

One can only hope to understand this enigmatic passage in the *Republic* about the idea of the Good by taking account of the problem it is intended to solve. In the *Phaedo*, Plato had used the general term "reflection" (*dianoia*) for the kind of thinking which proceeds by discovering hypotheses. But how can we know that the condition we have reached in going from hypothesis to hypothesis is itself no longer a hypothesis? Certainly not by the logical relation of dependence which all the others have to it, because that would not distinguish it from another hypothesis. We can only recognize it by a direct intellectual intuition (*noesis*) and a sort of vision; it cannot justify itself in any other way (*Republic* 511d).

From this results the rule of the philosopher, as he is described in the seventh book of the *Republic*. At the base of his intellectual development are the four sciences which use the "hypothetical method": arithmetic, geometry, astronomy, music. Plato takes the greatest care to indicate that he only accepts these sciences to the extent in which they use this method; he omits everything which might involve observation by the senses, everything which is not demonstrative. Arithmetic, for example, is not the art of counting —useful to the merchant or the strategist—but the science which discerns numbers in themselves, independently of sensible things (525e). In the same way, geometry is not surveying (526d), and Plato found an actual proof of this in a new branch of the science which he always considered very important. This new branch was stereometry or the science of regular solids, which is no longer a measurement of surfaces at all but is intermediate between geometry proper and astronomy (528a). Astronomy, which only admits combinations of uniform motions in order to explain the motion of the stars and planets, is therefore quite far from the observation of planets, which only presents irregular motions to the eye (530a–d). Finally, the musician who tunes his instrument by trial and error is not the scientist who discovers the simple numerical relations which make up the chords (531ab). By forcing us to rise to hypotheses by means of thought alone, apart from sensible things, these four sciences thus draw us toward Being, toward true realities (533ab).

But this is only a preparation. Above these sciences there is dialectic. The true dialectician is the "synoptic" thinker, the thinker who does not keep the sciences in a scattered state but sees their relationships with one another and with Being (537c); the thinker, in a word, who connects the many hypotheses with their one source, the Good, and by knowledge of the Good, the greatest knowledge of all, illuminates them and shows their reality.

VI *The Origin of Knowledge: Reminiscence and Myth*

In order fully to understand the mature Plato, it is most important to have these two planes of intellectual knowledge always in mind. A whole series of problems is bound up with their differentiation. In the first place, the purely Socratic Plato who contented himself with testing formulas or solutions given by his respondent left the origin of these formulas entirely vague. Yet, what chance did they have of agreeing with reality if they were wholly arbitrary? That is the meaning of the sophistic question put by Meno;[16] investigation is impossible if we are entirely ignorant about the thing we are seeking, as it is unnecessary if we know what it is. Therefore, the respondent's mind must already have been turned toward reality; he must therefore have already known this reality, and research and knowledge must be only a "recollection" (81d). If the mind can discover truths by simple reflection (guided or not by the master's questions) it is because it already possessed them in itself; it is by simple reflection that the slave questioned by Socrates discovered that the square which is the double of another is the one which is constructed upon the diagonal (82b–85b). But to discover a truth one already possesses is to recollect. The theory of recollection, moreover, is not at all an idle theory but a stimulating one. Because of it "we must be courageous and force ourselves to seek and to recover the memory of the things whose memory we have lost" (81d–86b). Because of it we become "better, more energetic, less indolent." Recollection was the first name given to the autonomy of the mind in its quest.

But this theory, in turn, implies solemn affirmation of the pre-

[16] *Meno* 8od.

existence of the soul (81b). The immortality of the soul, which Plato doubted in his first dialogues,[17] now becomes a condition of knowledge. A dry and abstract assertion of pre-existence is not enough. Plato doubtless thought that this belief would take shape only if it could be presented in a myth. In its first form in the *Gorgias* (523a) the myth of the soul existing separately from the body was quite removed from the problems of the *Meno*. It only told how the work of justice continued after death. In the dialogues that followed, the myth undoubtedly preserves the same character for the most part and remains the story of a divine judgment. Yet a place is provided (and in the *Phaedrus* [248a–c] this is a very large one) for the way in which the soul, before entering into the body, acquired knowledge of realities which it will remember during its terrestrial life. While accompanying the gods in the heavens on their circular course, it has seen in "a place beyond the heavens" those realities "without color and without shape" which are ideas: justice in itself, temperance, knowledge. Having descended into a body, those souls whose circumstances have allowed them to see the best become the souls of philosophers, capable of recollection.

Thus, in the *Phaedrus* ideas become constituent elements of the myth of the soul. They are localized beyond the sensible world in the supracelestial place which the soul perceives. Possibly this tendency to give ideas a sort of mythical and imaginative reality is a stumbling block in the philosophy of Plato. But one can see how it depends on the theory of recollection which is itself a condition of knowledge. Myth and science, if science wants to go beyond mathematical hypotheses, are connected by an indissoluble bond.

VII *Knowledge and the Dialectic of Love*

In the *Meno* the recollection of ideas is very closely connected with the possibility of having right opinions without the ability to justify them; in other words, without having scientific knowledge of them (97c–98c). Thus the celebrated politicians of Athens—Aristides

[17] *Apology of Socrates* 29ab.

or Pericles—who governed the city ably had no political science; that is to say, no methodical knowledge meriting the name of art. Otherwise, they would have been capable of teaching and transmitting it; but they were not even able to make statesmen of their own children (93c–94c). But for practical purposes, when action alone is in question, right opinion is equivalent to science. As this opinion is neither innate in the individual nor acquired by instruction, it must come from divine inspiration (99c, 100b). This inspiration is among the favors conferred by the gods on the city of Athens. This is an idea which could not have surprised any of Plato's listeners; for a Greek, the city was necessarily under the protection of the gods it worshipped. Just as recollection in the *Meno* is embodied in the myth of the pre-existence of the soul in the *Phaedrus,* inspiration also calls forth its mythical complement, which will make the imagination grasp the influences which are at work in the soul; this is the myth of Eros in the *Symposium* and the *Phaedrus.* Plato connects philosophic inspiration with a whole group of facts of the same general kind. Philosophic inspiration is itself an aspect of amorous madness; philosophy for Plato was what it had been for Socrates, not solitary meditation, but creativity of mind in the soul of the disciple. "One engenders only in beauty" and under the influence of love (*Symposium* 206c). Love tends toward immortality, the love of beautiful bodies which continues the life of one individual in another as well as the love of beautiful souls which awakens the dormant powers of intelligence in the master as in the disciple (206d, 208b). The life of the mind is thus grafted, as it were, to the life of the body. From instinctive desire which impels the living thing to engender its like, up to the sudden vision of eternal and imperishable beauty, there is a continuous progress which is a progress in generality. This is the progress of being stirred not by the beauty of a single body, but by all physical beauty. Above physical beauty is the beauty of souls, of actions, and of science, and still higher is the immense sea of Beauty from which all these beautiful things have sprung (209e–212a).

Plato stressed at length the daemonic nature of love. It seems that daemons play a role of very great importance in religious worship; they are intermediaries between men and the gods, bringing to the gods the requests of men and to men the gifts of the gods. Eros is one of these daemons, the son of Poros and Penia who combines the poverty of his mother with the ingenuity and fruitful intellectual resources of his father: he is the type and, as it were, the artist's model of philosophers. He symbolizes all there is in them in the way of inspiration and impulse. In the emotional world he is what mathematics is in the intellectual world. He attracts toward the Beautiful as mathematics attracts toward Being (202e–203c).

Just as Eros personified is one of many daemons, amorous madness is also a species within a larger genus which comprises any "madness coming from the gods" (*Phaedrus* 245b). Here Plato was thinking in particular of religious beliefs and practices associated with a way of divination whose social importance was immense, the prophecies of the Delphic pythoness "who conferred so many benefits on Greece thanks to her madness, and who, when in her right mind, conferred none" (244b). The madness of the prophet who foretells the future is compared to the madness of the poet possessed by the Muses. It is with these two kinds of delirium, whose value every Greek accepted, that Plato proceeded to compare the delirium of the lover. Its value is as great, because it is the agitation of a soul who discovers in sensible things the image of eternal beauty which it contemplated when it lived in the company of the gods before its terrestrial life. Madness is therefore the point of departure of philosophy, and it gives back the soul its wings (249a–250e). It stings the soul just as Socrates, the perfect lover of the *Symposium* (216a), is in the *Apology* (30e) the gadfly that arouses the Athenians.

The theme of Eros and, more generally, the theme of divine inspiration lays bare the emotional basis of Platonic knowledge. For Plato philosophy is not a purely and narrowly intellectual method:

The organ by which we understand is like the eye, which cannot turn toward the light unless the whole body turns. In the same way the whole soul has to be converted from becoming to being. . . . There are wicked persons who are clever and whose small soul has a sharp and penetrating vision . . . ; but the more penetration their soul has, the more evil they do! [*Republic* 518e ff.].

The vision of these mediocre men is contrasted with the vision of the Beautiful, which originates in love and which completes the initiation in love.

Moreover, myth connects the philosophic life with the whole of human destiny and so with the whole universe, which is its stage. The fall of the soul from heaven to earth, its avatars on earth, its conversion, and its return to the vision from which it set out; these are fundamentally the things that make up the myth of the *Phaedrus* and the allegory of the cave in the *Republic*. The fallen soul of the *Phaedrus* (246c) is the prisoner in the *Republic* who, placed in a dark cave, his back turned to the daylight, sees nothing but a fairly steady succession of unreal shadows on the back of the cave until dialectic comes to convert him toward the light (514a–516a).

VIII *Developments of the Hypothesis of Ideas*

Let us now return to the development of Plato's philosophy proper. We have seen how the method of hypothesis uses discursive reasoning, which is content to see how consequences are linked to hypotheses. But this method would still be incomplete if, having used hypotheses, one were not to examine them in themselves to see whether or not they are justified. Thus in the *Phaedo* Plato used ideas and participation in ideas as a hypothesis, in order to solve the problem of physical causality and to prove the immortality of the soul. But once these problems are solved, the value of the hypothesis itself must be tested.

Plato subjects the theory of ideas to a test of precisely this kind at the beginning of the *Parmenides* (130a–135c). And, before examining it, Plato actually posits it as a hypothesis enabling him to solve the difficulties which Zeno, the disciple of Parmenides, raised against the existence of multiplicity (128e–130a). If we posit

separately on the one hand ideas, and on the other hand things which participate in them, we can indeed easily conceive how the same thing can be one and many. The one and the many exist separately from the thing, and the thing participates in these two ideas at the same time. It is thus that the same thing can be without contradiction like and unlike, large and small.

Plato shows us the aged Parmenides smiling before the earnestness of the young Socrates, who expounds this solution. Parmenides does not say whether it takes into account the difficulty Zeno raised against the many, but he examines it in itself. First, the participation of things in ideas is impossible. For if several things participate in one and the same idea, either the idea is completely in each of them, and then the idea is separated from itself, which is absurd; or, it exists only in part in them, and then one would have to say that an idea, such as that of the small, is necessarily greater than each of its own parts, which is absurd (131a–e). Besides, the purpose of the theory of ideas is to affirm each idea as one; the idea of the "great," for example, beyond the multiplicity of terms which are all great. But this unity is impossible; for if we have the right to posit a greatness in itself beyond the many greatnesses, on grounds of their similarity, it will be necessary for the same reason to posit another greatness in itself beyond the many greatnesses and the first greatness, and thus ad infinitum (131e–132b). Shall we say, in order to answer the first difficulty, that the relation between the thing which participates in the idea and the idea is not the relation of part to whole but of a portrait to its model? Then, inversely, the model will have to resemble the portrait; the idea will have to be similar to the thing. But according to the principles of the theory there is resemblance only where there is participation in one and the same idea; it will therefore be necessary to posit beyond the thing and the idea another idea in which they both participate, and so to infinity (132a–133a). Finally, there is an inconsistency between the nature of the idea and the function for which it is designed. It is to be an object of knowledge. But it is evident that it cannot even be known by us, for if it exists in itself, it cannot exist in us; a reality in itself can only be known by knowledge in itself, in which we have no part. Inversely, to attribute to God knowledge in itself or knowledge of ideas is to deny him knowledge of things external to ideas (133b–134e).

According to this critique, everything that seemed to give value to the hypothesis of ideas vanishes. An idea does not explain things, since participation is impossible.[18] It is not a unity in the many, since it is dispersed into an infinity of ideas. It is not an object of knowledge, since it is completely separated from us. The whole hypothesis of the *Phaedo* is called in question.

It was in all likelihood about this time that Plato, by way of counterpart, was led to undertake in the *Theaetetus* a review of all the conceptions of knowledge which other philosophers had developed. Plato first aimed at those who said that sensation is knowledge (151e). In the *Republic* (478a f.) he had postulated as self-evident that sensible things, which are forever disappearing and in perpetual flux, could not be objects of knowledge, because they have opposite characteristics at the same time. Here he proves this directly, without the slightest reference to his positive theory. Plato is here attacking a special form of sensualism. He is not attacking those tough men "who believe only in what they can grasp with their hands" (155e) but the more subtle philosophers who, following Heraclitus and Protagoras, reduce all positive knowledge to the immediate consciousness each man has of his own present sensations. On their view, man, as Protagoras said, is the measure of all things (160c) in a perpetually moving world, where rest and fixity would be death and would cause the disappearance of both being and knowledge. As the spark flies from the rubbing of two bodies, the sensible quality and the sensation actually arise simultaneously

---

[18] *Phaedo* (100d) already contained doubts concerning the nature of participation, asking whether it is the presence of the idea in the thing or communion of the thing with the idea.

from a sort of friction of an agent on an object; they arise together and are nothing apart from one another (156a–157a). No quality is a reality in itself, no sensation is lasting. Swept along in universal movement, both have a complete and total evidence at each instant, which, however, disappears at each instant to make place for another (179c). These are some of the consequences of the universal mobilism of the old Ionian natural philosophers. Here Plato finds adversaries on whom the Socratic approach has no influence (179e–180b); for that approach implies that one can acknowledge certain fixed postulates, and how could this be possible if the adversary changes immediately and disappears as soon as one tries to understand his words?

Plato, who had such a keen sense of the flux of sensible things, made every effort to point out the strong points of his adversaries. He brushed aside disdainfully the common objections; for example, that Protagoras does not have the right to teach other men because each man, being the measure of things, is as wise as any other. If his wisdom can no longer be said to consist in the passage from error to truth, it still has a major role to play in setting aside harmful opinions and in favoring useful opinions (160e–162de).

So he aspired to refute this thesis by entering into it and following it to its end. If man is the measure of things, the universal opinion of mankind has to be taken into account; and all men are afraid of being mistaken in the subjects in which they know themselves to be incompetent and in which they recognize the competence of those whom they are addressing. Protagoras, if he remains true to himself, is forced to admit that he is wrong. The fact that men recognize masters—physicians more skilful than themselves in the matter of diseases to be feared, political counselors able to foresee what is useful to the city—is sufficient refutation of Protagoras. Such knowledge, of course, has reference to the future. The fact remains that the immediate evidence of present sensation is only attained by the one who experiences it. Plato replies that this evidence is ineffable; for to state what is moved, to say what one sees, is to stop motion or to immobilize sensation. One does not therefore have the right to say either that one sees or that one knows. Before one can say it, the present evidence is replaced by another (169d–172b, 182d).

To know is not, therefore, to feel. Is it not rather to judge and, more precisely, to make true judgments (187b)? The judgment or true opinion here in question certainly has sensible things as its object. But in judgments about sensible things, there is necessarily something which cannot be perceived by sensation. If we judge that objects exist, that they are identical or different, like or unlike, then the qualities themselves of the objects are certainly perceived by the senses. But existence, same and other, similar and dissimilar, are general or common terms, relations which cannot be given by the senses. It is therefore in reflecting on the data of the senses that the soul judges. If this reflection ends in truth, if we state a precise relation, we attain knowledge (184b–186d). But if this thesis is to be defensible, we would first have to be able to distinguish true from false judgment. Now (here Plato takes up the well-known thesis of the Eristics) any false judgment or error seems impossible. Error cannot consist in confusion; one cannot confuse two things, whether one knows them both or is ignorant of them both or knows one while not knowing the other (188a–189a, 189a–190c). Nor does it consist in judging that what does not exist, exists. That would be tantamount to opining non-being, which in the sense Plato takes it would be taking as the object of one's opinion something without knowledge-content, something entirely indeterminate, and so not opining at all. This twofold criticism of error (whose first part is repeated in several different forms) implies that Plato now calls in question what he had admitted in the *Republic,* namely, an intermediate state between knowledge and ignorance, corresponding to an intermediate reality between being and non-being. For if false opinion is impossible, it is because one can only know or not know and because, if one judges, one can only judge being. What gives force to the argument in the *Theaetetus* is that opinion is not considered there as intermediary between knowledge and ignorance but either as knowledge or as ignorance. It is presented as knowledge in the criticism of error, and fundamentally that is what makes false opinion impossible. One can only opine being; this comes down to saying that, if opinion is knowledge, then all opinions are legitimate. In the last part of the discussion (201a–c), on the contrary, it is presented as ignorance, since an able orator may convince his listeners of facts which they are not acquainted with directly and which nevertheless are accurate; they judge truly without having knowledge.

It is not sufficient, therefore, to judge truly in order to have knowledge. But wouldn't it be sufficient to add to this true judgment the enumeration of the elements which compose the reality spoken of and the manner of their composition (201d)? One knows a syllable when one knows the letters with which it is composed. This conception of knowledge as logical analysis of the meaning of words seems to have been the one Antisthenes held; and the argument by which Plato refutes it is quite instructive. In effect there would be knowledge only of the composite and not of the simple elements; this would mean that our knowledge consists entirely in a collection of things we do not know. In other words, knowledge, for Plato, cannot consist in a pure and simple juxtaposition which is not justified by the natures of the juxtaposed elements (203a–204a).

Thus, according to the *Theaetetus*, none of the hypotheses that have been made about the nature of knowledge are tenable. But according to the *Parmenides* the hypothesis of ideas is also full of difficulties. None of the hypotheses of the preceding dialogues are sustained: all views about intermediaries between knowledge and error, between being and non-being, collapse along with the theory of ideas. There can no longer be half-knowledge, inspiration, or love.

IX *The Dialectical Exercise of the* Parmenides

Or rather, one thing remains: the methodological impulse which had given birth to these hypotheses and which by continuing further is going to renew and rejuvenate them. It is not the dogma of ideas but this methodological impulse which constitutes Platonism. That is the meaning of the *Parmenides* as a whole. The theory of ideas

once overthrown, Parmenides exhorts the young Socrates to continue to practice the method of hypotheses, the one which Plato
valued so highly in the *Meno*. It is necessary, "having posited the
hypothesis, not only to examine what follows from this positive
assertion" but also to see what results from the negative (135a). It is
an exercise of this kind which comprises the second part of the
Parmenides. All the consequences of the Eleatic hypothesis, that
the One is, are sought; then the consequences of the opposite
hypothesis, that *the One is not*. The outlines of this search are of
prime importance, because they have a quite general value, independent of the hypothesis examined. In regard to each of the two
hypotheses one must first seek the consequences for the One, then
the consequences for the things other than the One. To seek the consequences is to seek the attributes which one must assert or deny
of the One in each of the two hypotheses. For this purpose it is necessary to have a list of the most general attributes (those common
terms mentioned in the *Theaetetus*) which can be affirmed or denied
of any subject whatever. Plato arrived at a sort of list of categories,
where each term contains two opposites: whole and part, beginning,
middle, and end, straight and circular (shape), in another thing
and in itself, in motion and at rest, same and other, similar and
dissimilar, equal and unequal, older, younger, or contemporary. But
it is very important to notice that the order in which we cite them
is not at all arbitrary for Plato; it is not arbitrary in the sense that
the attribution or non-attribution of each of them to the subject of
the search is always a logical consequence of the attribution or non-
attribution of the preceding one. Thus in the first hypothesis it can
be demonstrated that the One has neither beginning nor end, because it has already been demonstrated that it has neither parts nor
whole (144e–145b); it is demonstrated that it has no geometrical
shape, because it has neither beginning nor end (145b). These categories are not like outlines prepared beforehand but emerge, so to
speak, as they are demonstrated. The notion of the One is thus
gradually enriched, just as the notion of a mathematical figure is
enriched whose properties are discovered by means of implication.

The results of the search are disconcerting enough to have made the interpretation of the *Parmenides* a very difficult problem. In fact, from the hypothesis *the One is* Plato showed that a double series of consequences can be deduced by reasoning. In a first series of consequences, it is shown that we must deny of the One each of the pairs of opposite terms which we have cited, that consequently it has neither parts nor whole, neither beginning nor end, etc. In a second series, it is shown that on the contrary we must attribute each of these pairs to it. From the same hypothesis it is concluded, with reference to things other than the One, that each of the opposites must be attributed to them at the same time. From the hypothesis contrary to the first, *the One is not,* it is logically concluded that we must first attribute to the One, then deny of it, the pairs of terms which we had denied and affirmed of it in the first hypothesis and afterward attribute to things other than the One, and then deny of them, the same pairs of terms. In a word, Plato seems to undertake to demonstrate that one and the same hypothesis has contradictory consequences and that two contradictory hypotheses have identical consequences.

It was to remove this contradiction that the Neo-Platonists gave the complicated interpretation of the *Parmenides* which we shall see later on. They assumed that in each series of consequences the word *One* and the word *is* did not have the same meaning; contraries can then be affirmed of the One because they are not affirmed in the same respect. But nothing justifies such an interpretation. The meaning of Plato's strange dialectic appears to be quite different. If one considers attentively the critique of ideas at the beginning of the dialogue, one sees that it dealt less with the thesis of ideas, taken in itself, than with the relation of participation between sensible things and ideas. It was because of this participation that ideas either divided into parts or were separated from themselves and multiplied to infinity. A way out of this difficulty was to disregard, at least for the time being, that aspect of ideas in which they explain sensible things and rather consider them in themselves; in short, to establish that dialectic already so clearly defined in the *Republic* (511b) which "without relying on anything sensible uses only ideas in order to proceed from ideas to other ideas, and to end in ideas." It is this program which the *Parmenides* begins to carry out. It assumes relations between the One and being and deduces all the possible consequences from them, remaining in the purely intellectual sphere without making the slightest allusion to sensible things of which these ideas may be models. It is no longer a matter of explaining phenomena by ideas, as in the *Phaedo,* but of passing from a realm where knowledge is not possible, where hypotheses are powerless, into a realm where knowledge is possible. The *Parmenides* shows how fruitful hypotheses can be when they concern relations among ideas.

x *The Communication of Ideas*

What the *Sophist* proceeds to show in turn is that the method of hypothesis is absolutely necessary. The real object of the dialogue lies in the difficulties raised by defining the Sophist. If we say in effect that he is someone who has only an appearance of knowledge (233c), he will elude us by telling us that error is impossible, since it would consist in thinking non-being; but is it not true that non-being is not (236e–237a, 241d)?

In order to solve this problem, Plato made a critical examination of the opinions of philosophers on the definition of being. But this criticism led to a surprising result, namely, the impossibility of defining being in itself apart from every other thing. Here is his line of reasoning. When the Ionians and Parmenides sought to define being, the former defined it as many and the latter as one. They thus gave it characteristics which it does not have as being. First, in what sense is the being of the Ionians a pair of terms? If it is neither the one nor the other of the two terms in particular, there are no longer two terms, but three; if it is both at once, there are no longer two terms but only one. As for Parmenides, in what sense did he posit being as one? As it is not identical with unity, there is a whole constituted by being and the One. Either this whole exists, and then being is no more than a part of being; or else it does not exist, and then being is not the whole. The Ionians and Parmenides mixed being with something other than itself by not separating it from these quantitative determinations (243e–245e).

From the opposite point of view, those "terrible" men who only believe in the existence of what they touch and "who identify being with body" and the idealists, who see in sensible things only ceaseless flux and becoming and who only find being in "certain intelligible and incorporeal ideas," both make the mistake of restricting the meaning of being. First of all, can it be reduced to body alone? But one is forced to admit realities such as justice which effectively exist, since they appear and disappear in the soul. Do we want, like the "friends of ideas," to restrict being to these fixed and motionless realities which ideas are? But they could not claim to lay hold of "total being" in them; "total being necessarily contains intelligence, and consequently soul and life; being intelligent, animated and living, it is not motionless" (246a–249a). This twofold polemic against materialists and idealists is aimed at contemporary philosophers whom it is difficult to identify. Some believe they see Antisthenes in the first part; they also see Antisthenes earlier, in the *Theaetetus*. As for the second, the difficulty is great; the only idealists we know about at this time are Plato himself and his school. Can we not believe that he was criticizing a conception of ideas which had been his own, the very one he examined at the beginning of the *Parmenides* and which he had now gone beyond? Against the multiplicity of isolated and fixed ideas, such as appeared in the *Phaedo,* he would now oppose total being (248e), this rather mysterious term which seems to include not only the idea or the object which is known, but the subject which knows it—intelligence and the soul in which it resides. We have here a rough sketch which the *Timaeus* will later develop more precisely.

In any case, the direction of his thought remains clear. He reproached the materialists as well as the idealists for having failed to see in being this power of action and passion, this life which he put into it. But this reproach caused him in turn to fall into the difficulty which he had pointed out in *Parmenides* and the *Ionians*.

"Is it not just," says the stranger from Elea who leads the discussion, "that they now ask us the questions which we ourselves asked those who said that the whole was the warm and the cold?" (250a). We necessarily waver between too restricted a notion of being and too extensive a notion. When we try to limit it to itself, it is too barren; finding it too barren, we give it attributes—movement, life, intelligence—which go beyond it.

The impossibility of conceiving being in itself and without relation to any other term than itself reveals to us the necessity of communication and intermixture among terms such as being, motion, rest, etc. What thought grasps are never isolated elements but combinations. The object of thought, like words composed of vowels and consonants, like music composed of high or low tones, is formed by concepts which unite with each other. The attempt to define concepts apart from this union is perhaps what caused the consistently negative results of the Socratic dialogues. We can only grasp a concept together with the relations it bears to other concepts. Hence a new way of looking at dialectic: dialectic is the art which makes the rules by which concepts combine, as music makes rules for the harmonious combination of sounds. (253a–d).

This conception of dialectic is no doubt close to what Aristotle's logic will be. It is nevertheless distinct from it. In the first place, it is not a process of combining previously defined concepts. Plato indicates this with remarkable force: it is true of every attribute we can give to a notion that the notion does not have the attribute through itself but through participation in another idea: "to separate things from one another is to make all discourse disappear completely; we cannot formulate anything except by connecting ideas with one another" (259e). Hence thought passes from the indeterminate to the determinate; it is not content to explicate relations between notions that have already been defined. In the second place and for the same reason, the art of dialectic does not proceed by an application of general rules to particular cases but by a direct examination of each notion, which refers us from itself to the notions with which it must be united: thus rest and motion combine with being, but they cannot combine with one another (254d). But if motion is being insofar as it participates in being, it is non-being insofar as it is other than being; that is, insofar as it participates in the other (255e). It seems clear that in the direct and immediate knowledge of these relations the primary role is played by that intellectual intuition which Plato, in the *Republic,* had placed at the summit of the hierarchy of knowledge. For the method consists in grasping what the idea one is examining "wants"; in obeying what one sees in ideas (252e). And, for this reason, Platonic dialectic differs as much from discursive thought as the Cartesian method differs from logic.

XI *The Problem of Mixtures: Division*

From this time on, all Plato's effort will be spent on the art of understanding the rules of mixture, or blending. A strangely diverse effort, which extends from school exercises in division to the majestic synthesis of the *Timaeus;* an effort which results in giving directions and encouraging the impulse of thought rather than in creating a doctrine. In the *Phaedrus* (265d), Plato had already defined dialectic in terms of two successive phases: first, "manifold things are united in a single idea; then, inversely, one divides, idea by idea, according to natural divisions." It should be noticed that analysis or division here follows synthesis and that synthesis, far from being the termination of thought and following analysis, is on the contrary meant to serve as a starting point for division, which is thus the essence of dialectic. The exercises in division found at the beginning of the *Statesman* (258c–267c) and the *Sophist* (218d–231c) undoubtedly show how Plato had his students at the Academy practice dialectic. Division is there presented as a process which serves to determine a concept more and more precisely; it finally ends in a definition. Politics, for example, is a science; but the sciences divide into those whose end is knowledge and those whose end is action. Politics falls in the first class. The sciences of knowledge divide in turn into sciences which prescribe and sciences which judge; politics is one of the former. Thus, from division to division, one succeeds in fixing the concept more and more. It is clear that Platonic division is not a purely mechanical procedure; otherwise it would be open to Aristotle's criticism that it is entirely arbitrary whether we put the thing we are investigating in one member of the division or in the other.[19] It is actually intuition, not a logical procedure, which guides us. Moreover, if it is almost a general rule that division has to be binary, the rule for carrying out this division is not at all clearly defined and raises great technical difficulties which Plato knew very well but which he failed to solve. One of the greatest difficulties is knowing how to distinguish arbitrary divisions, such as the division of men into Greeks and barbarians, from legitimate divisions, such as their division into male and female. In one case, only the first group (Greeks) is determined, and the second is only determined by exclusion from the first. In the second case, we have two opposed characteristics that are equally positive (262e, 263b).

But what is the relation between these two conceptions of dialectic: dialectic as the art of composing mixtures in the *Sophist*, and dialectic as the art of division? This question is answered in the *Philebus*. This dialogue shows how the art of composing mixtures results in classification and division into species. The association of the two aspects of dialectic, elsewhere separated, to some degree transforms the notion of it. The blend is presented in a new form; every mixture worthy of the name is not an arbitrary combination but a quite stable combination of two elements: an indeterminate or unlimited element and a limit or fixed determination. The indeterminate is a pair of opposites such that each member of the pair can only be defined in relation to the other; that is, each member of the pair is entirely indefinite in itself. For example: larger and smaller, higher and lower, warmer and colder. These are purely relative and perpetually fluid terms, since what is larger than one thing can be at the same time smaller than another. The limit or determination is a fixed numerical relation, such as double or triple. Mixture, as can readily be seen, results therefore from the introduc-

[19] *Prior Analytics* i. 31.

tion of a fixed relation into the pair of opposites. Thus musicians demonstrate that a relation of one to two, introduced into the unlimited dyad of the high and of the low, creates the octave. In the same way we can speculate that a fixed relation of slow and fast creates a regular motion or brings out the forms of a fixed relation of largeness and of smallness.[20] This conception of mixture allows and even implies division of concepts: division starts from something unlimited, such as the voice with its infinite shadings of high or low; it introduces a certain number of fixed intervals—chords, characterized by fixed numerical relations such as $1/2$, $1/3$, etc. Knowledge will consist in recognizing the number and the nature of these fixed relations (18b).

This conception of mixture and division is no longer quite that of the *Sophist*. First, there is no longer a uniformly binary division; in the most perfect of all examples, music, the number of terms is determined by the possible numerical relations or chords. We see another example in the *Timaeus* (54a ff.), where division into four elements depends on the number of possible regular solids. Moreover, in the *Sophist* the mixture of one kind with another comes from its own nature. Being, in order to be what it is, has to participate in the same and in the different; there is here the rudiment of a relation of logical necessity. But the unlimited and the limit neither name nor imply one another; to unite them there has to be a fourth kind of being, different from them and from mixture; this is the cause of mixture (26e). In other words, considerations of harmony, fitness, beauty, and goodness are now substituted for the relation of logical necessity which the *Sophist* inclined toward. The idea of the Good, which dominated dialectic in the *Republic* and which was kept in the background in the middle dialogues, here resumes, along with mathematics, a role of prime importance. And, not being able to define the Good in its unity, Plato sets in its stead an equivalent made up of three terms: beauty, symmetry, and truth (65a). He thus posits three primordial conditions to which every mixture has to conform. Each of these three terms expresses

[20] *Philebus* 23c–27c; especially 23d, 26ad.

under a different aspect what he called in the *Republic* the unconditioned, the Good, in which explanation ceases.

XII *The Cosmological Problem*

The notion of mixture comprising beauty, proportion, and truth
was the real incentive of Plato's last studies. It enabled him to return to the problem of understanding sensible things by ideas, the
problem he had abandoned in the face of the difficulties concerning
participation raised in the *Parmenides*. That is the purpose of the
Timaeus. But to understand properly this renewed interest in natural philosophy, it must be clearly understood that sensible things
no longer seemed to him an ever vanishing flux, as in the *Theaetetus,* but as parts of a cosmos which is itself the most beautiful of
sensible mixtures; in other words, a compound ordered in accordance with fixed relations.[21] If such is the case, the problem of
understanding the physical world offers no inherent difficulty; it is
an instance of the dialectical problem in general, which, according to the *Philebus,* consists in determining the way mixtures are
formed. The problem of participation is therefore solved.

The world arose by a transition from disorder to order under the
action of a Demiurge (30a). The state of disorder prior to this action
is essentially the domain of "necessity"; the domain of a brutal
necessity, an aimless causality, which is not subject to any considerations of purpose (47e–48a). But this disorder and this necessity by
no means signify a radical unintelligibility; the necessity is a kind
of mechanical necessity analogous to the kind accepted by Democritus but injected by Plato, if not with the goodness of the Demiurge,
at least with a certain element of geometrical intelligibility. The
doctrine of atoms and the doctrine of elements appear in it but
pervaded by the geometrical approach; elements are composed
of corpuscles, and the corpuscles of a given element are distinct from
each other, not by their qualities, but by their geometrical form.

---

[21] 26a; cf. 30b, the world is a living being endowed with soul and intelligence.

The elementary corpuscles of each kind have the form of one of the four regular polyhedrons, cube, icosahedron, octahedron, and tetrahedron, corresponding respectively to earth, water, air, and fire. Plato's mathematical ingenuity, guided by the new discoveries of Theaetetus in stereometry, had no difficulty in demonstrating that the surfaces of the cube can be formed by four rectangular isosceles triangles and that, whenever the surfaces of a polyhedron are equilateral triangles, these surfaces can all be formed by six rectangular triangles, whose hypotenuse is twice the short side of the right triangle. The transmutations of the elements become perfectly intelligible (leaving aside earth) when it has been demonstrated that a corpuscle of water contains as many triangles as two corpuscles of air, plus one of fire, and that a corpuscle of air contains as many triangles as two corpuscles of fire (53c–57c). There is reason at the very heart of necessity. Brute necessity appears in the arrangement of these corpuscles, which depends on the way they react to the irregular shaking of the receptacle or space in which they exist. Like substances shaken in a sieve, they tend to unite according to their similarities and affinities (57bc). The source of necessity is therefore not in the elements but in the ambiguous nature of the receptacle, "this bastard concept, hardly believable" (52b). The receptacle appears indeed to be one of the indeterminate terms of which the *Philebus* gave examples; precisely speaking, it is both the geometrical indeterminate, in the sense that it has no determination of largeness and of smallness and has them all (50cd), and also the mechanical indeterminate, in the sense that its motion, its slowness and swiftness, has no uniformity (52e). It is the receptacle which first the elemental triangles, then the polyhedrons forming from them, begin to determine by introducing into it fixed relations of largeness and smallness (53c). It is into the receptacle that the intelligence of the Demiurge is going to introduce other determinations and in particular mechanical determinations.

For the creator or Demiurge is primarily the creator of the world-soul (34cd), and the soul is a source of motion (*Phaedrus* 245c; *Laws* 894d), not in the sense of brute mechanical force as the receptacle is, but the source of all that is regular and fixed in a motion. The world-soul is prior to the body which it is destined to animate and which houses it, but it is itself a mixture in which all the arithmetical or geometrical relations that will be realized in the world are in some way formed. Every mixture is composed of a limit and an unlimited, and one mixture is only distinguished from another by the aspect presented by these two terms. The limit and the unlimited which compose the soul prove to be the *indivisible essence* and the *divisible essence* in bodies (35a); every numerical and geometrical determination requires two terms of this kind. We learn from Aristotle that, according to Plato's oral teaching, numbers arise from the action of the One on the indefinite dyad of the large and the small.[22] Every number, every shape, are the result of a determination of something that was first indeterminate. Once the mixture of these two essences is produced, the Demiurge blends in the *same* and the *other;* that is to say, two terms which are also related to one another as the limit and unlimited of the *Philebus.* Plato is careful to tell us that the other enters into the mixture only by force; as we shall see, it continues to be the source of indetermination. The soul is thus made of three things: a mixture of two substances, divisible and indivisible, then the same, and finally the other. The Demiurge then divides the soul according to certain determined numbers which are the terms of the two geometrical progressions 1, 2, 4, 8 and 1, 3, 9, 27, between which mean proportionals are inserted. Next he divides it into two parts which intersect each other at acute angles in the manner of the letter X and are then bent back into two circles having the same center, one of the circles being inclined toward the other like the ecliptic toward the equator. The *circle of the same,* impelled by a motion toward the right, that is to say from east to west, remains whole; the *circle of the other,* impelled by a motion toward the left, that is to say from west to east, is divided into seven. We can see well enough that under the name of the world-soul Plato was striving to show how one can make a sort of rational construction of the astronomical

[22] *Metaphysics* M. 7. 1081a 14–15.

system as he conceived it. The principles of the system were that there are only circular motions, that these motions are uniform, and that the apparent irregularity of the motion of the seven planets is explained by the fact that, in addition to their diurnal motion, they are impelled by a motion of their own in the opposite direction. The soul is only a schematic diagram of the astronomical system (35a–36d).

The *Timaeus* is a story, a myth. The Pythagorean Timaeus tells there how the different mixtures were formed—the world-soul, the world, the elemental corpuscles—without trying to go beyond prob· able conjecture (29c–e); the modest tone inspired by Parmenides contrasts with the dogmatism of the Ionians. It is clear, moreover, that in the physical applications of mathematical diagrams Plato is guided by considerations of harmony and beauty. The sole reason for the formation of the world is that the Demiurge "was good" (29e); the Good continues to be the unconditioned, on which every proof depends. The spherical shape of the world and its uniqueness derive from an effort to imitate the perfection of the model (32b, 32ab). Time, divided into regular periods of days, months, and years which are linked to the celestial revolutions, imitates the eternity of the model as much as possible by its incessant cycles (37d). In the details of the physiology which he expounds at the end of the work, Plato was as passionate a teleologist as the Stoics will be. The tenth book of the *Laws* also strongly asserts that divine providence is not only general but penetrates to the very last detail of the structure of the universe (903bc). The theory of the universe preserves its arbitrary and intuitive character because it is primarily the story of the work of providence. The human mind can only surmise the intentions of the Demiurge; it is never sure of them (29e–30a). Besides, in bending necessity to intelligence (47e–48a), in striving to make it obey, the Demiurge meets with ever increasing resistance. If the first mixture, the world-body, is made so harmoniously that it is imperishable though engendered (41ab), the partial mixtures formed by the gods in imitation of the Demiurge, the bodies of animals, are subject to death (41c , 43a); the series of mixtures keeps on decreasing in perfection, and their conservation is less and less assured.

By an obvious paradox, arbitrariness was introduced into the science of physical things to the same extent as mathematics was introduced into it; arbitrariness, but also a freedom which liberates the mind from the illusions of immediate observation and allows it a fruitful play of hypotheses. It was probably because of this freedom of mind that Plato was able to suggest, in passing, the explanation of diurnal motion by the rotation of the earth around its axis.[23]

XIII *The Oral Teaching of Plato*

The dialogues do not acquaint us with all of Plato. Aristotle[24] has fortunately preserved for us something of his oral teaching, although it is often difficult to disentangle the thought of Plato in Aristotle's exposition, which was written with a critical intent and often mingles Plato's thought with theses of his successors in the Academy. According to Aristotle, Plato conceived ideas as numbers toward the end of his life, but as numbers different from those the mathematician uses. What are the *ideal numbers?* Why did Plato substitute or at least superimpose them on ideas? And first, how are they to be distinguished from mathematical numbers? Mathematical numbers are those formed of units all equal to one another and resulting from the addition of these units. Now we see in the *Philebus* and *Timaeus* that Plato had a clear predilection for some way of generating numbers other than addition and, in particular, for a way of generating numbers by progressions or by the insertion of three kinds of mean proportionals—arithmetical, geometrical, or harmonical.[25] His attention tends to be directed toward numerical

[23] Such was, from antiquity, the interpretation of the word εἰλλομένην (*Timaeus* 40b) by Plutarch (*Platonic Questions,* qu. viii); but this interpretation is not certain, and the sense may concord with the immobility of the earth.

[24] Metaphysics M. 7, 8.

[25] *Timaeus* 31c ff.

relations rather than toward numbers themselves. Pythagorean music made him see the essence of things in numerical relations rather than in numbers. The theory of ideal numbers seems clearly to be an attempt to find the most general types of relation. Aristotle tells us that these numbers do not result from addition, since their units cannot be added up, but from the union of two principles, the One and the indefinite dyad of the large and the small.[26] This dyad is nothing but the fully indeterminate and fluid relation of which the *Philebus* (24c–25a) gave us examples. As for the One, we know by a famous tradition that Plato identified it with the Good.[27] Now the function of the Good, according to the *Philebus,* is to introduce fixed relations between things, which is possible by measure. The One of Aristotle and the Good of Plato's lecture appear to be identical with measure, which the *Statesman* (284d) treats as the starting point of dialectic. The One is what makes it possible to measure and is the unconditioned term which we do not go beyond. Thus it is, according to Aristotle, that the large and the small, unequal as they are, can be equalized by the application of the One. And this is how the ideal dyad will be obtained, composed of the two terms of the relation; not by adding one unit to another, but by equalizing the indeterminate relation with the unit. Without pursuing the complicated method of producing ideal numbers[28] which Plato follows up to the ideal decade, the example of the ideal dyad shows that the ideal numbers are primarily fixed relations. It is natural enough to think that these ideal numbers are the principle of the eternal model of the world which he told us about in the *Timaeus* (28b), just as the soul formed by geometrical figures combined according to certain numerical relations is the principle of the sensible world. The Living in itself (30a) seems to denote the whole of intelligible reality beneath the ideal numbers and to comprise the intelligible species, just

---

[26] *Metaphysics* 7. 1081a 14.

[27] According to Aristoxenes (a contemporary of Aristotle), in his *Elements of Harmony* ii. 30 (ed. Meibom).

[28] There exists, moreover, no reliable interpretation of the obscure texts of Aristotle upon the question (cf. L. Robin, *Théorie platonicienne . . . ,* pp. 276–86).

as the world—living, animated, and intelligent—comprises, below the soul, the body. In any case, it is certain that Plato directed his studies toward the laws of the combination of mixtures.

xiv *Philosophy and Politics*

One can only separate Plato's politics from his philosophy by an abstraction. His greatest works are at once philosophical and political: the *Gorgias* points out the dangers of politics not based on reason, and the *Republic* uses philosophy as the sole means of arriving at viable politics. The trilogy consisting of the *Sophist,* the *Statesman,* and the *Philosopher,*[29] whose last dialogue remained in the planning stage, undoubtedly led to a demonstration of the political capacities of the philosopher. The trilogy consisting of the *Timaeus,* the *Critias,* and the *Hermocrates,* only the first and the beginning of the second of which were written by Plato, was to treat the revolutions of cities, their ruin, and their restoration, beginning with the formation of the world described in the *Timaeus.* Finally, the *Laws* is a veritable manual for the legislator. It is no more legitimate to separate philosophy from politics in Plato than in Auguste Comte. How can one forget that the impulse toward philosophy came to him from Socrates, who in the *Apology* stressed his social mission with such force?

Like Socrates, Plato firmly believed in the social mission of the philosopher. After describing, in the *Republic,* the government of the ideal city, he wonders what conditions might actually bring about a form of government approaching the ideal. A single change would be enough "but one which is neither small nor an easy one, although it is possible . . . , that philosophers be kings in their cities, or kings and rulers be good philosophers, that political authority and philosophy might coincide" (473b). This demand has to be understood in a wholly practical sense; he calls for the political authority of the philosopher just at the point where he crosses from theory to practice. Plato never wearied of insisting on the active role

[29] Cf. the indication of the whole plan, *Sophist* 217a.

befitting a philosopher. He must be compelled to come down from his contemplation of intelligible things and concern himself with the affairs of the city (519d); public opinion must also be prepared for this reform, since the people are inclined, just because of the vices of governments, to consider philosophy as useless to the city (500b). The philosopher will proceed with the state as the artist does with the wall he is painting; first he will carefully clean it, then he will outline the form of the state on it, constantly comparing his drawing with the model of justice he is capable of contemplating (501a).

xv *Justice and Temperance*

Before appearing as a reformer of the city in the *Republic*, Plato seems to have first reflected on justice as a moralist, in the manner of Socrates, rather than as a political reformer. He showed that men must become just, that is law-abiding, in order to be happy, before proving that only the philosopher can conceive and realize just laws. He is a moralist before being a politician, and so the opposite of the ambitious young men in Athens, immortalized by Callicles in the *Gorgias*, who gave themselves to politics without preparation. The two poles, so to speak, of Platonic ethics are in the *Gorgias*, which upholds justice against political banditry, and in the *Phaedo*, in which the philosophic life consists in purifying one's self from the body.

Let us begin by looking at the first of these two themes. In the *Crito*, Socrates was represented as respecting the laws to the point of death; everyone knows the famous exhortation where the laws of Athens point out to Socrates all he owes them (50a). Plato had a very strong feeling that not only security but all moral growth depends on them. But are not laws, Callicles objects, mere conventions which the common run of men have made in order to protect themselves from the greediness of the powerful? Does not natural justice consist in force, and should not the strongest have authority (*Gorgias* 482c–484c)? What then is this force which Callicles talks about? Is it physical force pure and simple? Then it belongs to the people, if they have the force to impose the laws (488b–e). So it is force accompanied by wisdom and skill or, more precisely, rational knowledge of politics and courage to realize one's plans (491a–d). But courage, which gives a man authority over others, implies that inner form of courage which is authority over one's self, or temperance. For the good is not identical with pleasure, and if it is necessary to choose the useful, good, and healthy pleasures, one can only do it with the help of temperance, which introduces a certain order into the body and soul, by eliminating the desires opposed to this order (504c–505b). This development of temperance or the virtue of control, a relative of geometrical equality, is the culminating point of the *Gorgias* (508a). In this virtue, which he had already tried to define in the *Charmides,* he found the basis of all the others —piety, justice, happiness. Temperance is action ruled by order and is directly opposed to the brutal and unrestrained action of Callicles. Here Plato glimpsed a truth which he made the basis of his philosophy and which he will develop forcefully in his old age;[30] the activity we call art, which chooses and acts according to rules, is prior to that so-called nature which is disorderly and unregulated, which Callicles wants to follow. The primacy of art at the very heart of nature and the order of the universe is a postulate of Plato's whole politics, as of his whole philosophy. Order is not a human conquest over unregulated forces; order is rather the basis of reality and is revealed to us by an intellectual intuition.

If temperance with the technique which discerns and orders is the fundamental virtue, the asceticism of the *Phaedo* and the government by philosophers in the *Republic* will be two inseparable aspects of this virtue. If it does not seem to occupy the central place it holds in the *Gorgias* in these two dialogues, the idea of the higher and dominating value of intelligence which inspires it remains the point of departure. In the *Phaedo* (82e ff.) the search for truth is accompanied by abstinence from pleasure: the soul is fastened to the body by desire and is forced to look through the body where it

[30] *Laws* x. 889e.

is, as it were, imprisoned. But philosophy teaches it that sight and the other sensations are full of errors; it tells the soul to believe only in itself and in its own thoughts. Thus philosophy disengages the soul from the body and is the cause of its abstaining as much as possible from pleasures, desires, and sorrows. True virtue consists in freeing one's self from all affections; justice, courage, and prudence are purifications, just as much as temperance (69a).

But, on the other hand, temperance is also a virtue which prescribes order. It has no less importance as a positive technique than as an ascetic rule. In this connection the conclusion of the *Gorgias* is significant, and it prepares the way for the *Republic*. Men will only be made better with the help of a scientific technique which neither the illustrious politicians of Athens nor the Sophists who came there to instruct the young ever possessed (513c–515d). In short, justice no longer appears to be merely the individual's obedience to the laws of his country, as in the *Crito,* but rather a demand for complete political reform under the direction of philosophers.

XVI *The Political Problem*

It is from this time on that Plato gave major attention to political thought, subordinating to it both ethics and psychology. Political thought is not like dialectic, which stays in the world of ideas; on the contrary, it continually comes in contact with facts. Plato, let us repeat, did not want to be a utopian but a reformer; he had to take into consideration the nature of men and the nature of things as they are.

The strange thing about this reformer was that, in total contrast to the Sophists, he was far from believing in progress. He meditated a great deal on the history and evolution of societies, as he did on the history of individual souls, mixing myth and legend with strict psychological observation. But like myth, observation always reveals the double conclusion that justice and virtue in an individual or in a society depend primarily on external conditions, on a stroke of fortune, and that, if there are changes in society, change always takes place for the worse or, at best, according to a cyclical rhythm which causes society to repeat the same stages. Legislation, were it up to the philosopher, aims at making the best possible use of existing conditions and also at arresting or delaying changes, giving society the greatest possible stability. Never, indeed, do we find in Plato the idea of a positive reform, of real social invention. He is always concerned with maintaining and preserving or with eliminating and suppressing. Very significantly, he tells us the myth that man only escaped complete decadence because the gods acquainted him with fire, taught him the arts, and gave him seeds of grain (*Statesman* 274e). Man's own initiative could not have brought him this far.

The goal of the philosopher's reform can therefore only be to imitate as far as possible the most perfect state of society which he is able to conceive in his mind; to take hold, as it were, of society at the level where it now is, in order to prevent it from falling even lower (*Laws* iv. 713e). There is never any question of promoting real progress. If a society offers the conditions necessary for the application of philosophy, it happens by fortune, through a series of circumstances independent of human will such as favorable climate and soil (704a ff.), whether this fortune be attributable to chance or to divine providence.

Hence the positivistic, realistic, and at times even conservative character of Platonic politics; hence his taste, increasing as he grew older, for history and ancient traditions;[31] hence his condemnation of the whole policy of expansion which had made Athens great but had also thrown its customs and morals into confusion.[32] He remained attached only to the traditional form of the Greek city. In the *Republic,* for example, it is understood that the city he has to administer is a Greek city (470e). If later, in the *Statesman* (262c–d), he considered the division of humanity into Greeks and barbarians ridiculous, it is nonetheless true that he wanted above all to strengthen Hellenism, to restore peace among the cities, and to

[31] Preface to the *Timaeus* and *Critias*.
[32] *Gorgias* 508e–519b.

end the practices of pillage and enslavement which accompanied the victories of one city over another.[33]

XVII Social Justice

The essence of social justice, in Plato, is to bring about the unity of society (*Republic* iv. 423d). Justice in cities imitates as far as possible the ideal essences that are "well-ordered, always preserving the same relations, without inflicting any harm on one another, disposed by order and reason" (vi. 500c). The just city gives us one of those examples of well-ordered multiplicity, of those mixtures whose nature it is the business of the dialectician to discover. When we know what this mixture is, we can determine what the just soul is, since justice in the soul is an ordering of parts which is in every respect analogous to the disposition of the parts of society constituting social justice. The *Republic* differs from the subsequent political writings of Plato in that it lays more stress on the conditions of this unity. He presented his study in the form of a history of society, in exactly the same way as the *Timaeus* expressed the conditions of the stability of the universe in a history of the formation of the universe by a Demiurge. And in this history of society his view extends far beyond the reform of a Greek city, back to the fundamental conditions of any human association.[34]

The state arises from needs and the discovery of a rational method of satisfying them. This method is the division of labor. There is a city as soon as four or five men come together who each agree to supply one of the elementary needs of all the others, in food, clothing, and shelter. The husbandman who produces food for all will in return have his shelter and clothing provided by the others. Specialized in his calling, each one will produce more and better. In its elementary form, therefore, the city is not a coming together of equal and similar individuals, but on the contrary a coming together of unequal and dissimilar individuals; it will remain so in its highest

---

[33] *Republic* v. 469b ff.
[34] 369b, on the division of labor.

forms, and this is what will guarantee the solidarity of its parts and its unity (370ab). As the size of the city increases and needs multiply, functions will become more complicated. Alongside the husbandman, for example, there will be a special maker of plows and agricultural implements (370c). Alongside the producers will be the class of those who barter, merchants by land and sea (371ab). But the principle always remains the same. It even remains the same in the state which has reached completion, where functions are grouped into a small number of classes: the class of artisans who are engaged in supplying material needs, the class of soldiers who defend the state against its neighbors (373c), and the class of "guardians" who are intrusted with enforcing obedience to the laws. These three classes represent the three essential functions of every state: production, defense, and internal administration (434c).

How these functions can best be carried out was for Plato the sole social problem. There can be no question of using the resources of the state for the happiness of an individual or a class. "We build the city," replies Socrates to Adeimantus who reproaches him for the very hard life he makes the "guardians" lead, "not in order that one class may have a greater happiness, but in order that the whole city may be happy." [35] The individual who is a part of the state is created to carry out his social function, not for something else. This is what justice consists in: to be just is to carry out one's own function (434c).

XVIII *Nature and Society*

Here Plato was confronted with a formidable question. The needs of the ideal society must reckon with nature. In fact, the exercise of each social function assumes not only an acquired education but also natural aptitudes. Love of gain in the artisan, the great passion needed by the soldier, prudence and reflection in the guardian of the city; these are based on innate character which no social order could produce (455b). Furthermore, the different proportions in which

[35] 420b; compare 465e ff.

these characters exist depend on the nature of the geographical environment. "One region," he said toward the close of his life, "is not as well qualified as another to make men better or worse." [36] The study of numbers which leads some men to philosophy and dialectic will produce cheating and not knowledge among Egyptians, Phoenicians, and many other peoples.

Plato attached utmost importance to nature. In particular, when he came to speak of the real leaders of the city, the philosophers, he repeatedly recommended selecting those who were capable of receiving instruction in dialectic on the basis of their natural aptitudes. And he made a very detailed list of indispensable innate qualities: love of truth and ease in learning, lack of desires that obstruct the pursuit of knowledge, courage and nobility of soul, and, finally, an accurate and extensive memory.[37] The union of these qualities is very rare, since there is almost an incompatibility between the necessary qualities, especially between the subtlety of a ceaselessly active mind and quiet seriousness and between the inertia of the man unconcerned with dangers and the piercing eye which sees through them.[38] The nobility of an old Athenian and the subtlety of a Sophist; those are the qualities which the philosophical nature has to combine.

Now there is not necessarily harmony between the demands of an ideal society and the material nature supplies; here we have a whole aspect of reality which eludes human art. No thinker has ever been more aware of this than Plato. In order to explain this fundamental fact, this reality of human character which resists reason and which nevertheless fixes our destiny, he appealed to a mode of explanation which is itself irrational: the myth of the choice of lives. After this life, souls undergo punishments or receive rewards according to the justice they have shown; then they assemble to choose a new life. This choice is entirely voluntary and the gods are not in the least responsible for it. But once the choice is made it

[36] *Laws* 747d.
[37] *Republic* 490c.
[38] 503b.

is sanctioned by necessity and the Fates, and the soul will be power-less to escape its destiny. Before its reincarnation it passes through the water of Lethe which takes away all memory of its choice; then its new life unfolds according to what it has willed. We can see the political concerns this myth deals with by its place at the end of the *Republic* (617d–621b), even though it deals only with individual destiny. Up to a certain point there is a conflict between mythical explanation which attributes our fate to a voluntary choice and naturalistic explanation which accounts for human character by geographic environment. And perhaps it was to unite these that, in the final form he gave to the myth, Plato appealed to the action of providence and universal justice which so organize the world that each soul is spontaneously attracted to the place it deserves to go.[39] His intention remains clear: it is to postulate character as an ultimate fact.

On the other hand, stability of character is to a certain extent a guaranty of social stability and, consequently, of justice. Thus, if social art cannot produce characters to order, it should at least pre-vent them from deteriorating from one generation to the next. And here, to give the legislator a hold, Plato introduced an additional explanation, based on heredity, that was incompatible with the mythological or naturalistic explanations. If this explanation is true, the leaders of the city can maintain the characters appropriate to each social class in a pure state by skilfully regulating marriages, just as the stockbreeder is able to keep strains pure (*Republic* 459b, 460e). And it will be negligence in applying marriage regulations that will bring about the decline of the philosophic aristocracy and, along with it, the decline of the entire city (546c). It must be stressed that no human method of re-establishing the primitive condition is given. For Plato, laws do not create; they conserve. For a return to the point of departure he relied on the cycle which governs change, an oscillatory development in which each phase repeats in reverse the preceding one.[40]

[39] Laws x. 903d, 905b.
[40] Myth in the *Statesman* 269a ff.

xix *Social Unity*

If, through good fortune or divine providence, the founder of the city has at his disposal the characters he needs, he can then establish a just city. To achieve this it is enough to regulate the activity of the citizens in such a way that "each devotes his efforts to a single function, the one for which he is naturally qualified, so that having his own occupation each may be not many but one, and so that there can thus arise a city which is one and not many" (*Republic* 423d). Thus wealth, for example, must be strictly regulated in order to hold the artisan to his craft: "Will a potter who has become rich still want to devote himself to his trade? Obviously not; he then becomes a bad potter" (421d). Nor must he be so poor that he cannot provide himself with the necessary tools. Hence the extraordinary laws concerning the guardians of the city; everything is subordinated to the necessity of maintaining perfect unity among them. The greatest misfortune for the city is division. Now one of the greatest causes of division is the system of separating the city into families, with the result that each family experiences its pains and pleasures separately. Community of women, children, and property is the only way of binding the guardians together: kept in ignorance of his natural filiations by strict regulations of public nurseries, everyone will have, depending on his age, the feelings of a son or a father toward everyone else (462a ff., 464d).

On the other hand, since the city does not take into account differences between persons, but only differences between their aptitudes, and since the citizen is defined wholly by his relation to occupations, it follows that women need not be given a different role than men in the city; from the social point of view there is no difference whatever between them. Some women will be artisans; others will have the noble passions of a defender of the city; others, the wisdom of the guardians (454b–457b).

Finally, if we only consider the functions and not the subjects who perform them, then by a very simple transformation Platonic sociology will become a psychology and a morality. There will be as many faculties in the individual soul as there are functions in the city. Primitive desires for nourishment correspond to the function of the artisan; the passion of anger to that of the soldier; reflective intelligence to that of the guardian. Just as each of these functions has its virtue or excellence—temperance for the artisan, courage for the soldier, and prudence for the guardian—so each faculty will have its own virtue. And in the same way that justice in the city consists in each one doing what he is suited for—the higher class ordering, the lower class obeying—so justice in the individual consists in holding each part of the soul to its natural role. Thus, the study of society enables us to see more clearly into the soul of the individual (453a, 443e ff.)

xx *Decline of the City*

The whole of morality, like the whole of politics, consists in fixing these natural relationships in the most stable possible way. But absolute fixity is impossible; for "all that is born is subject to destruction" (546a). Once the complex harmony which makes the unity and justice of society is disturbed, there is a more or less rapid decline. Passing through a regular sequence of governments where each one arises from the preceding one, the city gradually goes from the most just government to the most unjust government. For Plato there is no natural and spontaneous evolution other than this decline. Books VIII and IX of the *Republic,* which contain so many features drawn from his political and psychological experiences, hold out no hope for arresting the movement, once it is set in motion by the negligence of the chief magistrates of the city (545d). The state of harmony is followed by a state of partition and struggle, whose successive degrees are marked by different forms of government. Moreover, struggles and civil dissensions are accompanied by a corresponding state of agitation and instability in the soul of each citizen; to each type of society there corresponds a psychological type.

The best constitution is first of all followed by a struggle between "a race of gold and silver," which attempts to uphold virtue and tradition, and "a race of iron and bronze" totally enslaved to the pursuit of profit. This struggle ends in a sort of agrarian law by which lands and houses are distributed and appropriated; the regime of private property begins and, with it, the enslavement of agricultural workers. The dominant cast becomes that of the warriors, who care little for study but much for gymnastics and war, who are ambitious and jealous of one another, and who little by little acquire the taste for wealth (546d–549d).

The domination of the rich characterizes the third form of the city, which Plato calls an oligarchy. A certain position or rank is the condition of admission to the magistracy. The precarious unity of the preceding government is destroyed again; within the city there are two distinct cities, that of the poor and that of the rich—indigence on one hand, luxury on the other. The noble passions no longer predominate everywhere, as in the preceding governments, but base desires. Moreover, the poor, whom the rich are obliged to arm in order to defend the city, are a constant worry to them (550c ff.).

An insatiable desire for riches brings about the fall of oligarchies. In order to grow rich through usury, they encourage intemperance among the rich and noble youth. These young people, reduced to indigence, but nevertheless retaining all the pride of their origin, are the real supporters of the revolution which leads to democracy: hardened by the life they lead, they have no difficulty in overcoming the rich who are softened by luxury. Democracy is essentially the victory of the poor; its watchword is liberty. There, everyone leads the kind of life that pleases him. Nothing is more varied or less unified than a democracy like that of Athens, a real "emporium" of constitutions, where the politician can come to look for models; the democratic man is interested in everything, even in philosophy. From liberty arises equality, meaning that "equality for the unequal" which is due to the absence of authority (557–563).

An insatiable desire for liberty causes the downfall of democracy and changes this social form into its opposite, tyranny. Those who preside over the destinies of the city cannot taste power without wanting more and more of it and without becoming tyrants. The tyrant is the very antithesis of the guardian of the ideal city. He is the perfect example of the completely isolated individual, who breaks every tie with society; he banishes the good men he fears and lives among bodyguards he has obtained by freeing slaves. The dissociation of the city here reaches its extreme limit. The tyrannical man is the man who gives free rein to the most savage passions, to those which the well-bred man knows only in dreams. He is the individual who considers himself absolute, "friendless, always a despot or a slave, but ignorant of true liberty and true friendship."

xxi *The Myth of the* Statesman

The constant danger of decline which threatens cities is an indirect way of proving the necessity of government by philosophers who can arrest the downward trend. The highly pessimistic view of society, which emerges from the law of the debasement of cities, is not counterbalanced in Plato by a belief that political technique could succeed in effecting progress in the opposite direction. It is balanced only by a non-rational but very lively belief in the cyclical form of change; change, making a full circle, leads back to the primitive state. But Plato never gave this belief the philosophical and scientific form which he gave to his description of the directly verified fact of the decline of governments. He gave it the form of a myth, which he expounds in the *Statesman;* a myth undoubtedly designed to help understand the exact place and limitations of the art of politics in an evolution whose course as a whole escapes the grasp of rational art. Plato imagined, in effect, that in the happy age of Cronos, when the sun and stars were moving in an opposite direction from their present course, the whole development of beings was also in an opposite direction; in other words, development went from death to birth instead of from birth to death. The earth produced all the products useful to man spontaneously and without human work, and, in general, each being reached its state of perfection without effort; technical work and therefore political union were unnecessary. But when the sun changes the direction of its course, when, simultaneously, beings reach their completion slowly and with difficulty amid obstacles of every sort, then techniques of all kinds and in particular social techniques are necessary. Most of the arts are gifts the gods give to men in order to sustain them in these difficulties (268e–275b).

Hence the rather singular and novel features assumed by social art in the *Statesman*. All human art manipulates changing and heterogeneous things and, for that reason, proceeds less by general rules than by clever tricks which adapt themselves to circumstances. The same holds true of the art of politics; "the differences in men and in their actions and the complete absence of rest in human affairs resist any simple rule applying to all cases and valid at all times" (294b), just as in the other arts. It follows that the statesman, the political technician, is a living law and that he is absolute sovereign of the city like the shepherd with his flock. Thus Plato came to grant the politician a providential and superhuman character, the early germ of the theory of power in the Roman Empire and the Papacy. Here again we see no rational hope for natural progress, and myth is regularly substituted for knowledge wherever there is a question of returning to a condition better than ours (293–300).

XXII *The Laws*

This sense of the relativity and instability of human affairs is particularly strong in the *Laws,* the unfinished work of Plato's old age. It is filled with detailed instructions, indicating a clear intention to carry out his reform, perhaps in the Sicilian towns which were to be restored after the death of Dionysius. The problem of the *Laws,* like that of the *Timaeus,* is a problem of mixture. Here one searches for the proportions which will make the most stable possible society, just as the earlier dialogue discovered the proportions which would give the cosmos imperishable duration. For Plato, stability and perfection are the same thing: "It is of utmost importance that the laws be stable" (797a). Everything down to children's toys must stay the same from one generation to the next; every change is a disturbance, whether in the organism or in the city. Laws are only truly respected if no one has any recollection of a time when things were different than now, "and the legislator must contrive every means to produce this state of things in the city."

Some of these means are beyond his control; they are provided by nature itself: an environment favorable to the development of character and a region sufficiently isolated from the sea and from other cities to run no risk of contamination by commerce and by influence from others. These are happy accidents which are due only to the gods. On the other hand, the legislator can limit the number of citizens, by selecting a number which is rather small, but which is a multiple of as many other numbers as possible.

But, above all, he is master of the mixture which will produce the most stable constitution (691 ff.). History shows us the example of a constitution which has withstood time; that of Sparta, which has observed the rules of measure and avoided any excess. The powers of the two kings are limited by each other; their authority is limited by that of the senate, in which the restraining influence of the old is combined with the impetuous vigor of the young; it is also limited by the power of the Ephors. "In this way royalty, mixed as it had to be with other elements and being limited by them, has preserved itself and has preserved the rest." On the contrary, history shows the decline of the Persian constitution, that liberal monarchy which changed into a tyranny, and the decline of the democratic constitution of Athens, where liberty led to an unrestrained anarchy. Thus there are two antithetical constitutions, despotism and democracy, "mothers of all the rest." Isolated, they are injurious; but their well-proportioned mixture produces the best constitution (693d).

What prevents decline (for always, and here also, it is a matter of restraint which arrests and not of positive progress)? What prevents it is the harmony between feeling and judicious intelligence (689a); the cause of downfall is taking pleasure in what one judges to be wicked or unjust and feeling pain at which one judges to be just. It is because of this disposition of the mind, which is the worst of errors, that the city is no longer, as it ought to be, "a friend of itself" (701d).

Plato was well aware that pure intelligence is not enough; inclination is also required, and a free and voluntary inclination. The legislator should therefore not obtain consent by violence, but by persuasion (887a ff.); hence the use of prologues setting out motives for obeying the laws (719c–723b). This exposition of motives, which is also an ethical sermon, was an innovation in legislation.

The results of this way of assuring social stability by a faith implanted in minds, are especially clear in Book X, which is concerned with religious beliefs. Here impiety is treated primarily as a social danger; the atheism Plato combated was that of the Sophists, who considered the gods as human inventions (891b–899d). Those who denied providence and whom he refuted are not theorists but people who give free rein to their passions because they do not believe that divine justice enters into the details of human affairs (899d–905d). Finally, the erroneous belief that God is seduced by prayers is connected with a whole series of cult and religious practices involving private associations dangerous to social life (905d–907b).[41] Also, if it is first necessary to try to forestall impiety by rational arguments, as Plato did, it is then necessary to prescribe serious penalties for those who do not want to be convinced. As the case may require, temporary or life imprisonment removes these dangerously impious people from the city (908a ff.).

The last word of the political Plato was that contemplative serenity of the sage who sees the hidden motives which make men act. "Human things are not worth taking very seriously. . . . Man is God's toy, a mere piece of machinery for him" (803b). The legislator is above all the one who is familiar with this machine and who knows how to lead men.

---

[41] Cf. 909b, concerning the danger of religious associations independent of the city.

XXIII *The Academy of the Fourth Century (after Plato)*

After Plato, the Academy had successively as its head Speusippus, the nephew of the master (348–339), Xenocrates (339–315), and Polemo (315–269). The history of the teachings of the first two is scarcely known except by some allusions of Aristotle. They seem to have consisted in free developments of certain suggestions of the master. There was no orthodox Platonism at that time, and this was even the occasion for a sharp reproach brought by the Neo-Platonists against the direct successors of Plato.[42] Also Platonism, undermined by differences of opinion in the school, was overthrown by the attack of the new dogmatisms then forming. Aristotle, the Stoics, and Epicurus acted together in combating it.

The central problem for his successors as for the aging Plato seems to have been the formation of mixtures. As in the *Philebus* and *Timaeus,* the problem was to explain the different forms of reality by the introduction of a measure or a fixed relation into a reality primitively indefinite and without fixity. But this kind of explanation was only a vague scheme which did not exclude different interpretations. On the one hand, the scheme was actually most valuable for explaining numbers; the One determines the multiple or indefinite dyad of the large and the small, the equal determines the unequal. But what should be said about other realities such as mathematical magnitudes or the world? Speusippus thought that each of them implied a new pair of principles, different from those out of which numbers arise; in the same way that number comes from the union of the One and the multiple, for example, mathematical magnitudes originate from the mixture of the indivisible with unlimited space. Since different realities will each have its own special principles, they will no longer depend on one another, and the sum total of reality, according to Aristotle's objection, will be

[42] Numenius (2d century A.D.) in Eusebius *Praeparatio evangelica* xiv. 5. 2.

like a bad tragedy, made up of episodes.[43] But although he introduced distinct pairs of principles for each degree of reality, Speusippus must have insisted on an analogy or similarity between these
successive pairs; for example, although intelligence, the principle
of unity in the world-soul, has a special nature absolutely distinct
from the One, the source of the world,[44] there is nevertheless an
analogy of role between the One and intelligence. Analogies of this
sort were perhaps what Speusippus was looking for in his treatise on
Homologies, whose fragments concern the classification of living
things.

It follows equally from Speusippus' theory that the first stages of
reality contain nothing like the richness and plenitude of the subsequent stages. The Good or Perfection does not exist at the beginning but at the end. Likewise the living germ does not contain any
of the perfections which one finds in the fully developed animal.
Thus it is wrong, according to him, to assimilate the One, which is
the source, to the Good which is posterior.[45]

It is apparent how much of the Platonic dialectic Speusippus has
sacrificed. In abolishing the continuity linking the forms of reality
to their source by a deductive chain, he denied the existence of the
Good as a source, the existence of ideal numbers, and even the
existence of ideas. When he considered the series of composites—
mathematical numbers, mathematical magnitudes, soul—he used the
Platonic scheme in order to construct each of them; but he ignored
their connection.

In perfect contrast with Speusippus, Xenocrates seems to have
wanted to stress the unity and continuity of the series of forms in
being. He identifies ideas with ideal numbers,[46] and he finds these
numbers again in the series of beings which depend on them: in
lines and ideal surfaces which he demonstrates to be indivisible, in
the soul which he defines as a self-moving number and elsewhere

[43] Aristotle *Metaphysics* Z. 2. 1028b 21; cf. 1075b 37 and 1900b 13.
[44] Diels, *Doxographi Graeci,* p. 303; he is opposed on this point to Xenocrates.
[45] Aristotle *Metaphysics* A. 7. 1072b 30; cf. 1075a 36; 1092a 22; 1091a 29.
[46] Aristotle *Metaphysics* Z. 1028b 24.

as a combination of unity and multiplicity, and finally in the heavens and in all sensible things.[47] Whereas Speusippus refused to assimilate the One to the Good, because it would then be necessary to identify its opposite, multiplicity, with evil, Xenocrates did not hesitate when faced with this conclusion. And it follows that if all beings except the One are composites of unity and multiplicity, then they all participate in evil. His theory of indivisible lines is his best known one, thanks to the apocryphal treatise of Aristotle *On Indivisible Lines*.[48] The ideal line (and the same argument applies to surfaces and to bodies) must be indivisible, because it is prior to all the others and because it is their unit of measure.

Xenocrates sought to deny everywhere the apparent discontinuity of things. Plato had already indicated in the *Timaeus* that every sensible body must be composed of the four elements; the substantial unity of the different regions of the world, so contrary to the doctrine which Aristotle was to uphold, was taken up again by Xenocrates when he viewed the solidity of terrestrial bodies as imitating that of the sun and moon.[49]

Thus, the doctrines of Speusippus and Xenocrates diverged, but the problem they solved was the same. Also, the two disciples found themselves in agreement when it came to interpreting the *Timaeus*.[50] According to them, when Plato described the genesis of the soul and the world, he was not describing an actual development. The world is eternal; it was for the sake of convenience that Plato supposed it came into existence, just as the geometer produces by construction figures which he knows to be eternal, for the sole purpose of bringing out more clearly the elements which compose them.

The Platonic method thus became fixed in a doctrine with his successors; the bold imaginativeness of the myths was to end in dogmas. This transformation is connected with the intense interest

---

[47] Plutarch *Creation of the Soul according to the Timaeus* chap ii; Cicero *Dream of Scipio* i. 14; and *Tusculanes* i. 20.
[48] Aristotle *Metaphysics* N. 1091b 35.
[49] Plutarch *Concerning the Face of the Moon* chap. xxix.
[50] Plutarch *Creation of The Soul* chap. iii.

in the Orient shown by the fourth century, even before the time of Alexander. The titles of certain treatises of Democritus on the sacred writings of the Babylonians and Egyptians, and his admiration for the wisdom of the orientals whose moral maxims he may have translated,[51] are evidence of this interest. Plato himself or perhaps one of his immediate students, Philippus of Opus, wrote as sequel to the *Laws* the *Epinomis,* which contains the first codification of astral theology known to us among the Greeks. By locating the heavens farther from the earth, by sharply distinguishing celestial bodies from meteors, by pointing out the uniformity in the motions of the planets, the astronomers of the fourth century gave a new setting to this theology originating in the Orient (*Epinomis* 986e, 987b). The order which reigns in the heavens is proof of the intelligence of the stars and of the divinity of the souls animating them (*Epinomis* 982b). The world is divided into parts arranged hierarchically, each with its living things; between the earth, the abode of disorder, and heaven, the abode of the visible gods (984d), there is the air, where those transparent and invisible beings, the daemons, live. Endowed with a marvelous intelligence, with knowledge and with memory, they love the good and hate the wicked; for they know our thoughts. They are not, moreover, impassive like the gods but capable of pleasure and pain (984d–985b). Xenocrates accepted a theological hierarchy analogous at every point to the one in the *Epinomis:* at the summit, the highest gods who are unity and the dyad; unity is male, father, king of the heavens, Zeus, intelligence; the dyad, a feminine divinity, is mother of the gods and soul of the universe. Below them are the heavens and the stars, which are the Olympian gods; still lower, the invisible sublunary daemons who enter into the elements.[52] We can see the crucial identification made at that time between the rational picture of the cosmos and the old mythical and theological pictures. The daemons in and through whom the bond and unity of the world are realized

---

[51] Diogenes Laertius *Lives of the Philosophers* ix. 49; Clement of Alexandria *Stromateis* i. 16, 69; cf. R. Eisler, *Arch. für die Geschichte der Philosophie,* 1917, p. 187.

[52] Diels, *Doxographi Graeci,* frag. 304.

naturally occupy the central place in this cosmic religion, whose extraordinary development will be seen in Stoicism and in Neo-Platonism.

But Speusippus and Xenocrates seem to have concerned themselves especially with morality. Nine of the thirty-two works of Speusippus whose titles Diogenes (iv. 4) has preserved, and twenty-nine of the sixty works of Xenocrates (iv. 11), refer expressly to morality. Their successor Polemo is known chiefly as a moralist, and his contemporary, Crantor, wrote a short treatise *On Grief* which Panaetius, the Stoic, two centuries later recommended learning by heart.[53] Two features characterize this moral doctrine, in other respects little known. First, a certain naturalism: there are primitive natural tendencies inclining us toward soundness of body, health, and intellectual activity. The ultimate good, according to Speusippus, consists in attaining perfection in the things consonant with nature and, according to Polemo, in "living according to nature"; in other words, in enjoying primitive natural endowments by joining virtue to them.[54] The second feature, derived from the *Republic,* is the precept which demands regulation and discipline of feelings rather than their suppression.[55] That *metriopathia,* advised by Crantor in times of grief, contrasts with the savage impassivity preached by the new sects of that time. It will continue to be the tone of those writings for special occasions, the *Consolations,* which are to become so numerous in the following centuries. Certain themes (for example, the argument that death is not to be feared, whether it be annihilation or whether it be a journey of the soul to a better region) which are found in all these writings go back to Plato's *Apology* (40c); from there they passed, by way of Crantor, to all his imitators.[56] Seen in this light, the Academy had a role of some importance in the growth of that humanistic and undogmatic moral preaching which we will see developing in the third century and which will more or less transcend the disagreements among sects.

[53] Cicero *Academica Priora* ii. § 135.
[54] Clement of Alexandria *Stromateis* 418d, and Cicero *De Finibus* ii. 11. § 33.
[55] Cited by Plutarch *Consolation to Apollonius* iii.
[56] Gercke, *De Consolationibus;* cf. Cicero *Tusculanes* i. 49. 117–18.

Works

Text: Ed. J. Burnet. In *Scriptorum classicorum Bibliotheca Oxoniensis*. 5 vols.
Translation: *The Dialogues of Plato*. Translated by Benjamin Jowett. 4th edition. 4 vols. Oxford, 1953.

General Studies

A. Fouillée. *La philosophie de Platon*. Paris, 1869. 2d edition, 1888–89.

L. Robin. *Platon*. Paris, 1935.

A. Diès. *Autour de Platon*. Vol. II, *Les Dialogues et Esquisses doctrinales*. Paris, 1927.—*Platon*. Paris, 1930.

P.-M. Schuhl. *Platon et l'art de son temps*. Paris, 1933. 2d edition, 1952.—*L'Œuvre de Platon*. Paris, 1954. 2d edition, 1958.—*Études platoniciennes*. Paris, 1960.

A. J. Festugière. *Contemplation et vie contemplative selon Platon*. 1936.

R. Schaerer. *La question platonicienne*. Paris-Neuchâtel, 1938.—*Dieu: L'homme et la vie d'après Platon*. Neuchâtel, 1944.

J. Moreau. *La construction de l'idéalisme platonicien*. 1939.—*Réalisme et idéalisme chez Platon*. Paris, 1951.

S. Pétrement. *Essai sur le dualisme chez Platon, les Gnostiques et les Manichéens*. Paris, 1947.

V. Goldschmidt. *Les dialogues de Platon, structure et méthode dialectique*. 1947.—*Le paradigme dans la dialectique platonicienne*. 1947.—*La religion de Platon*. 1949.

H. Raeder. *Platons philosophische Entwickelung*. Leipzig, 1905.

W. Pater. *Plato and Platonism*. London, 1909 (French translation, Paris, 1923).

C. Ritter. *Plato, sein Leben, seine Schriften, seine Lehre*. Vol. I. Munich, 1910.

P. E. More. *Platonism*. Princeton, 1917.

U. von Wilamowitz-Moellendorf. *Platon*. 2 vols. Berlin, 1919. 2d edition, 1920.

P. Friedländer. *Platon*. Vol. I, 1928. 2d edition, Berlin, 1954. Vol. II, 1930. 2d edition, 1960.

J. Burnet. *Platonism*. Berkeley, 1928. See *Revue philosophique*, 1931, p. 283 ff.

Special Studies

C. Huit. *La vie et l'œuvre de Platon*. Paris, 1893.

J. Chevalier. *La notion du nécessaire chez Aristote*. Lyon, 1914. Pp. 191–222: summary of the works on the chronology of the dialogues of Plato.

V. Brochard. "Les mythes de Platon." *Études de philosophie ancienne et moderne*. 1912. P. 46.

P. Frutiger. *Les mythes de Platon*. Paris, 1930.

J. Bidez. "Les couleurs des planètes dans le mythe d'Er," *Bull. de l'Acad. roy. de Belgique*, August, 1935.

A. Diès. "La transposition platonicienne," in *Annales de l'Institut de Louvain*, II (1913), 267. Reproduced in *Autour de Platon*. Pp. 400–451.

P.-M. Schuhl. *La fabulation platonicienne*. Paris, 1947; *Le Merveilleux, la Pensée et l'Action*, Part II. Paris, 1952.

J. Pépin. *Mythe et allégorie*. Paris, 1958.

E. Milhaud. *Les philosophes géomètres de la Grèce*. Paris, 1900.

G. Rodier. *Mathématique et dialectique dans le système de Platon*. Reproduced in *Études de philosophie grecque*. Pp. 37–49.

R. Robinson. *Plato's Earlier Dialectic*. 2d edition, Oxford, 1953.

G. Rodier. "Évolution de la dialectique de Platon," in *Année philosophique*, 1905. Reproduced in *Études de philosophie grecque*. Pp. 49–73.

J. Rolland de Renéville. *Essai sur le problème de l'Un-multiple et de l'attribution chez Platon et les Sophistes*. Paris, 1962.

L. Robin. *Les rapports de l'être et de la connaissance d'après Platon*. Paris, 1957.

L. Robin. "Sur la doctrine de la réminiscence," *Revue des études grecques*, XXXII (1919), 451. Collected in *La pensée hellénique des origines à Épicure*. Paris, 1942. Pp. 337–42.

L. Robin. *La théorie platonicienne de l'amour*. Paris, 1908. 2d edition, 1933.

V. Brochard. "La théorie platonicienne de la participation d'après le Parménide et le Sophiste." *Études*. P. 113.

Sir David Ross. *Plato's Theory of Ideas*. Oxford, 1951.

A. Diès. *La définition de l'être et la nature des Idées dans le Sophiste*. Paris, 1909.

J. Souilhé. *La notion platonicienne d'intermédiaire dans la philosophie des dialogues*. Paris, 1919.

P. Kucharski. *Les chemins du savoir dans les derniers dialogues de Platon*. Paris, 1949.

N. J. Boussoulas. *L'être et la composition des mixtes dans le Philèbe*. Paris, 1952.

L. Robin. *La place de la physique dans la philosophie de Platon*. Paris, 1919. Collected in *La pensée hellénique des origines à Épicure*. Paris, 1942. Pp. 231–336.

J. Moreau. *L'âme du monde de Platon aux Stoïciens*. 1939.

W. J. Verdenius. "Platons Gottesbegriff," *Entretiens de la Fondation Hardt sur l'Antiquité classiques*. Vandoeuvres–Geneva, 1952. I, 241.

P.-M. Schuhl. "Platon et la médecine," *Revue des études grecques*, 1960, I, 73 ff.

E. Amado Lévy-Valensi. *Les Niveaux de l'Être, la Connaissance et le Mal.* Paris, 1963. Chap. L.

A. Brémond. *De l'âme et de Dieu dans la philosophie de Platon.* In *Archives de philosophie,* Vol. II, No. 3 (1924), p. 24.

L. Robin. *La théorie platonicienne des idées et des nombres d'après Aristote.* Paris, 1908.

P. Kucharski. *Les principes des Pythagoriciens et la dyade de Platon.* In *Archives de philosophie,* Vol. XXII (1959), Nos. 2 and 3.

V. Brochard. "La morale de Platon." *Études.* P. 169.

J. Gould. *The Development of Plato's Ethics.* Cambridge, 1955.

L. Robin. "Platon et la science sociale," *Revue de métaphysique,* 1913.

A. Espinas. "Origines et principes de la politique platonicienne." (Introduction to the edition of Book VI of the *Republic.* Paris, 1886.)

P. Lachièze-Rey. *Les idées morales, sociales et politiques de Platon.* Paris, 1938.

P.-M. Schuhl. "Sur le mythe du politique," *Revue de métaphysique,* 1932, p. 47.—"Platon et l'activité politique de l'Académie," *Revue des études grecques,* 1946, pp. 46 ff.

W. Jaeger. *Paideia,* 1947. Vols. II and III.

K. R. Popper. *The Open Society and Its Enemies.* Princeton, N.J., 1950.

R. B. Levinson. *In Defense of Plato.* Cambridge, 1953.

M. Vanhoutte. *La philosophie politique de Platon dans les Lois.* Louvain, 1953.

R. Weil. *L'archéologie de Platon.* Paris, 1960.

P. Lang. *De Speusippi academici scriptis.* Bonn, 1911.

R. Heinze. *Xenokrates, Eine Darstellung der Lehre und Sammlung der Fragmente.* Leipzig, 1892.

H. Cherniss. *The Riddle of the Early Academy.* 1945.

C. J. de Vogel. "Problems Concerning Later Platonism," *Mnémosyne,* 1949, pp. 197 ff., 299 ff. Cf. *Revue philosophique,* 1953, p. 463.

Special Studies in English

F. M. Cornford. *Plato's Theory of Knowledge.* London, 1935.—*Plato's Cosmology.* London, 1937.—*Plato and Parmenides.* London, 1939.—*The Republic of Plato.* n.d.

R. Demos. *The Philosophy of Plato.* New York, 1939.

G. C. Field. *Plato and His Contemporaries.* London, 1930.

R. C. Lodge. *Plato's Theory of Ethics.* London, 1928.

W. Lutoslawski. *The Origin and Growth of Plato's Logic.* London, 1905.

R. L. Nettleship. *Lectures on the Republic of Plato.* London, 1898.

C. Ritter. *The Essence of Plato's Philosophy.* London, 1933.

P. Shorey. *The Unity of Plato's Thought.* Chicago, 1903.

J. A. Stewart. *The Myths of Plato.* Oxford, 1905.

A. E. Taylor. *Plato: The Man and His Work.* London, 1926.

John Wild. *Plato's Theory of Man.* Cambridge, 1946.—*Plato's Modern Enemies and the Theory of Natural Law.* Chicago, 1903.

ARISTOTLE AND THE LYCEUM

ARISTOTLE was born in 385 in Stagira, a town located on the northern shore of the Aegean, east of the Chalcidice. He could not have come under the influence of his father, a physician, since Aristotle was very young when his father died. He spent many years in Plato's school, which he entered in 367. At the time of the master's death he, along with some other students of Plato, including Xenocrates, found himself at Assos in Aeolia with the tyrant Hermias of Atarneum. He lived there several years, not without profiting from the political experience of Hermias who had to maneuver between two powers of the day, Macedonia and Persia. In 343 he was at Mitylene on the island of Lesbos. From there he was called by King Philip of Macedonia to the court at Pella, where he was intrusted with the education of the young Alexander. He acquired powerful friends among the Macedonians; one of them was Antipater. His own nephew Callisthenes was among the friends of Alexander, later to become his victim. When in 335 he returned to Athens where the nationalist party, silenced after the political fall of the city, nevertheless still existed, this alien must have been known as a partisan of Macedonia. He did not return to the Academy but founded a new school, the Lyceum, where he taught for thirteen years. When Alexander died (323), the national Athenian party which Demosthenes still led forced him to leave the city. He withdrew to Chalcis in Euboea, to an estate inherited from his mother, where he died in 322 at the age of 63. His was a life very different from Plato's. He was not the Athenian of high birth, political to the very depths of his soul, who did not separate philosophy from the government of the city. He was the student who isolated himself from the state in speculative pursuits, who made politics itself an object of scholarship and of history rather than an opportunity for action. In the case of Plato, we only know the writings he intended for the public and are almost entirely ignorant of his teaching. In the case of Aristotle, on the contrary, only insignificant fragments of the works written for a wide public remain. What we do have are the courses he wrote out either for instruction at the Lyceum or possibly for the lectures he must have given at Assos before becoming Alexander's tutor; notes written out by a professor for himself, with no attempt at literary perfection. Sometimes they are mere outlines for oral development, into which students' notes may even have been inserted when these collections were published after his death.

These works can be classified as follows:

1. Early works intended for a wide public (which Aristotle himself calls exoteric discourses), the dialogues which Cicero could have had in mind when he praised the golden flow of Aristotle's eloquence. Of these only a few fragments remain, collected by V. Rose. They are the *Eudemus,* a dialogue on the immortality of the soul, the *Protrepticus,* addressed to a prince of Cyprus, Themison, to which the discourse *To Demonakus* by a student of Isocrates appears to be a reply (the author of this discourse complains about those who engage in disinterested study and turn away from practical affairs), and last, the treatise *On Philosophy* or *On The Good,* which dates from the time Aristotle withdrew from Plato's school. It already contained, in addition to a history of philosophic thought, a critique of the theory of ideas. And it concluded with an astral theology demonstrating the divinity of the stars.

2. The corpus of scientific works. (*a*) The collection of logical works known as the *Organon:* the *Categories; On Interpretation* (on judgments); the *Topics* (on the rules of discussion); *Sophistical Refutations; Prior Analytics* (on the syllogism in general);

Posterior Analytics (on demonstration). To these we can add the *Rhetoric* and the *Poetics.*

b) The collection on first philosophy entitled *Metaphysics.* This work, consisting of twelve books (numbered by capital letters of the Greek alphabet) plus a supplementary book to the first (α), is not all of a piece. Book α has to be considered separately; it is a kind of preliminary to physics by Pasicles, a nephew of Eudemus. Book Δ is a lexicon indicating the various meanings of philosophical terms. Books H, Z, and Θ comprise a treatise on substance, to which I is added and which is continued by M (chaps. 1–9, to 1086a 20). Books A, B, Γ, E, M (from 1086a 20), and N date from an earlier period, when Aristotle still counted himself a Platonist, although he criticizes the theory of ideas. Book K (1–8) appears to be a student notebook; it belongs to the same period as the preceding group and sums up the books of this group. Finally Λ is a theological treatise, a synoptic treatise on the various kinds of substances which is self-contained (with the exception of chap. 8, a very specialized inquiry into the number of celestial spheres needed to explain the motion of the planets, which refers to the astronomer Callippus who reformed the Attic calendar in 330).

c) The works on nature: the *Physics,* whose earliest parts appear to be Books I, II, VII, and VIII; *On the Heavens,* where a reference to the dialogue *On Philosophy* (i. 9) proves a rather early date; *On Generation and Corruption;* the *Meteorology,* where the authenticity of the fourth and the last books has occasionally been questioned; the *Mechanics* (whose authenticity is still a possibility according to Carteron's *La Notion de Force dans le Système d'Aristotle* [1923], p. 265).

d) The collection of biological works, very important for the history of science: the *Parts of Animals; On the Generation of Animals,* along with the short treatises *On the Progression of Animals* and *On the Movement of Animals; the History of Animals.* The great treatise *On the Soul* belongs to this collection and also the short works following it: *Sensation and the Sensible, Memory and Recollection, Sleep, Dreams, Divination by Dreams, Length and Brevity of Life, Youth and Old Age, Respiration.*

e) The collection of ethical and political works: the *Eudemian Ethics,* the earliest and the closest to Plato; the *Nicomachean Ethics; the Politics.* The *Politics* shows two different orientations: on the one hand, that of Books H and Θ which contain the theory of an ideal state, to which A, B, Γ are an introduction; on the other hand, that of books Δ, E, Z, which embody factual political research based on a vast historical induction. The latter group belongs to Aristotle's last period, the period when he described the constitutions of some hundred cities; only the first one, the *Constitution of Athens,* has been recovered.

Finally, it is necessary to add some apocryphal works which have crept into the collection of his writings and which are the products of the work of his school. One of these, the *Problems,* has an interest of the highest order; another is the *Magna Moralia.*[1]

1 *The Organon: The* Topics

Aristotle was the inventor of formal logic; that is, the part of logic which gives rules of reasoning independent of the content of thought. But in spite of their appearance, the logical writings collected under the title of the *Organon* (instrument) do not give a systematic exposition of this logic. In appearance, they are arranged according to the chapter titles of the classical manuals of logic: (1.) *Categories,* containing the theory of terms; (2.) *On Interpretation,* or the theory of propositions; (3.) *Prior Analytics,* or the theory of syllogism in general; (4.) the *Posterior Analytics,* or the theory of demonstration, the syllogism whose premises are necessary; (5.) the *Topics,* or the theory of dialectical and probable reasoning,

---

[1] The problem of classification is different from that of the chronology of the works, concerning which W. Jaeger and F. Nuyens arrived at rather different conclusions. The principle lies in the progressive detachment which Aristotle shows toward the Platonic theory of the soul.

where the premises are only generally accepted opinions; (6.) the *Rhetoric,* the theory of rhetorical reasoning or enthymeme, whose premises are selected to persuade the audience. The syllogism, whose elements are presented in the first two treatises, is examined carefully in the third treatise; it is the common instrument used equally by scientists, dialecticians, and orators, although each with different premises.

In point of fact, Aristotle wrote the *Categories* and the greater part of the *Topics* (ii–vii) before he discovered the syllogism. He only reflected on the rules of reasoning after thinking about the rules of a sound discussion. We have already seen in Plato's *Sophist* and *Parmenides* how the idea of logical outlines (division and classification of terms, definition of the highest genera, relations of the predicate to the subject) arose from the conditions of discussion; the overriding problem was to get the better of misologists or eristics. It was in this environment of ardent dialecticians that Aristotle's logic was born. Now the dialectician does not use the methods of the professor who lectures and still less the methods of the scholar who creates knowledge. Dialectic is a dialogue in which a speaker first proposes a thesis to another who examines it; this examination proceeds by means of questions which have to be answered yes or no. The purpose of the examination is generally to refute the respondent by leading him to contradict himself.

We have seen the transposition by which Plato turned dialectic into the whole of philosophy. Aristotle must have abandoned this hope early. He reduced dialectic, or the art of discussion, to the level of an exercise which does not yield certainty because it does not take into consideration things themselves but men's opinions about things. What defines dialectic as such is really less a logical structure of reasoning than the human relations it involves. In a sound discussion, one has to be careful to take as starting points only propositions that are generally accepted, either by all men or by competent men if a technical thesis is at issue. Moreover, the questions asked should neither be too easy, since an answer would be unnecessary, nor too hard, since one has to give an immediate answer.[2] Such methods lead only to analysis and comparison of judgments in order to show their agreement or disagreement.

But this exercise is indispensable, and we are going to see first the outlines of logic and then Aristotle's whole philosophy grow out of it. His first concern had to do with vocabulary: confusion in discussion arises from designating different things by the same name (homonyms) or the same thing by different names (synonyms), and the indispensable preliminary is to enumerate the different senses given to words used in the discussion. Nearly the whole of the *Categories* and Book Δ of the *Metaphysics* are devoted to these lexicographical studies; they are less concerned with distinguishing things themselves than with distinguishing various senses of a single world.

The same is true of the theory of propositions which is the basis of Aristotelian logic. When he asserted that every proposition consists of a subject and a predicate, Aristotle asserted a thesis of immense importance, not only for logic, but for metaphysics. He did not borrow this thesis from the analysis of language as has sometimes been said (actually, he was well acquainted with verbal forms, such as those of vows and prayers, which he assigned to rhetoric) but rather from the analysis of dialectical problems. In reality, every dialectical problem consists in asking whether or not a predicate belongs to a subject. The misologist made dialectic impossible by denying the possibility of asserting a predicate of a subject; inversely, it was the demands of dialectic which led Aristotle to his theory. This is why he usually states propositions, not in the classic form, A is B, but in the form, B belongs to A. A proposition is a *protasis,* that is to say an assertion presented for the approval of a listener. So it is with the classification of propositions. The classic division into universal propositions (affirmative or negative) is first presented as a division of problems. Every problem really consists in asking whether a predicate belongs (or does not

[2] *Topics* i. 9, 10.

belong) to all (or to a part) of a subject; this gives the formula of four propositions.[3]

Moreover, in order to grasp the meaning of a dialectical problem, it is important to know the kind of predicate that is demanded. Does the predicate state what the subject is, or does it only set forth a property of the subject? Does it set forth a property which belongs to it necessarily or only accidentally? These are cases to be distinguished in order to make discussion possible, for many errors come from thinking that one can reverse propositions; in other words, from holding that because A belongs to all B, B belongs to all A. Now, conversion is only admissible if A is a property of B; that is to say, belongs to it necessarily and exclusively. From considerations of this kind springs the famous division of predicates into five classes: genus, species, difference, property, and accident.[4] The first three are obviously connected with the Platonic practice of division; division was intended to show what a subject is (its quiddity) by first determining what the most general class it belongs to is, and then dividing this class into a number of classes. In Aristotle the largest class (animal) becomes the genus; differences (rational) are what permit its division into subordinate classes; the synthesis of genus and difference is the species (man). For Aristotle, as in Platonic division, each of these predicates answers the question "what?", genus and difference each indicating a part of the essence of the species, when taken separately, and indicating the entire essence, whose formula is the definition, when taken together. Property and accident, on the contrary, are predicates which do not form a part of the essence of the subject, predicates which do not answer the question "what?" Property necessarily depends on the essence of the subject to which it belongs exclusively, as the equality of angles to two right angles belongs to the triangle alone among the polygons; accident, on the other hand, need not belong to the subject.

[3] *Ibid*. ii. 1.

[4] *Ibid*. i. 4; cf. the commentary of Porphyry *Introduction Concerning the Five Voices*.

The *Topics,* in their practical applications, give ways of testing which of these classes a given predicate belongs to; for example, a predicate will be identified as the genus of a subject only if one verifies the fact that it belongs to all the species falling under the subject; everything belonging to the subject must also belong to it (iv. 1). These are rules enabling us to discuss whether a predication conceded by the respondent is valid, whether what he has stated to be the genus is not rather a property, etc., but they are in no sense rules for discovering.[5] Such is the character of the famous rules of definition given in the *Topics;* dialectic is incapable of answering the question "what." For the only questions admitted are those which can be answered by yes or no. Incapable of establishing a definition, dialectic can proceed to test a proposed definition by inquiring, for example, whether the definition applies exclusively to the thing defined, whether a property may not have been surreptitiously introduced in addition to the proximate genus and the specific difference, or whether homonymous or metaphorical terms may not have been used, as was done by those who defined only by analogy.[6]

It was his experience in these discussions which led Aristotle to pose three problems which came to dominate his logic: the problem of converting propositions, the problem of categories, and the problem of opposites. The first is suggested by the spontaneous employment, in discussions, of propositions that are the reverse of those which the respondent was made to admit; if, for example, it has been conceded that every pleasure is a good, we are inclined to think it has been conceded that every good is a pleasure. Now, such a reciprocity is possible only if the predicate belongs exclusively to the subject; in other words, is either one of its properties or else the formula of its definition. But in the general case the universal affirmative converts to the particular, since the predicate can belong to terms which are not in the subject. On the other hand, the uni-

[5] *De Interpretatione* xi. 20b 8.
[6] *Topics* vi. 2; vii. 2.

versal negative and the particular negative are not changed by conversion.

The second problem, that of categories, is also suggested by the needs of discussion.[7] The ten categories are the different senses which terms (subjects and predicates) can assume. They can either indicate a substance (man, horse) or when and where a thing is found (adverbs and objects of place and time) or the quality of a thing (qualifying adjectives) or what it is relative to (double, half) or someone's situation (he is seated or lying down) or his possession (he has shoes or arms) or his action (he cuts or burns) or what he suffers (he is cut or burned). Although this classification does use the analysis of language, it does not entirely reduce to it, since in spite of linguistic form the substantive *whiteness,* for example, can designate a quality and not a substance. These distinctions arise rather from dialectic. For clarity of discussion, it is not enough to know whether a predicate is genus, difference, species, property, or accident. It is also necessary to know which of the ten categories it belongs to; for if a term is a genus and if this genus is a quality (color), for example, its difference and its species will also have to be qualities.[8] This precaution is all the more necessary because a single word can have several meanings, each of which belongs to a different category. The term *good,* for example, can come under the category of producing (remedies which produce health) or of quality (virtuous) or of time (good opportunity) or of quantity (good measure). In certain cases, it is because of the categories that the dialectician is able to keep the distinction between property and accident; if I alone am seated in a company, then even though being seated is in itself an accident, it becomes a property with reference to those present and as long as their gathering lasts.[9]

The problem of opposites is pre-eminently a problem of Platonic dialectic. If a discussion is even to be possible, then (since every problem consists in asking for a yes or a no) the "no" must at least

[7] *Ibid.* i. 7; *Categories* 2.
[8] *Topics* i. 15, 107a 3.
[9] *Ibid.* i. 5, 102b 11.

have a meaning in relation to the "yes." Error must at least have a meaning in relation to truth; otherness must have a meaning in relation to sameness. This is Plato's question in the *Sophist*. Aristotle, with the experience of discussion uppermost in his mind, sought to determine which theses require and which exclude one another. When one proposition asserts of the whole subject what another one denies of the whole subject (all men are just; no men are just), they are called contraries and cannot be true at the same time. Two propositions are contradictories when one asserts what the other denies (all men are white; it is not true that all men are white; or, some men are not white). Of two contradictory propositions one must be true and the other false.[10] It was also necessary to determine what the pairs of predicates are in which one term requires or excludes the other. There are four oppositions of terms: relatives (double and half), contraries (good and evil), possession and privation (clear-sighted and blind), and contradiction (ill and not ill).[11] The meanings of the first and fourth are easy to understand; two relatives imply one another, and two contradictory terms exclude one another, so that one of the two must necessarily belong to the subject. On the other hand enormous precautions have to be taken in using the two other groups of opposites. First, we have to determine what genus the opposites belong to (white and black belong to the genus color; even and uneven to number) and restrict the discussion to this genus. Then, we have to distinguish two cases; the case where contraries have no mean, so that predication of the one entails exclusion of the other (even, uneven), and the inverse case (white and black, not-white not necessarily being black). In this second case, the determination of contraries will be difficult; if the contrary of white is black and not another color, the reason is that, in the genus color, black is the thing furthest removed from white. Terms that are as far apart as possible; this is the rather vague definition of contraries which Aristotle ends up with. As for possession and privation, it is obvious that they only have meaning

[10] *De Interpretatione* 7.
[11] *Categories* 8.

when they are applied to a subject which possesses by nature something it can be deprived of. A man is blind, not a stone; otherwise the sophism that man has horns because we cannot say when he lost them would be true.

.II   *The Organon (continued)*: *The* Analytics

Aristotle drew his whole theory of the syllogism from these logical constructions, so plainly made for discussion. He came to see that the necessity with which we deduce consequences from theses that are first laid down is completely independent of the facts being discussed. The professor who lectures, the dialectician who discusses, the orator who persuades, all use equally rigorous reasoning, however different their starting points may be. This reasoning is the syllogism, in other words the process which causes thought to see the connection of a predicate with a subject where this connection is not recognized immediately. It is therefore permissible to make an independent study of this reasoning "in which, certain things being laid down, another follows necessarily from them solely because the former have been laid down." [12] This study is the aim of the *Prior Analytics,* and it contains three parts: the genesis of syllogisms (chaps. 1–26), the means of devising syllogisms (27–30, and the reduction of all valid reasoning to syllogisms.[13]

It was Platonic division which may have given Aristotle the idea of the syllogism; for division is indeed a kind of syllogism. It "brings together" a predicate (e.g., mortal) with a subject (e.g., man), after it is conceded that this subject belongs to a genus (e.g., animal) and that this genus is divided into two species, mortal and immortal, in the first of which comes man. There are, therefore, clearly three terms here, forming a logical hierarchy. And thanks to this logical hierarchy, two of them are brought together by the third. But this is a "weak syllogism" incapable of drawing a necessary conclusion, because it provides no way of discovering in which

---

[12] *Prior Analytics* i. 1. 24b 18.
[13] *Ibid.* i. 32 (beginning).

of the two species, mortal or immortal, man should be placed, and because on the other hand it makes the middle term, animal, a more extended genus than the predicate mortal.[14] But let us keep the idea of a logical hierarchy, and assume there are "three terms" which are so related to one another that the last (minor) is in all the middle and that the middle is in all the first (major).[15] From this will result a "syllogism of extremes." If A is asserted of all B (major), and B of all (or some) C (minor), then A is necessarily asserted of all (or some) C. Likewise if A is denied of all B, and B asserted of all (or some) C, A is denied of all (or some) C. Such is the perfect syllogism (first figure) which concludes immediately from inspection of the logical hierarchy between A, B, and C. Let us note also that the hierarchically arranged concepts need not, as in Platonic division, be part of the quiddity of the subject of the conclusion; they can also be properties and accidents, provided they satisfy the conditions indicated.

Would a different logical hierarchy among three terms make possible a syllogism of extremes? Yes, certainly; and it is not necessary that the middle term be included in the major term and include the minor. If, for example, the middle term is asserted of all the major term and denied of all the minor term, it follows that the major term is denied of all the minor term (second figure). This is a syllogism, but an imperfect syllogism, because it does not rest on immediate inspection of the hierarchy of terms. It must therefore be demonstrated, in other words reduced to a syllogism in the first figure. This demonstration is effected by converting the minor; being a universal negative (the middle is denied of all the minor), it converts to a universal negative (the minor is denied of all the middle), and the syllogism then belongs to the first figure (second mood). This demonstration, which can serve as an example of the three other moods, is clearly motivated by the desire to find underlying every syllogism one and the same conceptual relation which locates the middle between two extremes.

[14] *Ibid*. i. 31; *Posterior Analytics* ii. 5.
[15] *Prior Analytics* i. 4. 25b 32.

There is, moreover, a syllogism in the case where the major term and the minor term both belong to all the middle term; we are then justified in concluding that the minor sometimes belongs to the major (third figure). In this case, the hierarchy is the inverse of that in the preceding figure, since the middle term is more general than both the major and the minor terms. It will be easy to transform this imperfect syllogism into a perfect syllogism by converting the major, which, being a universal affirmative, converts to a particular affirmative and becomes the following: the middle belongs to a part of the major. In this way the hierarchy of concepts which gave rise to the syllogisms is restored.[16]

In Platonic division, all propositions were necessary propositions because the predicate expressed the quiddity of the subject. As soon as we are free from that restriction, there is no reason to think that syllogisms contain only necessary premises. Propositions can be merely contingent and possible or else state a factual truth which is not necessary. There are thus three modalities of propositions. This gives rise to a new problem: the problem of determining the modality of the conclusion in each of the three figures when the modality of the premises is known. With the exception of syllogisms in the first figure with necessary premises, where we can see immediately that the conclusion is necessary, Aristotle demonstrates the modality of the conclusion in all possible cases, using either conversion or *reductio ad absurdum*.[17]

The complicated mechanics of the syllogism are the outcome of dialectic: conclusions are really problems to be solved. They are put forth as questions prior to the syllogism which provides an answer to them. The syllogism often arises from long previous investigations: once the question whether a predicate belongs to a subject or not is asked, it is necessary to find the middle term which will answer it. That is why it is necessary to make two lists, one of all possible subjects of the major, and the other of all possible predicates of the minor (without, however, going back beyond the proximate genus in the case of predicates indicating quiddity). The middle term will necessarily be in the common part of these two lists.[18]

This groping search for the middle term makes a complete contrast with the rigid mechanism of the syllogism, once it is discovered. This contrast is most evident when Aristotle shows how we can deduce truth from falsity; the truth of the conclusion in no way guarantees the truth of the premises. There is even a case where deduction is fallacious in spite of the perfect correctness of the syllogism; this is the case of circular proof, where we use as a premise the conclusion of a syllogism which itself had for one of its premises the conclusion we are now trying to prove.[19] The problem now is to know how to justify the premises. The syllogistic art does make it possible to connect the conclusion necessarily with the premises; it provides no way of laying down premises, in cases where these premises are not themselves conclusions of preceding syllogisms.

In this context we find a distinction between the three arts all using the syllogism: the apodictic art or art of demonstration, dialectic, and rhetoric. It is to the apodictic art that the *Posterior Analytics* is devoted.

The syllogism giving knowledge or demonstration is not merely one whose conclusion follows necessarily from the premises (a feature common to all syllogisms) but one whose conclusion is necessary. Now the conclusion can only be necessary if the premises are themselves necessary; it is a rule of modal syllogisms that, if the middle term belongs necessarily to the major term, and the minor term necessarily to the middle term, the minor term belongs necessarily to the major term. The scientific syllogism or demonstration is therefore characterized by the nature of its premises. They must be true; they must be primary and immediate and hence undemonstrable, since if they had to be proved and so back

---

[18] *Posterior Analytics* ii. 13.
[19] *Prior Analytics* ii. 2–7.

to infinity, knowledge would be forever impossible; they must contain the cause of the conclusion; finally they must be logically prior to the conclusion and easier to know than it (i.1, 2, and 6).

What are these indemonstrables? First, there are the common axioms such as: "It is impossible for a predicate to belong and not belong to the same subject at the same time and in the same respect." But such axioms are universal conditions or common principles of all knowledge and do not contain the cause of anything in particular. The indemonstrable propositions containing a cause are those that tell us what the thing is whose predicates we are trying to demonstrate; in other words, definitions, which are the "very principles" of demonstration.[20] The middle term must be taken from the quiddity of the thing; there is a sort of parity between the middle term, the essence or quiddity, the reason, and the cause. Thus, astronomers have discovered that the essence of a lunar eclipse is the interposition of the earth between the moon and the sun. This interposition is the middle term through which we will demonstrate that the moon is eclipsed. If every body thus separated from its luminous source is eclipsed and if the moon is thus separated from it, it follows that it is eclipsed. It is always because the middle term constitutes part of the essence of the major term and because it is asserted of the minor term that the major term can itself be asserted of the minor term. It is because a right angle is formed by half of two right angles, and the angle inscribed in a semicircle is half of two right angles, that it is equal to a right angle. It is because you cannot attack an adversary without his attacking you in turn that the Athenians who first attacked the Medes were in turn attacked. It is because walking produces easy digestion, and the man in good health has good digestion, that this man takes a walk. The middle term, therefore, always brings out the essence or an aspect of the essence of the main term. The minor premise may be a simple statement of fact which asserts this essence of the minor term; the conclusion will necessarily follow.[21]

[20] *Posterior Analytics* i. 9–11.
[21] *Ibid.* ii. 10.

It is certain that in a demonstration the effect is linked analytically to the cause, since the effect (eclipse of the moon) is the same thing as the cause (interposition of an opaque body). Yet, the expression "analytical connection" is inadequate to characterize demonstration; for the same connection holds in every syllogism, demonstrative or not. When we really see the connection peculiar to demonstration, we see that there is a connection of derivation between the middle term and the effect, a connection of source and consequence implying the real and effective priority of the middle. The syllogism of the cause or reason goes beyond a mere play of concepts; it makes contact with reality itself.

But it is precisely at this point and for this reason that the theory of knowledge here begins to run beyond the *Organon*. In fact, it is not possible to demonstrate the truth of a definition; it is impossible to make a definition the conclusion of a syllogism. Here the *Organon* is inadequate. At most, it can point out this impossibility. Every demonstration shows that one thing is true of another, but a definition states the essence of a thing and does not assert one thing to be true of another.[22] For such a demonstration to be made, the cause of the essence would have to be different from the essence itself; but it is not different, since a thing is what it is immediately and because of itself.[23] The *Analytics* cannot give a positive method of discovering definitions, any more than the *Topics* can. The nature of this method is nevertheless indicated. The principle that we cannot learn anything except by starting from some previous knowledge is true without exception; although primary and immediate, a definition is not without an origin. This origin is sense perception, from which it is derived by induction.[24] Induction is the reasoning which Aristotle discusses in the *Topics* and which consists in predicating a property to a genus by showing that it belongs to the species contained in this genus. Thus the "ancients" showed that the absence of gall in an animal is a symptom of longevity, giving

[22] *Ibid*. ii. 3. 90b 25.
[23] *Ibid*. ii. 7. 93a 4.
[24] *Ibid*. i. 31. 88a 4; ii. 9. 100b 3.

the examples of solipeds and stags; more recent observations could add the dolphin and the camel. Nevertheless, induction (which we can see does not deal with individuals but with species) cannot make us see a necessary connection between longevity and the absence of gall, even when the induction is complete. This connection will only be grasped intellectually by a physiological analysis showing the role of the liver in the preservation of life and showing gall to be a secretion, excremental in nature, which affects the liver and consequently life. Induction can therefore only prepare the way for knowledge of essences.[25]

This conception of demonstrative knowledge only applies to instruction, a method first made for discussion. Indeed, knowledge is primarily the art of the professor who teaches; in other words, the art of one who excludes all premises that are not certain and then proceeds deductively like the geometrician, and not by questioning like the dialectician. But the certainty of these propositions cannot itself be an aim or subject of knowledge; they would then have to be conclusions of syllogisms and so back to infinity, and this would make demonstration impossible. If knowledge is to be possible, premises are therefore needed which are themselves indemonstrable and which are not subjects of knowledge. How can we discover these premises? The dialectician or the orator appeals, as the case may be, to common or enlightened opinion; but these do not achieve certainty. Where will the scientist get them? This question is central to the whole philosophy of Aristotle and above all to his metaphysics.

III *Metaphysics*

The metaphysics of Aristotle occupies in effect the place left vacant by his rejection of Platonic dialectic. It is "the science of being as being, or of the principles and causes of being and of its essential attributes."[26] It raises this very concrete question: what makes a

---

[25] Compare the *Prior Analytics* ii. 25 and *Parts of the Animals* iv. 3.
[26] *Metaphysics* E. 4. 1028a 2; Γ. 1 (beginning).

being what it is? What makes a horse a horse, a statue a statue, or a bed a bed?[27] The problem is to know the meaning of the word "is" in definitions stating the essence of a being. As a result the *Metaphysics* turns out to be mainly a treatise on definition. In reality, the problem of definition which Plato thought he had solved by dialectic belongs neither to dialectic, which simply judges the value of definitions formed, nor to demonstrative science, which uses them as principles, but to a new and still unknown science, first philosophy or the hoped-for science, which is occupied with being as being.

To be sure, the word "is" has other senses than the one it has in definitions. It can serve to designate an essential attribute or a property (man *is* laughing), or even an accident (man *is* white). And an accident can be taken in any one of the nine categories. But the being of a property, like that of an accident, assumes the being of a substance; if we can also speak of the being of a quality and ask what it is, the reason is that there is first a substance. All these senses of being are derived from the first sense. The first and essential aim of metaphysics is therefore to determine the nature of being in its primary sense. But it broadens to include all the derivative senses, since all these senses are related to the primitive sense.

This is why metaphysics must first prove the axioms, since without them we could not speak of being in any sense. These axioms are that one cannot simultaneously assert and deny something, that one cannot say a thing both is and is not, and that one cannot say a predicate belongs and does not belong to a subject at the same time and in the same respect. The negation of these principles is equivalent to Protagoras' thesis in the *Theaetetus,* where he asserts that whatever seems true is true. The proof of these indemonstrable principles cannot, moreover, be a positive demonstration, but only a refutation of those who deny them; a thoroughly dialectical refutation consisting in showing the adversary that, when he seems to deny them, he actually accepts them. That there is no middle ground between affirmation and negation is a condition of thought.

[27] Z. 1. 1028a 12–20.

To say the contrary, to say that what is, is not, and what is not, is, is to deny there is any truth and falsity. The refutation also consists in showing the inadequacy of the examples given by the opponent to support his thesis. In particular, the variation of sense impressions according to circumstances affords him no proof; for, if wine, sweet for a healthy man, is bitter for a sick person, at the very moment when the wine seems bitter to him it does not also seem sweet to him. The sense impression itself verifies the axiom (Γ 5–7).

Moreover, the task of metaphysics is new. The problem is no longer, as with the natural philosophers, to reach the component elements of beings by decomposition nor, as in Plato, to ascend to a supreme reality, an object of intellectual intuition, by a dialectical regression. The problem is rather to determine, by generalization, the features common to all real things. Thus metaphysics is neither a science of the Good or final cause nor a science of the moving cause, since the Good and the moving cause do not include unchanging things such as mathematical entities; metaphysics is the much more general science of quiddity which leaves out nothing.[28] It does not investigate all substances one by one and collectively but investigates what they all have in common.[29] But, once again, what they have in common are not concrete elements like fire or water, but the fact that each has a quiddity which allows it to be classified in a genus and determined by a difference.[30] In this respect no distinction need be made between sensible substances and insensible substances nor between corruptible and incorruptible substances. The domain of metaphysics is not limited to the category of insensible and incorruptible things; it is more extensive.[31] Not that the metaphysician, investigating being as being, imagines he has found the supreme genus. That is the error of Platonists and Pythagoreans who speak of a kind of supreme genus of being (or of the one, which comes to the same thing since *one* can be said of anything that *is* can be said of) and then determine all

[28] B. 2. 996a 18b 26.
[29] *Ibid.* 997a 16–25.
[30] B. 3. 998a 20b 14.
[31] B. 4. 1000a 5.

classes by the method of division, by means of differentiae of being. This is a logical error, since it is a rule of logic that a differentia (for example, biped) should not include in itself the genus (animal) of which it is the differentia, whereas in the case of every so-called differentia of being, we can say that it *is*. Being, a universal attribute, is not therefore a genus of which the other beings are species. The first genera are the categories, and being, like unity, is above them and common to all (i. 2).

In order to make unity or being the genus and hence the generator of every real thing, Platonic dialectic started not so much from being as from pairs of opposites—being and non-being, one and many, finite and infinite—by whose mixture it generated all the forms of reality. Metaphysics prevents dialectic from escaping this way, too; opposites are not primitive principles, but modes of being of substances. Something is substance before being finite or infinite. But substance, in other words a man or a horse, "has no contrary." This first principle cannot therefore be a starting point of dialectic. The theory of opposites is only a subordinate part of metaphysics.[32] We will see what a prodigious role it continues to have as a principle of physics.

If being is neither a supreme genus nor one term in a pair of opposites, it is only a predicate. The only real things whose predicate it is, when taken in its primitive sense, are individual realities: Socrates, or this horse (τοδε τι). These realities are the ones investigated by the metaphysician, not as particulars, but insofar as they are something. But isn't there a serious difficulty here? Are these moving, vanishing, sensible things really something? Is knowledge possible except by reaching their intelligible and unchanging model? Hence the famous dilemma: either an object is an object of knowledge, in which case it is universal and therefore not real, or else it is real and therefore sensible, without true being, and so not an object of knowledge, for there is "only knowledge of the universal."[33] That is what led Plato to postulate the unchanging

[32] N. 1. 1087a 29b 4.
[33] B. 4. 999a 24b 16; A. 6. 987a 34b 14.

reality of ideas that are objects of knowledge, beyond the realities of becoming that are objects of opinion. This way out was closed to Aristotle, and one of his principal concerns was to show the stable and permanent elements contained in the essence of becoming.

IV Critique of the Theory of Ideas

In one sense, this conception of metaphysics stays faithful to the Platonic spirit; if knowledge is possible, even though individuals are the only real things, the reason it is possible is the presence of stable and so intelligible realities in these particular things. Plato's fallacy was to consider these unchanging realities as separate from sensible things. In setting ideas apart, Plato, according to Aristotle, was only trying to conceive a substance which could be the object of the kind of knowledge invented by Socrates. The latter had located knowledge in inductions leading to definitions. Plato, extending the method Socrates had used in ethics to the whole of nature, saw in ideas substances corresponding to the quiddities stated in definitions, and he explained sensible things by their participation in these substances.[34] Aristotles' critique is of course thoroughly dialectical; it is less concerned to show that ideas do not exist than to show that Plato's philosophy is not primary philosophy. It is concerned to show, in other words, that Plato left separate the two things he thought he had united: knowledge and substance. Elaborate as it is, Aristotles' critique can therefore be reduced to two main heads: either ideas are objects of knowledge, and therefore not substances; or they are the substances of things, and therefore cannot be objects of knowledge.

Let us consider the first point. We know the three arguments by which Platonists proved the existence of ideas; the one beyond the many (a multiplicity of objects possessing the same property, "beauty" for example, requires this property to exist beyond and above all of them), the arguments drawn from the sciences (because a definition of geometry implies the existence of its object), and the persistence

[34] A. 6. 987b 1–10.

of the representation of a thing once the thing has disappeared, implying the stability of an object of knowledge which is not subject to the flux of sensible things.[35] Supposing now these three arguments were true, they would prove too much. The many things whose unity is asserted, the things that are defined, and finally the things represented in thought after they have disappeared can well be something besides substances; they can be quantities, qualities, and relations. These arguments thus prove the existence of ideas of qualities or relatives as much as they prove ideas of substances.[36] But how could the idea of a thing which is not a substance be a substance? Because if the idea of a quality is, as is admitted, the very being of this quality,[37] it follows that it itself is a quality. We have to go further: even the idea of a substance cannot itself be a substance, because every substance is one, and if ideas are objects of definition, as they have to be in Platonism, they cannot be one. Every definition is really composed of a genus and a difference. For example, man is defined as a two-footed animal. This composition should not be an obstacle to the unity of the thing defined, since two-footed animal designates a single being. But if the theory of ideas is true, composition is incompatible with unity; the terms *animal* and *two-footed* each designate an idea and therefore a substance. There are therefore two substances in man, and man loses both his unity and his substantiality.[38] But even further, the unity of the genus animal is no better preserved than the unity of the species; if it were one, then in order to form species, the genus would have to participate in contrary differentiae at the same time and in the same respect. For example, animal would have to participate in two-footed and many-footed.[39] If this is impossible, the genus must be many, and its unity must be in our thought and not in reality.

Finally, if Plato's line of argument were pushed further, it would prove, not one idea for each class of things as it intends, but

---

[35] A. 9. 990b 11–15.

[36] *Ibid*. 16, 22–34.

[37] Cf. the consequences of the contrary supposition, Z. 6. 1031a 29.

[38] M. 4. 1079b 3–9; compare Z. 12. 1037b 10–17; Z. 13. 1039a 3–6; 1038b 16.

[39] Z. 14. 1039b 2–6.

an infinity of ideas. For if there must be an idea corresponding to every multiplicity of similar things, the same rule should apply when we envisage sensible man and the idea of man. To these two terms, since they are similar, there must correspond a third man. To the group formed by these three men, there must correspond a fourth, and so on to infinity.[40] In this way the substantiality of the idea vanishes.

So if ideas can be defined, they are not substances; inversely, if ideas are substances, they can neither be objects nor means of knowledge. Throughout the argument that follows, Aristotle attributes to Plato an intent to make ideas principles of explanation of sensible things. They are nothing but the fully realized quiddity of these things,[41] and they claim to solve the problem of metaphysics. What makes a (sensible) man a man is the fact that he participates in man in itself. But this explanation is illusory. First, since ideas are fixed substances they must always be causes in the same manner, and they do not therefore explain the becoming of sensible things, the why of their origin and disappearance. The idea, being motionless, can be the cause of immobility but not of motion.[42] Besides, how would ideas act? Most certainly not like nature, which is immanent in things, since they are separated from things. Nor can they be moving causes. And, as a matter of fact, nothing abstract, nothing universal can produce a particular thing. It is always a particular existing thing which generates a particular thing. The architect makes the house, and "man begets man."[43] This concrete and direct vision of becoming, or rather of many becomings, is opposed to the Platonic fiction of alleged models of things which in reality are nothing but these very things with the expression *in itself* added, which far from explaining things merely doubles them.

Nothing essential is added to this criticism by the argument Aristotle directs against other related theories: first against the theory of mathematical entities, conceived by Plato as intermediaries between ideas and sensible things, next, against the theory of mathe-

[40] Z. 13. 1039a 2.
[41] M. 9. 1086b 9; A. 9. 991b 1–3.
[42] A. 7. 988b 3–4.
[43] A. 9. 991a 8–11; Z. 8. 1033b 26–32; Λ3. 1070a 27.

matical numbers erected into supreme realities by Speusippus, and finally against the theory of ideal numbers in Xenocrates. Yet, one objection is no longer valid; unlike ideas, Aristotle cannot say that mathematical essences only duplicate sensible things, since their natures are different. But this difference in nature is precisely the starting point of a criticism opposite to the one he directed against ideas; namely, the completely arbitrary character (which he especially points out in the advocates of ideal numbers) of the relation between a number and the thing it is supposed to explain.[44] But couldn't one say that sciences like astronomy, which substitutes a mathematical construction made of circles or spheres for the visible sky, come closer to reality than those staying with sensation? These sciences were really the strength of the Platonists; Aristotle himself[45] admits that, in sciences like harmonics, arithmetic gives the reason or essence of the chords which the senses acquaint us with. Does it follow that mathematical realities are distinct from sensible ones? If the astronomer's sky is a reality distinct from the sensible sky, there will have to be a motionless sky in the very place where we see the sky move.[46] Mathematical being does not have a separate reality; it results from an abstraction which views shapes and outlines by separating them from their contents. So Aristotle certainly does not think that mathematics makes real substances intelligible. In the last analysis the forms and regular motions of the heavens have physical causes for him. Similarly, he rejects the mathematical constructions of phenomena like vision which were then being attempted. Mathematics deals only with predicates of things, with quantity, and does not consider substance, being as such. We will not find metaphysics in this area.

v *The Method of Substance*

When he rejects the doctrine which states that the quiddities or essences of things are eternal substances realized outside the things whose essences they are, Aristotle certainly does not mean

[44] M. 8. 1084a 12–27.
[45] *Posterior Analytics* i. 9.
[46] B. 2. 997b 12–24.

to deny that there are quiddities; quite the contrary. But quiddity is in the thing itself. The quiddity of man exists in Socrates and Callias. In one of its aspects, metaphysics is the sum of rules enabling us to separate this quiddity from the remaining attributes. But in the nature of the case there is no room here for demonstration, since we do not demonstrate quiddity; hence Aristotle's frequent appeal either to experience or to opinion, a sign of the dialectic method.

If the substance in question is ourselves, then in a general way it is easy to eliminate from the essence attributes like musician, or dressed in white, which are acquired and do not belong to us as such. There remain, as a residue, the characteristics belonging to the definition. "Essence is of all things which have a definition." It includes only what is not derived but primitive in the thing. But we still have to distinguish definitions where the thing defined is in something else, definitions that only concern derived things and not substances, and definitions proper, which are definitions of an essence that do not refer to anything else. Thus evenness, defined as divisible by two, implies number; snub-nosed, signifying curvature in a nose, implies nose. Essence or quiddity only belongs to these things secondarily and not primarily as it does in the case of substance.[47]

The ground thus cleared, the principal difficulty remains: what makes the unity of the essence expressed by the definition, the unity without which it cannot be a substance? If the definition of man is two-footed animal, what makes two-footed animal denote a single essence and not a collection of two terms, whereas white animal is a compound of essence and quality?[48] This is a very serious question, since it raises the question whether, as the atomists have claimed, we can obtain the essence of a being by mere juxtaposition of elements, or whether the essence has a true unity. In order to answer it, we have to distinguish between the material parts of a being and the parts of its form or its essence. Thus, the material parts of a circle are the segments into which it is divisible; its formal

[47] Z. 4. 1030b 4–6.
[48] Z. 12. 1037b 10–18.

parts are the genus (plane figure) and the difference which define it. Now the circle does not originate from a juxtaposition of its material parts; in fact the circle is prior to them, since the concept of a semicircle implies the concept of a circle. Similarly, the acute angle is a material part of the right angle but is nevertheless logically posterior to the right angle, since it is defined as the angle smaller than a right angle. Likewise the hand is posterior and not prior to the essence of a living body, since it could not exist as a hand apart from that body. It is true that we do not always clearly distinguish the essential parts from the material parts. It is difficult, for example, to see that flesh and bone are not part of the essence of man. And the Platonists took advantage of this difficulty in order to reduce the formal essence of all things to numbers, rejecting everything else belonging to the material parts (Z. 11).

But assuming this distinction is made, it follows immediately that the unity of a being does not result from a conjunction or juxtaposition of material parts, since these parts are posterior to the being, but from the way in which its logical components, genus and difference, are united. There are two ways in which an attribute unites with a subject: either the subject participates in the attribute (man is white), or else the attribute is contained in the subject (the number two is even). But a differentia cannot belong to a genus in either of these two ways; how could a genus participate in several differentiae which are contrary to one another? How could differentiae be contained in a genus without everything being reduced to the unity of a genus? Genus and difference unite in a completely different and much more intimate way: *animal* and *two-footed* do not designate two beings but only one, which, first as animal, appears relatively indeterminate (in other words, matter or potential being), and then as two-footed is relatively determinate (in other words, form and actual being). A definition is, therefore, one single statement about one single being because it first determines the being incompletely by the genus (animal being two-footed potentially), then completely by the difference, two-footed.[49]

[49] Z. 12. 1037b 8–27

Here there is no trace of a juxtaposition of parts that are foreign to one another. When we speak of animal and two-footed, we do not speak of two different things but of a single being, first indeterminate, then determinate.

But it is clear that if this answer is to be valid, then the complete and actual concept of man must exist prior to its components; for the concept of animal can only be considered indeterminate in relation to a complete concept such as the concept of man. We should not, therefore, make definitions "as is customarily done," [50] meaning, no doubt, by the method of Platonic division which attempts to construct species synthetically by starting from the genus and so going from potential to actual being. We should define in another way; analytically, going from actuality to potentiality. The unity of essence is thus bought at the price of renouncing any genetic and constructivist method of arriving at concepts. Essence is not composed of elements as the syllable is of letters; it is simple and indivisible (the analysis of definition is not, we have seen, a true decomposition). "Simple terms can neither be inquired into nor taught; or at least the inquiry is of a different kind." [51]

There is no way of grasping these indivisible terms except by that immediate intellectual intuition which Aristotle calls thought ($\nu\acute{o}\eta\sigma\iota\varsigma$), and which is to essence as vision is to color and which can no more be mistaken about its object than each sensation can about what is felt. There can be error when we combine thoughts but not when we think in simple terms through this kind of immediate contact.[52] Let us observe, to be more precise, that intellectual intuition does not, as in Plato, come at the end of a long dialectical movement which takes us beyond sensible things. Thought is in sense perception; it is immanent in sensation, just as essence is in the thing.[53] "There is sense perception of the universal, of man in Callias, for example, not of Callias alone." [54] Thought, making use of

[50] H. 4. 1045 I. 20–22.
[51] Z. 17. 1041b 9.
[52] *De anima* iii. 6. 430b 14.
[53] Θ. 9. 1051b 24–30.
[54] *Posterior Analytics* ii. 15. 100a 16.

induction, produces the universal. Thought, far from separating it-self from sensible things, instead turns toward them in order to know essences. But in Aristotle there is not and cannot be a method of picking out essences; there is merely a general confidence in thought's ability to discover them.

VI *Matter and Form: Potentiality and Actuality*

It remains to be shown that essence (οὐσία) really is being as being, in other words that essence does not refer to a higher principle which is truly a fundamental principle. To understand the significance of the problem, we only need to think of the opposition Aristotle was to encounter both among Platonists, for whom a genetic construction of essences was the fundamental problem, and also among the natural philosophers or theologians who, in their own ways, claimed to deduce the diversity of beings. By denying the very possibility of raising the problem, Aristotle had an immense influence on the direction of philosophic thought: he put an end to all attempts to give a genetic explanation that were beginning to appear in Greek thought. And so it is particularly important to understand his doctrine on this point.

Here, because of the very nature of the subject which has to do with indemonstrable principles, Aristotle uses a method of analogy, intuition, and induction without demonstrative rigor. Metaphysical concepts concerning being, placed above the genera of being, cannot be defined; their meaning can only be suggested by analogy.[55]

This reasoning can be formulated thus: if essence (form or quiddity) is a first principle, it is because it is an actuality and because actuality is always prior to potentiality.

What is actuality (ἐνέργεια)? Actuality is to potentiality as the waking man is to the sleeping man, as the man who sees is to the man whose eyes are shut, as the statue is to the bronze, as the finished is to the unfinished.[56] The second term in each pair is

[55] Θ. 5. 1048a 36.
[56] *Ibid.* 1048b 1

"potentially" the first. The man whose eyes are shut is a potential seer, bronze is a potential statue; this means that eyes will see and bronze will become a statue, if certain conditions are realized. The man who sees and the statue are, properly speaking, actual beings; their actualities are, respectively, vision and the shape of the statue. Vision is an actuality in the sense that it continues to be vision during the whole time it occurs. Life, happiness, intellectual intuition are actualities for the same reason, whereas a march that progresses and is at a different stage at each moment is not an actuality but an action or a motion. Actuality (ἐνέργεια) is something like the work or the function (ἔργον) of an actual being; vision, for example, is the function of the eye.[57] Again, actuality is entelechy (ἐντελέχεια), in other words the final and finished state which marks the limits of possible realization.[58] It is clear that the notion of potentiality has no meaning in itself and that it is wholly relative to actual being. It is not by what it is but, on the contrary, by what it can become that potential being is known as such. Actuality, on the contrary, is the reference point in relation to which potential beings are assigned a place and set in order.

Now "essence or form is an actuality"[59] and the pre-eminent actuality; for quiddity is what belongs to a given being from the time of its birth to its extinction, integrally and without change or deficiency. It does not admit of more or less: one is not more a man or less a man. To express this unalterable permanence, Aristotle uses for essence the expression τὸ τί ἦν εἶναι, the fact of a being's continuing to be what it was. There is no becoming of essence or form. The form of the bronze sphere, which is the spherical shape, does not originate with the manufacture of a bronze sphere. What originates is the union of the spherical shape and the bronze.[60] Birth or becoming thus consists in the union of a form with a being capable of receiving it. This potential being that becomes actual

[57] Θ. 8. 1050a 21–22.
[58] Θ. 3. 1047a 30.
[59] Θ. 8. 1050b 2.
[60] Z. 8. 1033b 5–11.

being after having received form is properly what Aristotle calls matter (ὕλη). Matter is the sum of conditions which have to be realized if form is to appear. The potential chest, or, what comes to the same things, the matter of the chest, is wood.[61] Aristotle's thesis amounts to a declaration of the non-existence of indefinite being. Every actual being, such as this tree or this man, has as long as it exists a unique essence which makes it an actual being (τόδε τι); not to exist is (like the legendary goat-stag) to be nothing.

Now—and this is the most important of all Aristotelian theorems —actuality is prior to potentiality in the three senses of the word *prior;* logically, temporally, and substantially.[62] It is logically prior since, as we have seen, the notion of potential being implies that of actual being in relation to which it is said to be potential. It is temporally prior since an actual being only comes from a potential being by the action of another being that is already actual; for example, the potential musician only becomes an actual musician if he is trained by an actual musician: it is man who begets man. Finally, it is substantially prior since potential man, who is the seed, derives all his essence from an adult and actual man.

The great objection and perhaps fundamentally the only one that Aristotle made against his predecessors was their failure to recognize the truth of this theorem, beginning with the theologicans who made everything come from darkness[63] and continuing down to Plato who insists on having the kinds of being originate from the most indeterminate ultimate genera. Against all these opponents, Aristotle never wearied of repeating what can be asserted in different ways but can never be proved; namely, that existence can only be given in the form of substances that are actual and wholly determinate, and that the only indetermination or matter which can exist in the universe is not an absolute and intrinsic indetermination, but only an indetermination relative to more complete forms.

---

[61] Θ. 7. 1049a 18–27.
[62] Θ. 8. 1049b 19–21.
[63] Λ. 6. 1071b 26–28.

VII *Physics: The Causes, Motion, Time, Place, the Void*

Actuality, in other words the active function of a presently existing being, is thus always the final principle of explanation. The
eye will be explained when it is shown that its matter is selected
and arranged for vision; the animal will be explained when all
the organs are shown to be combined in order to make vital functions possible; the city, when the human activities which are its
materials are shown to unite to bring about a happy, convenient,
and good life. A good part of Aristotelian science will consist
in pointing out how the materials selected are organized with a
view to a certain function. Metaphysics has only sketched the outlines or conveyed the spirit of the sciences. It is for experience to
fill them out, and this is a collective, encyclopedic task, subject to an
infinite number of revisions. The rigidity of the outlines is equalled
by the variety and diversity of the matter put into them.

To guide ourselves in this encyclopedia, we should hold fast to the
following Aristotelian maxim: "We must proceed from the general
to the particular";[64] in other words, from those indistinct and confused wholes which, for us, are the first things known, to those detailed and distinct things which in themselves, though not to our
perception, are really the first. The science of Aristotle has the same
rhythm as his universe; it is a passage from the indeterminate to
the determinate. What effects this transition is actual thought; for
example, thought which knows how to actualize in a geometrical
figure lines that are in it potentially and will serve to demonstrate
a theorem. The science of Aristotle does not progress in depth;
rather, it grows by extension and expansion.

This is because the study of functions, actualities, or essences is
inseparably joined to experimental investigations of the material
conditions in which these functions can be realized. These investigations, which of course are unlimited, make up the greater part of
the works of Aristotle. General physics will be complete when, hav-

[64] *Physics* i. i. 184a 23.

ing defined natural beings in general, we grasp the mechanism of motion which brings them into being. The study of living beings will be complete when, having defined vital functions in general and the soul, we describe the thousand organic combinations which enable life to be realized. Thus form is always inseparable from matter, actual being from potential being.

The fundamental concepts of physics refer to this union. The theory of causes answers the question "What makes this kind of subject acquire this kind of form, the patient to be cured or the bronze to become a statue?" The causes are (1) the material cause, out of which the thing is made, e.g., the bronze or the patient; (2) the formal cause, or form, model, or essence illustrated by the idea of health in the mind of the physician or the idea of a statue in the mind of the sculptor; (3) the efficient cause, which is the physician or the sculptor, and (4) the final cause, i.e., the final or finished state in view of which the potential being has become actual being, illustrated by the shape of the statue toward which the bronze changes or the condition of health into which the organism changes (*Physics* II. 3).

Nature is also defined not properly speaking as form but by its relation to matter. When we consider first the products of the arts like a statue or a bed, and then natural beings like a stone or a man, we see that the latter have in themselves the principle of their motion or their stillness, whereas the former have this principle in a being outside them, the sculptor or the carpenter. In the case of nature we are dealing with an immanent active force ("the seed produces a work of art"); in the case of art, the active force which is a thought abandons the work once it is finished. What distinguishes them from one another is therefore clearly the relation of the form to the matter, internal in the one, external in the other.[65]

By taking into account the relation of form to matter, we can give a sense to the widely held notions of *chance* and *spontaneity,* which the natural philosophers tended to criticize as meaningless. These are popular and ready notions designating not the absence of a cause,

---

[65] *Physics* ii. 1; *Metaphysics* Z. 9. 1034a 33.

as the natural philosophers said, but on the contrary designating causes acting for our happiness or our misfortune. The man on his way to the market-place who has the good fortune to meet a debtor he was not thinking about and so collects his debt, rightly believes that luck is a perfectly real cause. It is in fact real, but only on the condition that we consider it wholly relative, in the same way that matter is only matter relative to form. Chance can only be defined in relation to acts done for a specific result. Chance occurs when an act done for one purpose has the consequences it would have had if done for another purpose. The creditor, coming to the market, collects his debts as if he had come for that purpose. Chance is not, therefore, a primary cause like will or intention. It is rather a cause by accident, in the sense that the act which results in a happy or unhappy outcome has not been done in order to produce that effect. But it is also true that this effect could have been willed. Chance is consequently an uncommon occurrence, whereas effects produced by definite causes are those which occur always or at least most of the time. Spontaneity is like chance, but its sphere is more extensive. It is to purposiveness in nature what chance is to the intentional ends of the human will. If a falling tripod lands so as to serve as a seat, we say that it has fallen this way spontaneously. It is, therefore, as great an error to deny these causes as to make them primary causes, prior to intelligence and to nature.

Finally, the connection between form and matter governs the idea of *motion* that Aristotle develops. It is essential to bear in mind that for Aristotle the word *motion* calls to mind changes in states of determinate beings. Locomotion, for example, is not a space traversed in a given time, a definition according to which any motion has an exact relation to another motion. It is the motion of a living being, a leap, a walk, a crawl or a flight, or the motion of a stone, a motion toward the center of the world, or the motion of a star, a circular motion.[66] These are motions of different kinds (because they belong to different substances) and are not just quantita-

---

[66] *On the Progress of Animals* iii (beginning).

tively different; they depend to a great extent on the nature of the subject that possesses them. There are many kinds of changes of state other than locomotion: qualitative change or alteration, like the change of color in the skin during intense emotion or in sickness, and quantitative change, increase or decrease, as when a child grows until he has attained his adult stature or when a patient becomes thin from consumption.

All movement is therefore limited between an initial state and a final state[67] ending in rest, when all or part of the possibilities contained in the initial state have been developed. This is the source of the famous formula, "Movement is the actualization of the possible *as* possible." [68] It is not insofar as he is a living being of a given height that a child grows; he grows insofar as he is a child, in other words insofar as he has the possibility of reaching adult height. Once this possibility is realized, movement ceases. Movement only has meaning, therefore, in the relation of form to matter, of the actual to the virtual.

Movements are usually named with reference to the final states toward which they tend; blackening is an alteration tending toward black. But we must not lose sight of the fact that movement starts from an initial state which is the contrary of the final state, or intermediate between the final state and its opposite.[69] If a thing blackens, it is because, at the beginning, it was white or at least gray; if it grows, it is because it was small; if a stone falls downward, it is because it was above. Consequently all movement takes place between opposites—from above to beneath, from white to black—since it only substitutes one thing for its contrary. Moreover, the initial state and the final state, being opposites, are necessarily in the same genus; there is only movement from a color to a color, from a place to a place. There will therefore be as many supreme genera of movement as there are genera of being which admit opposites. Now, among the categories only those of quality, quantity, and place

[67] *Physics* v. 1. 224b 35.
[68] *Ibid.* iii. 1. 201a 27–29.
[69] *Ibid.* iii. 2. 201b 22 ff.

admit opposites, and for this reason there are only three genera of movement: change, increase and decrease, and locomotion. These three genera of movement are just as irreducible to one common genus as the genera of being from which they are derived.[70] In each of these genera, movement has its starting point in the *privation* of a certain quality and its terminal point in the *possession* of this quality. Movement goes from the non-white to the white, from the non-musician to the musician. On the other hand, privation and possession must belong to a subject which does not change during the process of becoming, a man for example (*Physics* I.7).

To these three genera, Aristotle first added a fourth which he later excluded,[71] generation and corruption, in other words the birth and death of a substance. This passage from non-being to being and from being to non-being should not be called a movement, first because "no substance has an opposite," and second because it is abrupt and discontinuous. Generation is no doubt preceded by all kinds of movements which have modified matter so as to put it in a state to receive form, as in the preliminary work of the sculptor. The scientist even has as his principal object the study of these transformations; for example, the treatise *On the Generation of Animals* first studies the modifications of the seed which will render it capable of receiving form. But this series of modifications which are true movements must not be confused with generation itself, which coincides with the final state to which these movements lead and which takes place in an indivisible instant.

The aims of this theory of movement are easy to see if we think of the previous development of Greek philosophy. Movement was primarily indefinite unlimited flux, that element refractory to conceptual thought which the Platonists called the *other* or the *unequal*.[72] This universal flux which gives birth to and carries away incessantly changing forms renders all science and all knowledge impossible; there was nothing left but "to flee from here"[73] and

[70] *Ibid*. i. 200b 32–201a, 9.
[71] Compare *Physics* iii. 1. 200b 32 and v. 1. 225a 34.
[72] *Ibid*. iii. 2 (beginning).
[73] Plato *Theaetetus* 176a.

seek knowledge in a transcendent world. In place of this picture, which considers potential beings as absolute realities, Aristotle substituted his own, according to which potential being is wholly relative to actual being. There is no universal flux; there is only a collection of movements, each one limited in a precise way by an initial and a final state. There is no flux of substantial forms; the substantial form which, as final cause, has directed the series of modifications which have led to its being received by matter, remains permanent and identical. Knowledge, with its permanent concepts, penetrates changing things themselves.

There remain, however, some properties that are common to all movement and that are all characterized by infinity: continuity, existence at one time and in one place and perhaps even in the void. Do not these continuous media, time, place, and the void, introduce absolute non-beings, indifferent to form, not dominated by it? This is certainly the way the problem arises: how can these media which claim independence for themselves be made relative to form or essence? Or again, how can we get back from a mathematical theory of space and time which was beginning to emerge, to a physical theory of place and duration which connects place and duration with the essence of a being, just as its color and form are connected with it, and which sees in the concept of place not the intuition of a universal and indifferent medium, but a general concept arising from a comparison of places occupied by bodies?

The idea of the infinite, of place, void, time, and the continuum, was a rich source of objections to the metaphysics of substance. First, there was the old Ionian idea of the infinitely great where innumerable and ever recurring worlds can continually draw on matter to renew themselves; then the more subtle Platonic idea of the Infinite, which sees in the indefinite dyad of the great and the small an independent absolute which, combining with the One, forms essences; the related idea of a space or place, independent of eternal essences, where only the images of these essences can appear; the independent reality which Democritus gave to the void, making it that monstrosity of substance without essence; the Platonic theory of time as the image of eternity which forced a denial of the true substantiality of all temporal things; finally a theory of continuity which culminated in a view of the universe as a single movement. All these ideas seemed to Aristotle incompatible with his movement of substance.[74] And so his problem is not so much to study these notions in themselves as it is to develop them in such a way as to bring them into agreement with his theory of being; if agreement is impossible, he denies them.

So it is that the only argument he gives against the Platonic thesis of Infinity as a separate and absolute reality is that any reality of this kind is a substance and consequently an individual, whereas Infinity can only be divisible.[75] Here Infinity reduces to nothing but an attribute of a substance. How and in what sense can it be an attribute of substance without endangering the unity and indivisibility of substance is the question which dominates the whole theory. First, there cannot be a sensible body which is infinitely great. In fact, a body is something limited by surfaces. A body of this kind, moreover, could have no imaginable physical structure. If it were composite, it could only be composed of elements that are themselves infinite; for, assuming an element were finite, it would necessarily be absorbed by the Infinite elements which have an infinite power as a result of their infinite size. The elements of this alleged body are therefore all infinite. But then they each occupy the whole of space and mutually penetrate each other, which is absurd. Yet this body cannot be a simple one either; for then there would no longer be any change, since change only takes place between opposites. Nor can we say it is homogeneous, since perfect homogeneity abolishes distinctions of place, of above and beneath, and so abolishes natural locomotions which as we will see have no other cause than the tendency of a body to regain its own place. We cannot say it is heterogeneous, since as we have seen the elements that compose it would all have to be infinite and so would have to

[74] Cf., especially, *Physics* vi. 10.
[75] *Physics* iii. 5 (beginning).

occupy all places; but the elements can be heterogeneous only if each has its own place.[76]

Therefore, there is no infinitely great body. Does that mean that we can deny Infinity? We cannot do so without absurdity. Time extends endlessly into the past and into the future. The series of numbers is unlimited (infinite by addition), geometrical magnitude is indefinitely divisible (infinite by subtraction). But what does divisibility consist in? In the last case, for example, it consists in the fact that it is always possible, having taken half of a magnitude, to take half of that magnitude; each magnitude which one takes is always a finite magnitude, but different each time. It is the same with the infinity of time and with the series of numbers which does not consist in actually reaching an infinite number, but in always being able to take a larger number than the one at which we have stopped. The infinite by addition is in one sense the same as the infinite by subtraction, since it consists in maintaining the possibility of always assuming a greater size than it already has. Far from being, as some have said, that beyond which there is nothing, the Infinite is that beyond which there is always something. That is tantamount to saying that the Infinite is not an actuality, but a potentiality. Thus Aristotle liberates philosophy from the Pre-Socratic picture of the infinite container which would be an ever renewing source of worlds. The Infinite and the unlimited are terms relative to the finite, to the completed, in which they exist as matter and in relation to which they assume a meaning: for "it is absurd, it is impossible that it is the unknowable and the unlimited which contains and defines" (*Physics* III. 6).

But at what price is this liberation obtained? And are we not forced to deny at the same time the unlimited productiveness of becoming? This, however, Aristotle refuses to do. In his limited world, made of definite substances, becoming is inexhaustible and has neither beginning nor end. Such a thing is possible only if "the corruption of one being is the generation of another." If, in one

---

[76] *Ibid.* iii. 5. 205a 8.

sense, becoming proceeds from non-being to being and from being to non-being, it always proceeds in a more exact sense from being to being; an element can only be destroyed by giving rise to another. It is in itself and not in the Infinite that becoming finds the sources of its own renewal (III. 8, beginning).

The theory of place (IV. 1–5) is also made to protect the new substance metaphysics. Aristotle very profoundly observed that the problem of place would not arise for him, if there were no locomotion, in other words change of place; for then place would be an attribute of body in the same way as color. But there is change of place; "where there was air, there is now water." What is this peculiar attribute which are cannot displace, which it yields to water and which appears to form, as it were, a permanent substance? To make it, as the *Timaeus* does, an undifferentiated receptacle of things is to ascribe to it a very equivocal substantiality; to make it the inner space filled by a body, to identify it with the dimensions of a body, is to say that it changes its place with the body, which is absurd. The paradoxical problem it raises is that of connecting place with body in order to make an attribute of place, while leaving it separate. If we consider a body, we may regard the surface which belongs to it as in direct contact at all points with the limiting surface belonging to its surrounding. This limiting surface, a sort of ideal vessel in which the body is contained, is the place of the body. Thus the place of a celestial sphere is the internal surface of the greater sphere in which it is encased. The place of a body, at least its particular place, is therefore "the extremity of the body which contains it." It follows from this that "place exists at the same time as the thing; for the limits exist with the limited";[77] but it does not belong to the thing which is in it, but to that which contains this thing. If place is motionless, if things change place, it is because there are things which are motionless containers. Place is nothing separate; it is related to substantial realities. Any danger to metaphysics is averted.

Also dangerous is the concept of the void, especially since the

[77] *Ibid*. iv. 4. 212a 29.

atomists considered it indispensable to physics, demanding that physicists either admit the void or deny evident phenomena, like motion or condensation and rarefaction, which cannot take place in a plenum. Aristotle was not content with a mere reply; he took up the offensive. Taking a position on his adversaries' own ground, he pointed out that the physical structure of things known to us is incompatible with the existence of a void.[78] In the first place, we are acquainted only with directed locomotion, natural motions which are motions of bodies toward their proper place, above or beneath, depending on whether the body is heavy or light, and which stop once this place is reached, and with violent motions which cause bodies to move from their proper places and which stop as soon as the efficient cause ceases to act. These motions are necessarily limited between an initial state and a final state. Now, in the void, there is nothing of the kind since there is neither above nor beneath in it; there is therefore no reason why a body in motion in the void should not stop anywhere or continue to move indefinitely. It is indeed instructive to see how this consequence which, in the eyes of Aristotle, is absurd, is a rough statement of the principle of inertia which, in its turn, overthrew Aristotelian science. To acknowledge its validity is to assume we are justified in considering moving bodies independently of all their physical properties. Now for Aristotle, who made motion an aspect or a consequence of these properties, this is an absurdity. A body in the void would be a body without physical properties, and its motion could only be arbitrary. There is a still greater absurdity. A body in motion, moving in the void, would have to be impelled by an infinite velocity. For a modern physicist, a given velocity corresponds to a given force acting at one moment on a given mass; if this velocity changes, it is because other forces are applied to the body in motion, for example, the forces of resistance resulting from the environment. Aristotle is nowhere near so precise a dynamics. For him, force consists essentially in overcoming a resistance; for example, the force of the towman who is pulling a boat. Velocity is by no means

[78] *Ibid.* iv. 6–9.

proportional to the force, since experience shows that the boat, at first motionless, starts abruptly only after a certain degree of effort. Besides, the effort of pulling communicates no velocity to the boat, since the boat stops as soon as the effort ceases. It is therefore by renewed application of force that the body in motion continues to move. Velocity depends then on the resistance to be overcome. Suppose the resistance to be decreased, velocity will increase; suppose it to be non-existent, velocity will become infinite. What has been said of pulling may be said of pushing: a body which makes an effort to traverse a medium has a speed which increases as the resistance of the medium which it traverses diminishes. If this resistance becomes non-existent, the speed is infinite. Now, that is precisely the case in regard to the void.

There remain the difficulties raised by the advocates of the void. As for motion, the advocates of the plenum extricate themselves by the theory of motion in a ring, already suggested by Plato: each body in motion constitutes part of a circle of other bodies in motion, and all parts of the circle change place at the same time, which is possible without a void. As regards condensation and rarefaction, they admit that for every increase in volume by a change of air into water, for example, there corresponds an equal decrease by a change of water into air, so that the total volume of the universe remains the same.

If time is essentially the succession of days and nights, and in general of periods, it is linked to the regular motions of the heavens and originates, as Plato said, with the heavens.[79] This was both to affirm a clear notion of time and to eliminate the ancient and vague cosmogonic image of a primitive time prior to the world. Concerning this last point, Aristotle of course agrees with Plato; concerning the first, he admits that time is connected with motion, that it is something pertaining to motion; and he gives as proof of it the fact that as soon as we no longer perceive change, for example in the state of sleep and in the states in which the soul does not change, we no longer perceive time. But Plato was mis-

[79] *Ibid.* iv. 10–14.

taken in believing that it depended only on the motion of the heavens. To identify time with the day, with its multiples and its submultiples, is to confuse time with the unit of measure by which we measure it. It is to bring into being a time beyond the movements it measures; it is to make of time a numbering number, the number by which we calculate time, a number which is actually connected with the celestial motions. But time is in reality the thing which we count, the number numbered. It exists in every movement, of whatever kind; for each movement has its duration, as an attribute belonging to it; it is "the number of the movement according to the anterior and the posterior," in other words that which at a given instant, the present instant which is the end of the past and the beginning of the future, we can count as anterior and as posterior. We calculate it by means of the celestial revolutions, as we compute the length of a thing by means of the cubit, without making length any less a part of the thing itself.

In this way the efforts of Aristotle were directed toward transforming the notions of motion, of the infinite, of place, and of time. In refusing to conceive them as separated from substance, he rejected the whole spirit of the ancient physicists, and he inaugurated a movement of thought whose abuses and dangers we shall see later.

VIII *Physics and Astronomy: The World*

It is in the same spirit that Aristotle develops the picture of the world which came down to him from the geometrical astronomers of the fifth and sixth centuries.

To reach a true understanding of Aristotle's position, we must take into account the contrast between the mathematical view of the universe created by the astronomers and the view of the natural philosophers. There was complete disagreement between them. In one view there was a heaven of the same nature as the meteors, involved like them in an endless cycle of birth and corruption; a single eternal motion of which the present state of the universe is only one phase; a trend toward universal motion which gives no permanence to anything except motion. On the other hand, the astronomy of Plato and Eudoxus substituted for the sensible heaven a heaven of a permanent geometrical structure, composed of circles or concentric spheres, each with a uniform motion. It affirmed the existence of distinct and irreducible motions, since the system succeeds only if each of the spheres is animated by a motion of its own independent of the motion of the others; finally it shed light on the opposition between the almost perfect intelligibility of celestial things and the ceaseless change of sublunary things.

But the new astronomy is not merely a hypothesis for Plato. It aspired to restore and to justify rationally a very ancient religious idea whose negation was physics and which was furiously attacked by the last representatives of the Ionians in the fourth century; this was the idea of a religious kind of opposition between heaven and earth, heaven containing divine beings and being itself divine in nature. Astronomy, therefore, included all the passion of a religious conviction, and Plato, in the *Laws,* built on astronomy the religion which he imposed on the citizens. The soul, or self-moving motion, which initiates all other movements, was in fact, as he saw it, a necessary presupposition of the new system of the world. The soul, by its own movements which are called desiring, examining, deliberating, directs all things in heaven and on earth.[80]

Aristotle follows this movement of thought but transforms it. He accepted the astronomy of Eudoxus but sought physical causes for it. He accepted the close association of astronomy and theology, and it was truly an astral theology which he instituted; but in place of self-moving motion, in place of soul, he substituted a motionless mover with the nature of intelligence.

Let us look at the first point: Aristotle sought to establish the physical causes of the primordial character of circular motion, in other words of the uniform motions of stars according to the great circle of a sphere. This motion is the only one to realize a condition which the natural philosophers sought in vain in the other motions, namely, perpetuity. The natural philosophers made the

[80] *Laws* x. 893c, 896a.

mistake of attributing perpetual motion to qualitative alteration, a mistake since, as we have seen, motions of this kind necessarily have an initial and a final state, and since they proceed from one contrary to another, from the hot to the cold, for example. Moreover, these motions are necessarily posterior to locomotion or conveyance; there is alteration only when a patient undergoes the action of an agent. For example, nourishment is transformed into flesh by assimilation under the influence of a living being, but in order for this influence to take effect the patient must first be brought into contact with the agent by locomotion. Further, the capacity of a being to produce locomotion is the sign of its perfection. The superiority of the animal over the plant consists in this capacity, which it possesses only when it is completely formed and perfected; and the perfect is necessarily prior to the imperfect. But among locomotions all cannot be continuous. These motions are, in fact, of two kinds: (1) rectilinear motions, typified by heavy bodies which descend or by fire which ascends, and (2) circular motions. Now rectilinear motions cannot be continuous; the world not being infinite, they necessarily take place between an initial and a final state, contrary to each other, between above and beneath, right and left, in front and behind. Could we say that a body in motion may be conceived as moving without stopping from above to beneath, then from beneath to above, and so on to infinity? But this motion is not a single motion; since motion upward is the contrary of motion downward, it consists of as many motions as there are changes of direction. Moreover, it is not a continuous motion; there is in reality a halt each time the body in motion changes direction, since it cannot be conceived, for example, that the final instant of the upward motion is the same as the initial instant of the downward motion.

It is quite otherwise with circular motion in one direction; its initial point is also the final point to which it is directed; or rather any point in its course may be considered as its beginning, end, or middle; it is the only motion which at every instant is all that it can be. From this follows the conclusion which sounds so strange to modern ears: circular motion is the only one which can be at once "simple and complete." For if a rectilinear motion has a simple direction—for example, downward—it is not complete, since it excludes motion in the opposite direction; and, if it is complete, it is not simple, since the body in motion must follow successively different directions.[81]

This kinetics, from which modern thought will later have so much difficulty in freeing itself, has its source in Aristotle's conception of motion. Aristotle defined motion, not by what it is at each successive instant, but by what it realizes globally in the being that has the motion. For example, rectilinear motion upward, the natural motion of light objects, is the motion by which fire, returning to its proper place, fully realizes its essence. Motion is not that quasi-substance Protagoras said it was; it is an attribute of substance and, since it is natural or voluntary, it must have its cause in the substance itself. As the movement of the runner on the race track has its cause in his will to win the prize, so the motion of fire has its cause in the nature of fire which has its natural place in the upper regions. Thus, circular motion has its cause in the nature of the substance of the heavens, a fifth essence, different from the four elements whose essential property is the ability to move regularly. The simplicity of circular motion thus arises, not from the simplicity of its path, but rather from the unity of intention which it manifests; simplicity means unity of purpose and is independent of the complexity of motion itself.

It is in this sense then that circular motion can be a single, simple, and continuous motion, the only one capable of realizing the perpetual motion sought by the ancient physicists. This perpetual motion is absolutely necessary; for there is no time without motion, since time is the number of motion; and time did not begin—in other words there is no instant which we could say is the initial instant of time, since every present instant exists only as the limit between the past and the future. The circular motion of the heavens is, therefore, a perpetual and necessary motion without beginning or

[81] *Physics* viii. 7–9, especially 8. 264b 9 and 9 (beginning).

end; not being a motion between opposites, it has no initial point. There is no cosmogony; there is no temporal origin of the order of celestial things; the diagrams of the astronomer became reality; mathematical astronomy, founded upon observation and analysis, is transformed into a dogmatic physics.[82]

Theology is closely connected with this celestial physics. The substance of the heavens has the power to move in a circular motion; this power is its matter, its local or regional matter, in other words the simple possibility of changing place, without alteration or change of any other kind.[83] But who transforms this possibility which, as we have seen, must go on realizing itself eternally, into actuality? Who is the mover?

IX   *Theology*

Aristotle retains Plato's notion of the contrast between, on the one hand, apparently spontaneous motions, such as the motions of fire rising, stones falling, living beings moving and stopping as their desires dictate, and the indefatigable course of the heavens and, on the other hand, movements due to the action of pushing or pulling. Both affirm the original and primitive character of the first kind of motion and the derivative character of the second. The latter are in fact intelligible only by their relation to the former, since they consist in opposing them, principally by causing heavy bodies to move in a direction other than their spontaneous direction downward. Mechanics is properly speaking only the art of constructing machines such as the lever, the balance, the wedge, to produce these violent and unnatural motions for man's use. It follows that it is quite unintelligible and even contradictory to seek, as the atomists did, a mechanistic explanation of motions of the first kind. Ordinary perception and experience supported such a thesis and for a long time hindered the development of Democritus' inspired intuition, in which Aristotle's whole theology disappears.

[82] For Aristotle's own collaboration with the astronomy of the spheres and the modifications which he introduced, see *Metaphysics* Λ. 8.

[83] *Metaphysics* Δ. 8. 1069b 26; H. 1. 1042b 5–6.

These primitive motions have movers which are not bodies and whose action is not mechanical. For the Platonists they are souls, that is, self-moving motions. The Platonism of the *Laws* and the *Epinomis* is a true restoration of animism; soul, that spontaneous force existing not only in animals but pervading the whole universe, directs the universe down to the last detail, from the motions of the heavens to the changes of the elements. Aristotle protests against this confusion; where Platonism seeks unity and continuity, he differentiates and makes a hierarchy: the motion of an element attaining its proper place, the movement of a living being and the movement of the heavens, are not produced by movers of the same species. The motion of the falling stone has no vital motion, for it does not begin and end by itself but is produced as the result of an external circumstance, the removal of the obstacle which prevented it from reaching its proper place. It stops when this place is reached.[84] Locomotions of animals, on the other hand, originate in thought and desire; they conform to desire as far as the mechanical conditions of motion and the organic constitution of the animal permit. Animals have the power of starting and stopping according to desire, whereas an element can neither move nor stop by itself. Finally, the movement of the heavens is not comparable to that of an animal.

In a work considered as apocryphal, no doubt wrongly,[85] Aristotle criticises the analogy some had tried to make between them. It has been observed that the movements of an animal imply unmoved parts within the animal, fixed points around which the segments of the skeleton might turn. And they imply a fixed plane outside the animal, the earth, on which it found a point of support. Similarly, in the universe, the poles would constitute the fixed points around which the heavens revolve, and on which the earth rotates. This comparison, carried farther than Aristotle did, leads to the conclusion that the mover of the heavens is of the same nature as a living being, in other words of the nature of soul. But Aristotle

[84] *Physics* viii. 4.
[85] *On the Movement of Animals* iii and iv.

avoids this conclusion by pointing out the weakness of the analogy. In a revolving sphere, it is not true that there is a part which is motionless. The poles are mere mathematical points without physical reality. Besides, if we compare the relation of the earth to the heavens with that of the earth to animals, we will have to say that the earth is outside the universe. Contrary to Plato, Aristotle sees no resemblance between the heavens and a living organism.

Thus the natural mover of an element, the mover of an animal, and the mover of the heavens are of a different nature. They possess, however, a common attribute, which is that they are themselves motionless. Aristotle strongly opposes the Platonic idea that the source of motion can be another motion. There is no exception to the general principle that a mover, as such, cannot be moved; for the mover is that which is actually what the body in motion is potentially; for example, it is heat insofar as it warms; it is the scholar insofar as he instructs. If the mover were moved, as Plato would have it, it would have to be at the same time and in the same respect scholar and not scholar, heat and not heat. So if there is a being which moves itself, it is not simple; it necessarily divides into an immobile mover and a part moved by this mover (*Physics* VIII.5).

Each of the classes of motions (natural, animal, and celestial) refers us to a distinct class of immobile movers: nature, soul that represents objects, and mover of the heavens. There are a very great number of such movers, as many as there are distinct motions or at least distinct series of connected motions. Fundamentally, the notion of immobile mover completely coincides with the notion of form or actual being. The mover is actual being insofar as it has encountered a body in motion capable of passing from potentiality to actuality. The type of moving action is that of the physician who cures his patient or of the sculptor who sculptures—in other words, action which governs motions in such fashion that matter becomes capable of receiving a form actually existing in the mover; the action directs as well as moves. And that is why motion ceases when the mover no longer acts, as an army is without order when it is no longer commanded. It is not something that can be communicated to the body in motion and persist by itself; the moving body as such never possesses in itself anything but the possibility of moving.

Among these immobile movers it remains to be seen what the particularities of the mover of the heavens are. Since the motion of the heavens is continuous and uniform, it requires an eternally actual mover whose action is immutable and therefore a mover that is indivisible, since a divisible mover would necessarily exhaust its action at the end of a finite time.[86] How did Aristotle, starting from these purely formal characteristics of the mover of the heavens —eternality and indivisibility—derive from them the idea that this mover is an intelligence that is always actual, endlessly contemplating his goal, an eternal and perfect living being—in other words, God?[87]

The mediating idea is that of an actual being; the mover of the heavens is always in act. Now, a being fully actual, in which there is no trace of potentiality, of possible development, of matter, of privation, can be only a thought ($\nu\acute{o}\eta\sigma\iota\varsigma$). Aristotle imagines this pure act as the most divine and the most desirable state within us; this state is the contemplation of the scholar who, having attained truth, has a firm and definitive knowledge of it. If we assume this state to be permanent and complete and free from corporeal life, not transitory, partial, and connected with the body as it is in man, we picture to ourselves pure act, the act of intelligence, which is the eternal and perfect life of God, which is God himself. There is therefore no more trace in God of the intellectual operations which, in the human soul, imply change, such as sensation, image, exploratory reflection, discursive thought, than there is of the vegetative functions which are related to the life of the body; God is not a soul, a vital principle, but an intellectual thought.

But does not an intelligence always contain potentiality? For

[86] *Physics* viii. 6.
[87] *Metaphysics* Λ. 7. 1072b 27-29.

example, our human intelligence is only a faculty of thinking; to exist actually, it must undergo the influence of an intelligible object, very much as sensation can only exist actually under the action of a sensible thing. If God is intelligence, the intelligible object that enables him to think would then be superior to him. A serious question, since we see restored at one stroke, above the mover of the heavens, the whole intelligible world of Plato which the Demiurge contemplates as a model above him; the eternal actuality of the mover of the heavens is endangered if he can cease to think. Aristotle solved it in the following manner: since God is the superior being, it follows that he has no other intelligible object than himself; "he himself thinks himself; he is thought of thought." [88] Only in this way can he be self-sufficient. Is this a purely verbal solution? Aristotle knew very well that, even in man, all knowledge, whether sensation, thought, or reflection, is accompanied by self-knowledge; one cannot know without knowing that one knows. But the principal object of knowledge is not this consciousness of self; it is an intelligible or a sensible object, distinct from intelligence and sensation. What in man is an accessory becomes in God the principal or rather the only thing; he no longer has to seek the objects of his thought outside himself, and it is only thus that his thought can be complete and indestructibly perfect. Our highest sciences strain for this state of independence. In fact, in the theoretical sciences such as mathematics, the object is identical with the thought one has of it;[89] the thought exhausts all there is in the object. It is neither posterior nor prior to it; it is identical with it.

The theology of Aristotle is at the summit of metaphysics and physics. It solves both the problem of the mover of the heavens and of substance. It solves the problem of the mover of the heavens, for the perfect uniformity of their motions is explained by divine immutability. Besides, it is natural that intelligence be the mover, in other words that movable things tend to imitate this immutabil-

[88] Λ. 9. 1074b 33.
[89] *On the Soul* iii. 7 (beginning).

ity as much as they can; God moves the heavens as the beloved moves the lover.[90] The condition of this uniform motion is the unalterable fifth essence, or ether, capable only of circular motion. Its justification is this motion which is the end for which it exists. Thus God is not the Demiurge of the world, he does not even know the world; he is only the end toward which it aspires.

This theology also solves the problem of substance. With Plato, Aristotle admits a separate incorporeal substance, which is God. But God is very different from ideas. The great difference is that God, unlike ideas, is not the substance of all things, nor is he the object of knowledge. On the other hand, he is, one might say, pre-eminently substance as he is pre-eminently knowledge. He is pre-eminently substance, because what he is, his essence, does not have to seek support beyond itself to become an actually realized substance. The other substantial forms can actually become substances only if they find beyond themselves, in matter, the conditions of their realization; the statue can become a reality only through the marble; man, only through an organized body made of a multitude of elements. This is why the substantial form which is the essence of a being is still not its substance; substance designates, rather, the compound of form and matter. In God, who is pure act, the difficulty disappears. Thought has no other conditions than itself; it exists without matter. This eternal substance, identical with its essence, is the type which transitory substances, born of a combination of form and matter, strive to imitate. But it does not take the place of these substances. God is also pre-eminently knowledge but a knowledge inaccessible to man, who seeks his objects in the world. It is clear how greatly the place of theology in the doctrine of Aristotle differs from that of the world of ideas in the doctrine of Plato.

In order to understand this theology better, it is appropriate to mention the crisis which it seems to have undergone in the course of the development of his thought. Aristotle was in general extremely cautious in developing his theology.

[90] *Metaphysics* Λ. 7. 1072b 2.

Beings not engendered and incorruptible are unquestionably precious and divine, but they are the very ones which we know least . . . ; unquestionably, with the value that they possess, a slight contact with them is more agreeable to us than knowledge of the things which surround us, as it is better to see the least part of a beloved object than to be acquainted with many others in great detail; nevertheless the proximity of these beings, their kinship in nature with us, these are benefits received in exchange for the knowledge of divine things.[91]

These are words characteristic of the former Platonist: he no longer seeks in the suprasensible the object of an exact knowledge; theology is above man's grasp. From this comes his hesitation between monotheism and polytheism. He certainly leans towards monotheism, because the unity of organization of the universe can be attributed only to the unity of its final cause, and he concludes his theology by citing the verse from Homer, which will become the permanent text of pagan monotheism: "It is not good that there be several masters." [92] But on the other hand, God is the mover of the heavens and an immobile mover; his effects must, therefore, always be the same. Now astronomy discloses the existence of a great number of concentric spheres, each animated by its own motion, quite independent of that of the others; the principles of Aristotle here require there to be an equal number of distinct movers, and this leads to polytheism.[93]

Hence, the real function of Aristotle's theology; knowledge of God himself is in no wise its end, nor has it any role whatever in morals or politics. God is considered solely in his cosmic function, as the producer of the unity of the world, a unity which affords rational knowledge of it. There is a hierarchy between this immobile mover and the other immobile movers, down to the transitory and changing actions of souls, nature, and forms in general. The action of each of the lower movers is determined not spontaneously and at will but according to the order which comes from

---

[91] *On the Parts of Animals* i. 5.
[92] *Metaphysics* Λ. 10. 1076a 24 (*Iliad* ii. 204).
[93] Cf. *Physics* 258b 10; 259a 3, and *Metaphysics* Λ. 8. 1074a 31–38.

the first mover and which is transmitted by the motion of the heavens to the earth. Knowledge of natural things will consist primarily in distinguishing this hierarchy, where each term is the final cause which governs the lower term. The movement of the heavens strives by its circularity and uniformity to imitate divine immutability, just as, below the moon, the endless and ever recurring circle of generation and corruption imitates the movement of the heavens as far as matter permits. "All natural beings have thus something of the divine in them." [94] Theology is the guarantee that there are not only partial final causes each working in a limited sphere, but a universal final cause which regulates their action; "man engenders man, but the sun also."

x The World

The entire universe is, therefore, the sum of conditions necessary to the existence of the movement of the heavens. In fact, if there must be a circular motion, there must be in opposition a body at the center which remains motionless; this is the earth. Geocentricism and the immobility of the earth are thus demonstrated. Further, if there is earth—in other words a heavy body which displaced from the center tends to return to it—then by a necessary opposition, there must be fire, in other words a light body which tends to rise; for if an opposite exists, it is impossible for its opposite not to exist. If we consider, not the affinity of the element with its proper place, but rather the essential qualities through which it manifests its activity and passivity, we will see that the existence of intermediate elements, water and air, follows from the same rule; for earth, whose attributes are coldness and dryness, is opposed not only by fire whose attributes are warmness and dryness but also by water whose attributes are coldness and humidity. Fire, which is warm and dry, is opposed not only by earth but also by air, which is warm and humid.[95] Thus the four elements are deduced. We see that Aristotle, following a notion then current among physicians and physicists, recognized four fundamental active properties (paired in opposites): the warm and the cold, and the dry and the moist. If we combine in the same subject these four attributes (in pairs), excluding combinations which would unite opposites, there remain four possible combinations; dry-cold, cold-moist, moist-warm, and warm-dry. Each of these combinations characterizes an element, earth, water, air, or fire. It is easy to see that we pass from each one to the following one and that we return from the fourth to the first by substituting for a property of the pair the opposite of this property; thus we pass from earth to water by substituting the moist for the dry, in the pair which forms earth. There is therefore the possibility of a continuous passage from one element to another in a determinate order, earth being able to change into water, water into air, and air into fire. Each time, the passing away of one element is the generation of the next. Moreover, this becoming is circular, since in the same way the fourth element can give rise again to the first (the inverse order of the one we have chosen is equally possible). In this way becoming can be endless. This end-less movement of circular transmutation is not only possible, it is actual. If in fact the elements were not to change into one another, then, since they possess limited movements upward and downward, each would stop in its own place and motion would cease in the sublunary regions: the circle of transmutations imitates in its way the circular motion of the heavens. On the other hand, for this circle to be possible, there must be more than one circular motion in the heavens; a single motion such as that of the fixed stars, for example, would leave the elements in the same relation to one another. There must therefore be several concentric spheres, each endowed with its own motion and having its axis inclined toward that of the heaven of the fixed stars. As a result of the inclination of the ecliptic, the changeable effects which we call the seasons are produced, each one characterized by the predominance of one of the fundamental properties of the elements, the hot, the cold, the dry, or the moist, which temporarily prevails over its opposite ac-cording to the relative position of the sun.

This, briefly, is[96] the universe of Aristotle: all the particulars are governed by the whole. The outline of the physics of sublunary objects is thus determined. It is the study of the reciprocal actions and passions which take place either between the elements or between bodies already formed and which produce all the mixtures and alterations thanks to which new bodies can arise and new substantial forms can be fashioned in matter. And it must not be forgotten that all these changes, although they have their material conditions in the elementary forces, have their final cause, their true cause, in the form toward which they are directed. The remedy acts by a succession of changes in the living substance, but the true cause of these changes is the attainment of a state of health. We must refrain from believing that the production of a new body is due to combinations or changes which are only their conditions.

Still, these conditions can be studied in themselves. A body submits to the influence of a force only because it has matter, in other words, ultimately, the possibility of change. Thus when air changes into water, under the influence of cold, it is not the heat of the air which has been affected, since heat is a form; without matter, fire would be impossible. In reality its matter has been affected.[97] "First matter" is the name of that entirely indeterminate power of change which is implied by the transmutation of the elements. Second matter, the bronze of a statue, for example, is determinate in itself, although it is indeterminate relative to the change which it is still capable of undergoing.[98] It is, therefore, due to matter that the agent is able to act by assimilating the patient—for instance, fire when it warms. In order for there to be action, the agent must encounter a patient which is actually different from it but which is similar to it potentially. An especially important case is mixture, which comes about as a result of reciprocal actions and passions between two bodies; mixture is not a juxtaposition, as the atomists claimed, but a real union where every part, however small it may

[96] For an exposition of the whole, see *On the Heavens* ii. 3, continued by *On Generation and Corruption* ii. 9.

[97] *On Generation and Corruption* i. 7 (end).

[98] *Metaphysics* Θ. 7. 1049a 25.

be, is homogeneous with the whole. Here again we find that same absolute confidence in brute and unanalyzed sensation which is characteristic of the mind of Aristotle. The differences of mixtures depend both on the quantity and on the nature of the bodies which enter into them. The mixed body may disappear if it is in too small a quantity, as a drop of water in the sea, or if it is much more passive than the other, as, in an alloy of tin and of brass, the tin disappears leaving only its color.[99]

An initial application of this physics is made in the *Meteorology,* where Aristotle tried to determine the different actions which produce that group of irregular phenomena occurring below the sphere of the moon—the Milky Way, comets, fiery apparitions—and also the general states of the atmosphere—winds, earthquakes, lightning, and storms. The fourth and last book is devoted to the study of what might be called different states of matter under the influence of the two pre-eminently active causes, the hot and the cold. Special attention is given to the phenomena of cooking and congealing, as well as to states due to mixture, such as the soft, the flexible, the fragile, the breakable, etc.

All these studies are oriented toward the last chapter, which takes up the study of mixtures forming the various parts of living beings, bone, muscle, etc.

XI *The Living Being: The Soul*

The elements exist only for the purpose of forming these living tissues; these tissues exist only for the purpose of forming organs such as the eye or the arm; these organs themselves exist only for the purpose of performing certain very complicated functions, such as sight for the eyes or movement for the arms.[100] The vital functions at work are therefore one of the principal ends for which

---

[99] *On Generation and Corruption* i. 6–10.
[100] *The Parts of Animals,* ii. 1; that which we call the tissues are homoeomerous, composed of homogeneous parts, the organs being unhomoeomerous, composed of several homeomerous parts.

nature acts and brings about all the combinations and mixtures which will make the living being possible.

But life is not the product of these combinations and mixtures. The organized body possesses life only potentially; it will be alive actually—in other words, able to exercise the functions of a living body, such as nutrition, development to the adult state, and corruption—only when it has received the substantial form called the soul. The soul is "the first entelechy of a natural body which possesses life potentially," [101] in other words, of a body endowed with organs adapted to perform vital functions. It is therefore connected with this body as the cutting edge of steel is connected with the ax. It is the immediate condition of the activity of the body, almost in the same way that the knowledge which the scholar possesses is the immediate condition by which he contemplates truth. Just as the scholar does not always contemplate, so the soul does not always act and has its period of sleep; but it is always immediately qualified to act.

The soul in Aristotle is, therefore, primarily the principle of vital activity, the unmoved mover of this activity. Psychology is the introduction to the study of living beings, as theology is the introduction to the study of the universe. It no longer has any proper and separate object, as in the tradition of Pythagoras and Plato; the soul is no longer the wanderer who goes from body to body to fulfil its own destiny. It is connected with the body as sight is connected with the eye.[102] Nothing remains of the Platonic myth, which Aristotle seems to have accepted in his early writings. The problem of moral philosophy is as independent of psychology as it is of theology; soul and body arise and disappear together.

The result is that there is no study of the soul in general as Plato believed. The philosopher studies the soul in the way in which the geometer studies forms: the geometer does not study form in general, which does not name an essence, but the triangle, the polygon, etc., and thus a series of forms, from the simplest to the

[101] *On the Soul* ii. 1. 412a 27.
[102] *Ibid.* ii. 1. 412b 18.

most complex, each of which implies the preceding but not the following. Likewise, the philosopher studies the series of functions or faculties or powers of the soul, each of which implies the preceding but not the following: the nutritive, sensitive, thinking, and moving functions. Whatever possesses the sensitive function, for example, possesses the nutritive; but the reverse is not true and the plant, for instance, has only the capacity of nourishing itself. These functions do not constitute, for the things that possess several of them, so many different souls; they differ logically, since they imply different acts, but they do not differ spatially or constitute different substances; each living being has a single soul (*On the Soul* ii. 2).

The theory of the functions of the soul arose very obviously from the classification of living beings into vegetables, animals without reason, and rational animals. But this clear-cut classification should not make us forget that Aristotle is essentially a gradualist and that he sees in higher life not a pure and simple addition but rather the realization of something which was prefigured in lower life.

"In most of the other animals, there are traces of characteristics which are distinguished most clearly in men: sociability and unsociability, gentleness and harshness, courage and cowardice, timidity and self-confidence. In many of them there are even suggestions of reflective intelligence. It is by degrees that these animals differ from man and that man differs from many of them. Nature passes gradually from inaminate beings to animals, to such an extent that the continuity causes the limits to elude us and we do not know where to place intermediates; for example, with respect to certain marine beings, we may ask whether they are animals or plants.[103]

It is not that Aristotle is in the least inclined to favor an evolutionism like that of Empedocles; quite the contrary. For Aristotle it is an absolute rule (which he transfers from the domain of life to the whole of nature) that we cannot pass from one genus to another and that like always produces its like. As there is specific identity between the health of the physician and the health he produces in the sick room, there is always specific identity between

[103] *History of Animals* viii. 1.

the generator and the engendered. Living beings are divided into incorruptible fixed species whose form is transmitted from one perishable individual to another by generation; it is only in this way that the living being may imitate the eternal course of the stars and attain perpetuity. Thus the thesis of the immutability of the species is connected with the most profound tendencies of Aristotle, his search for fixed points in becoming. For him continuity is something quite different from evolution; it is not explanation of the higher by the lower but, quite to the contrary, explanation of the lower by the higher, of the plant by the animal, of the animal by man: only the perfect and full-grown enables us to understand the imperfect.

That is the leading idea of the study of the faculties of the soul, which may, then, be considered under two aspects. In the first place, the study of each of the faculties is like the introduction to a chapter on anatomy, which describes the tissues and the organs formed of these tissues enabling the faculty to exercise itself. Thus the nutritive function, which is the assimilation of nourishment by the body, so that the body grows to the adult state and maintains itself in it, controls a whole mechanism of corporeal action without which it cannot be known. This mechanism consists first in cooking the ingested food by internal heat emanating from the heart which, as the source of heat, is engendered first in the animal; nourishment liquefied or hardened by heat circulates in the veins, and it filters through them, as through a vessel of coarse clay; condensing under the effect of cold, its watery parts form flesh; its earthy parts, which still retain a little humidity and heat, lose these under the action of cold and become the hard parts such as nails and horns. Moreover, each living being has as much innate heat as it is needed for this purpose.[104] Similarly, the sensory function governs the anatomical and physiological study of the sense organs. In general, these faculties are in no sense idle explanations but resemble centers of direction in experimental research.

---

[104] Compare *On the Generation of Animals* ii. 6, and *On the Soul* ii. 4.

Secondly, the study of each function is oriented as it were toward the study of the higher function and especially of the one which is superior to all of them; namely, intellectual thought. This characteristic is especially evident in the study of the faculties of knowing or distinguishing the true from the false. This discernment takes place either with the aid of sensation or with the aid of thought. Aristotle remains quite faithful to this Platonic distinction and sharply criticizes the natural philosophers who reduce thought to sensation (*On the Soul* iii. 3); but its significance is changed, because Aristotle stresses opposition less than continuity. Already in the case of sensation he tries to show there is something permanent, fixed; real knowledge. Sensation is not a purely passive change, where the organ submits to the action of qualities which are sensible, perpetually changing, and mobile. To be sure, it is only under the influence of a sensible agent upon a sense organ that the faculty of sensing becomes actual. But sensation is not on that account reducible to an act of the sensible agent alone; the plant, for example, undergoes changes as a result of heat, but it does not feel the heat.[105] It must, therefore, be said that sensation is a joint act of the sentient being and of what is sensed; for example, of color and of vision, of noise and of hearing; and we must insist upon this jointness and upon the impossibility of attributing sensation to either of the two factors separately (*On the Soul* iii. 2).

Such an action already has something of the nature of thought; for like thought with respect to intelligible things, sensation, with respect to sensible things, affirms truly its proper object. In fact we call a sensible quality the proper object of a sensation when it causes this sensation to pass into action; color in the case of sight, sound in the case of hearing. Now each sensation expresses the complete truth in regard to its proper object; vision is not mistaken concerning white. Error begins only if it affirms that this white is such or such an object. The different kinds of sensations give an integral knowledge of these sensible qualities. There are no sensible quali-

[105] *Ibid*. ii. 12. 424a 32.

ties, in fact, except those that act by contact, like tactile qualities or tastes, or through an airy or liquid medium, like colors, sounds, or odors (*On the Soul* iii. 1).

In another aspect, this sensible knowledge is directed toward intellectual knowledge, since it apprehends things without their matter: "it is not the stone itself which is in the soul" when one perceives it, it is only its form.[106] Although it is confined to the knowledge of particular things, sensation separates them from their matter. Moreover, the multiplicity of the five senses has as its reason for existence the facilitation of the knowledge of qualities common to all the sensibles, such as motion, size, or number. Perception of these common properties would not be possible with a single sense, because it would not be able to free itself from its proper sensible object.[107] Finally, this multiplicity implies a common center, capable of apprehending and discerning all qualities, without which the sensations of each sense would be isolated from the others as those of so many persons unknown to each other. Now, this common center can perceive resemblances and differences and, in general, all sorts of relations between sensibles.[108]

Thought, in the broadest sense, includes all acts of knowing independent of the present influence of sensible objects; in other words memory images as well as opinions and scientific judgments.[109] Aristotle recognizes at both ends of the scale of knowledge an intuition which can only be veridical; at the bottom, the intuition of the proper sensible by sensation and, at the top, the intellectual intuition of indivisible essences.[110] Between these two lies everything else, that is, everything capable of being true or false, every proposition asserting that an attribute belongs, has belonged, or will belong to a subject. Aristotle did not make a very systematic study of these intermediary faculties. It seems clear that he considers each of them from three different points of view; in itself, in its

[106] *Ibid*. iii. 8. 431b 28.
[107] *Ibid*. iii. 1 to the end.
[108] *Ibid*. iii. 2. 426b 17–22.
[109] *On the Soul* iii. 3 (beginning).
[110] *Ibid*. iii. 6 (end).

relations to the lower faculty, and in relation to the higher faculty. Thus the representation or image (φαντασία) in itself is all that appears to the soul outside of sensation; it is generally false, without a corresponding reality; but it does not claim to be true, since, unlike opinion, it is not accompanied by belief.[111] Thus the sun appears to us to be a foot in diameter, but we know that it is larger than the earth. In relation to sensation it is the image of a past sensible thing, a sort of picture which results from the sensible object's leaving its imprint like a seal upon wax. This image is the recollection of the object, and there is memory only where there is an image. Contrary to what Plato said, we do not remember purely intellectual truths, we contemplate them afresh each time that we think of them.[112] Finally, in relation to intelligence, the image is the condition of thought; "there is no thought without an image," because the image is the material through which intelligence contemplates the universal. The geometer, in order to demonstrate the properties of the triangle, must draw a triangle of definite dimensions; but he does not think of these dimensions.[113]

The treatises of Aristotle contain many scattered references to complex intellectual facts, such as reminiscence or judgment. Reminiscence is like the orientation of the soul in the pursuit of a recollection; it proceeds from the existing state and arrives at the recollection sought for through a series of other states connected with the first either because they are similar to them or because they are contrary to them or else because they have been next to them; what was later called the association of ideas is thus presented as a means of recollection.[114]

At the other pole of knowledge is intelligence, whose action is the indivisible thought of intelligible essences that are themselves indivisible. Comparable in its certitude to the sensation of proper sensibles, it greatly differs from it. Between the intelligible and

[111] *Ibid*. iii. 3. 428b 2.
[112] *On Memory* i. 450a 22.
[113] *Ibid*. 449b 30
[114] *Ibid*. ii.

intelligence, there is indeed a relation analogous to that which exists between the sensible and the sentient. Intelligence is like a blank tablet which contains all intelligible things potentially and which only becomes actual when it undergoes their action.[115] But whereas the sentient organ is destroyed by a sensible object that is too intense, such as a dazzling light, intelligence on the contrary thinks more as the clarity of the intelligible object increases.[116] And whereas in the joint act of sensation the sentient always remains distinct from the sensible, in the intellectual act of contemplation intelligence is completely identified with the intelligible, and one cannot find in it, when it thinks, anything other than its object: it is, therefore, itself intelligible.[117] Finally, whereas sensation is divided among organs each of which is capable of apprehending only one particular kind of sensible object, intelligence is capable of receiving all intelligible things without exception. These three distinctive characteristics have a single explanation: intelligence perceives forms or essences without matter and free of all the particularities which accompany them in sensible objects; for example, it thinks not the snub-nosed, which is curvature in a nose, but curvature in itself. By abstraction, it causes the intelligibles which existed only potentially in sensible objects to become actual. Now, the knowledge of immaterial things is necessarily identical with these things; there is nothing in a geometrical or arithmetical notion but what we think in it.[118]

Yet, our intelligence is only a faculty of thought; it is all intelligible things, but it is these things only potentially. It does not always think. How does it act? It clearly does not act by the influence of sensible images; images are no doubt indispensable to its activity of abstraction (we cannot think without images), but actual intelligible things cannot originate spontaneously from images, since images contain them only potentially. In conformity with the general principle according to which a being cannot pass from potentiality to actuality except by the influence of a being already actual,

[115] *On the Soul* iii. 4. 429b 31.
[116] *Ibid*. 4. 429a 29.
[117] *Ibid*. 4. 430a 2.
[118] *Ibid*. 7. 431b 12.

Aristotle is therefore led to assert, beyond our intelligence which does not always think, an intelligence eternally actual and impassive, a fixed and indefectible thought which undergoes no change whatever and which is productive of all other thoughts, in the way in which light makes colors become actual. Exactly what is the significance of this intelligence? Is it a part of the human soul like the passive or potential intelligence? Apparently not, since Aristotle declares it incorruptible and eternal, whereas passive intelligence is perishable. If it is a substance separate from the human soul, is it not identical with the mover of the spheres, with God, who is the eternally existing thought? This seems the more likely as the intelligence within us is the most divine part of our being, the one whose activity places us above human nature and makes us participate in the life of the gods. But on this point Aristotle does not express himself formally, and he leaves his interpreters in a quandary whose consequences will be seen later (*On the Soul* iii. 5).

What remains certain is the particular place in the human soul which he gave to intelligence. If it perceives immaterial things, it is because it is itself immaterial; it has no need of any bodily organ whatever. If the generic definition of the soul, entelechy of an organized body, is still appropriate to it, it does not apply in quite the same sense as it applies to the nutritive or sensitive faculty. It is clear that the organized body is a condition without which intelligence cannot think, since it cannot think without images. But being in itself independent both of the functioning of an organ and also of images themselves, we must say that it joins itself to the soul by a kind of epigenesis, that it enters it from the outside and "through the door." [119]

The soul is thus conceived in a manner analogous to the world and, we may say, according to the same principle: a development of faculties which, supported by the organized body, orients itself toward an end, intelligence, which in certain respects transcends them. Psychology and cosmology, whose relationship was somewhat

[119] *On the Generation of Animals* ii. 3. 736b 27.

vague in Plato due to the myth of destiny which gave separate individuality to the soul, were united more closely than ever. In Aristotle's philosophy, the soul is formed so to speak only in order to be a spiritual image of reality. "The soul is in a way all things; for things are either sensible or intelligible, and knowledge is in a way the known and sensation is the sensible." [120] In this synthetic view of the soul only the two poles are presented; namely, sensation and intelligence. The interval between them, that is to say all the movements of thought in which we are ourselves reflection, opinion, imagination, are absorbed in their relation to one or the other of these fixed poles, where the soul becomes purely representative and intuitive of reality.

XII Ethics

The whole of Plato's thought rested upon a very intimate union between the intellectual, moral, and political life. Philosophy, through knowledge, achieves virtue and the capacity to govern the city. All these things are dissociated in Aristotle: the moral or the practical good is that which man may attain through his action and has nothing to do with the idea of the Good which dialectic places at the summit of beings.[121] Ethics is not an exact science like mathematics but an instruction which aims at making men better. It aims not only at giving them right opinions concerning the things to be sought or avoided but to make them actually seek after or avoid these things. "Where virtue is concerned, it is not sufficient to know; one must possess and practice it." The moralist should not entertain too many illusions about the effect of this teaching. Mere discourses are not sufficient to inspire goodness. They will be fruitful when they are addressed to young men of liberal and noble character, but they are quite incapable of leading ordinary people to virtue. Ethics, therefore, is instruction, but aristocratic instruction. It is not preaching to the crowd, but an invitation to reflection for

[120] On the Soul iii. 8 (beginning).
[121] Nicomachean Ethics i. 6.

the more gifted. Habit and the fear of punishment will suffice for others.[122] And it even seems that virtue may be developed fully only in the well-to-do classes. "It is impossible or difficult for a poor man to perform noble deeds; for there are many things which one can do only through the instrumentality of friends, wealth, or political power"; a very ugly man, of low birth, alone and without children, cannot attain perfect happiness.[123] Virtues as precious as courage, generosity, courtesy, and justice can be practiced only on a certain social level: "A poor man cannot be magnificent, for he does not have the means to spend appropriately; if he tries to, he is a fool." [124]

This morality is that of a well-to-do middle class which is determined to enjoy its social advantages wisely. In it one senses neither the popular inspiration of an awakener of consciences, like Socrates, nor the certainty which inspired Plato. It is in complete harmony with the rest of Aristotle's philosophy. In ethics, as everywhere else, the problem is to define an end and then determine the appropriate means of attaining this end. But it is a practical and human end, in other words an end which must be accessible to man through actions. To know it, therefore, we must avail ourselves of observation and induction; in other words we must try to discover for what end men act the way they do. There is no doubt that they all seek happiness. Pleasure, knowledge, wealth are only means of attaining this end which is not in turn subordinated to any other. The end, therefore, is happiness, but a human happiness, that is to say, one which is accessible to us by our actions and which lasts throughout the greater part of life. It is important to see that this happiness which gives direction to action as an end is neither a part nor a result of action (any more than intellectual intuition is a result of mental work, since it rather gives direction to this work). Happiness belongs to another category than action: happiness is an absolute and an activity, while action is relative to an end.[125] Happiness

[122] Ibid. x. 9. 1179b 1 ff.
[123] Ibid. i. 8. 1099a 31.
[124] Ibid. iv. 2. 1122b 25.
[125] Ethics i. 9 (beginning)

comes to us like a gift of the gods and a reward for our virtue; as the source of good things, it has something of the divine in it.[126] Moreover, this is the universal opinion of men, who consider happiness as a thing to be prized beyond all others, but not as a thing to be praised. It would appear that Aristotle struggled against that type of eudaemonism, so different from his, which prevailed after him and which reunited what he tried particularly hard to distinguish: the praiseworthy and the prized, the action and the end.[127]

It is a universal rule that a being attains its proper end only if it fulfils its proper function; excellence in carrying out this function is the virtue of this being. The notion of virtue in general goes far beyond the sphere of ethics. We may speak of the virtue of a living being and even of an inanimate object or of a manufactured implement. The word does not suggest a specifically moral quality. Besides, the virtue of a being is something acquired, superadded to its essence. In fact, essence does not admit of degrees. Aristotle is adamant on this point. One either is or is not a man; one cannot be more or less of one. But not all qualities of a being are deduced from its essence with the same necessity as the properties of a triangle are deduced from its essence. There are different degrees of perfection for a being of the same essence. There are tools of good and of poor quality, good or poor quality constituting no part of the essence. Virtue, therefore, is found in the category of quality, more specifically in the acquired qualities (*Ethics* i. 13; ii. 1).

Let us apply these principles to man: his proper and distinctive function is activity in conformity with reason. All human activity, good or bad, is rational; human virtue consists in the perfection or the excellence of this activity. To realize the meaning of this formula is the goal of the theory of the virtues. This meaning is extraordinarily rich and complex, if we try, as we should, to see it at work in all the particular details of human life; for ethics must teach us how to act and must consequently come down to particular cases:

[126] *Ibid*. i. 12 to the end.
[127] *Ibid*. i. 12.

"In matters of action, general notions are empty; and particular notions are truer because actions concern particulars" (iii.7, opening passage). Ethics, therefore, is a kind of concrete description of the way in which reason may penetrate and direct every human activity. No detail of emotional life or social relations is omitted, for it is due to such details that reason takes on a meaning. Ethics is oriented quite naturally toward the description of the passions, as, a little later, the new comedy of Menander (342–290) substitutes subtle character analysis for the violent diatribes of Aristophanes. These analyses give the *Nicomachean Ethics* all its value. It is not a matter of general rules but of inquiring into "when it is necessary to act, in what case, with respect to whom, in view of what and in what way" (ii. 7).

Virtue is a stable disposition from which virtuous action arises. This disposition is not natural and innate; man is born with dispositions to certain passions, anger or fear, for example. But these dispositions constitute neither vice nor virtue, and he is neither praised nor blamed for them. Virtue is an acquired disposition and acquired by choice, since it is praised. It really exists only when it has become habit, in other words when, although acquired, it produces actions with the same ease as an innate disposition. Man is truly just only if he has no difficulty, if he even takes pleasure in performing a just act. Such a habit, born of the will, at the same time makes the will firmer. All virtue in man, therefore, comes from his voluntary choice.

But what must this choice be in order to be rational and virtuous? On this fundamental point, Aristotle (this is characteristic of his method in ethics) appeals in part to an analogy, and in part to common opinion (ii. 6). He makes an analogy between virtuous acts and works of nature and art. These works aim primarily at avoiding excesses, the too much or the too little. Physicians know that health or the excellence of the body turns out to be a just proportion of actively opposing forces, hot and cold, which have an effect on the body. The sculptor and the architect also seek certain right proportions. Nature and art find their excellence when they have attained the mean between the two excesses. The material condition of this goal is that these men operate on continua which comprise the more and the less, one of those infinite multiples that Plato mentioned in the *Philebus,* where the warmer and the colder, the lower and the higher, form pairs. This condition is realized in the ethical life. The will works on actions and passions which include want and excess, the more and the less; these actions and passions appear in pairs, like fear and courage, desire and aversion, where the growth of one term is a diminution of the other. Virtue consists in attaining the proper mean in these continua. It is also common opinion that there is only one way of being good and a thousand of being bad. But the problem of the mean also takes on particular characteristics in the context of ethics. The problem is not to find the object of virtue, to define the mean, in a precise and absolute manner, as we define an arithmetical mean between two extremes. Ethics does not carry such rigor. It addresses itself in fact to men naturally inclined to opposite passions of every degree and of every nature; its effect is less to give men a theoretical definition of virtue than to produce it in them. It is obvious that courage will not be produced in the same way in the timid who must be urged on and in the audacious who must be restrained. Depending on the individual, the mean will be closer to one or the other extreme; it is the mean in relation to us and not according to the thing itself. The determination of the mean, inseparable from the means of producing it, is therefore a question of tact and prudence. In an arithmetical mean, the mean is posterior to the extremes and determined by them. In the ethical life, the extremes are at least ideally posterior to the mean and are extremes only relatively to it. The imperfect is conceived only in relation to the perfect. In a sense the mean is the true extreme, that is to say, the highest degree of perfection (ii. 6).

In sum, virtue is an acquired disposition (ἕξις) of the will, consisting in a mean relative to us, defined by reason, in other words as a man of sense may define it.[128] This is a very general outline,

[128] *Ethics* ii. 6. 1106b 36.

which ethical experience will proceed to fill in; there are as many pairs of virtues and pairs of vices opposed to one another and to virtue as there are pairs of passions. In regard to fear and daring, for example, there is one virtue, courage, and two vices, foolhardiness and cowardice. In regard to the pursuit of pleasure, virtue is temperance, and the opposed vices are intemperance and brutishness. It is the same when we find a pair of actions opposed to one another. In regard to the gift of wealth, virtue is liberality, the opposed vices are, on the one hand, niggardliness and, on the other, prodigality (ii. 7). These examples show us more clearly how virtue is a mean wholly relative to our human condition, and even to our social condition. Thus liberality, a virtue of private citizens of modest means, is quite different from magnificence, a virtue of the rich magistrate, patron of his city. What is generosity in the one will be niggardliness in the other.

If Aristotle defines virtue as a voluntary disposition, he is very far from seeing in it anything like intention. Disposition is envisaged only as a disposition to action. If the material conditions of action are absent, virtue no longer has any meaning. "The generous person needs wealth to act generously, and the just, exchanges of social intercourse; for intentions are invisible, and the unjust person also boasts of his strong desire for justice." Thus these are human virtues inseparable from the social environment, political virtues, which the gods, for example, do not possess at all. "How would they be just? Can one seriously imagine them making contracts with each other and returning deposits?" [129]

From this follows his analysis of the will (iii. 1–5). It is considered not in itself but in its relation to the action which it produces. The main problem is social education, the problem of knowing what actions the legislator will be able to encourage usefully by his praise or prevent by his reproach: one condition is that they be voluntary. This condition concerns their various causes, in other words their originating source, their end and their means. An action is voluntary (ἑκούσιος), in the most general sense, when its

[129] x. 8. 1178a 24 and 1178b 28.

starting point is internal to the being that performs it. What makes the act involuntary is either physical constraint, as when the wind carries us along, or else moral constraint, like that of a tyrant (but here there is no precise point at which a threat makes an act involuntary), or finally ignorance, not the ignorance of what is good or bad but ignorance of specific circumstances, knowledge of which would have modified our action. In this general sense, voluntary action is by no means peculiar to man; it is also found in animals. The properly human act is the act performed through reflective choice (προαίρεσις), in other words through choice preceded by deliberation (βούλευσις). Deliberation is the search which *con*cerns, not the end of the act, but rather the various possible means of attaining this end. It takes place, therefore, only where there is indeterminateness and contingency. It corresponds in the practical domain to discursive thought in the theoretical domain. It constructs practical syllogisms, in which the major premise implies a prescription and an end (light meats are wholesome), the minor premise, a verification of fact by sense perception (this meat is light), and the conclusion, a practical maxim which leads immediately to action or abstention. A general maxim, without particular knowledge of the facts, would never entail action. It is the proper role of "practical intelligence" to discover these particular facts expressed in the minor premises (here sense perception is really intelligence), whereas "theoretical intelligence" knows first principles.[130] But deliberation is always relative to an end; willing the end (βούλησις), very different from the deliberation which depends on it, is that which aims at the good or, at least, at that which appears to us to be the good.

This analysis of the will has as a consequence the distinction between two kinds of virtues: (1) the ethical virtues, which are related to character, in other words to our natural dispositions to this or that passion, in order to bring them within their proper limits, and (2) the intellectual virtues or virtues of reflection, which are qualities of practical thought resulting in action. It is impossible

[130] vi. 11. 1148a 35.

to confuse the first with the second, impossible to confuse the force of the will ruling the passions with the clarity of intelligence seeking the right course. The unity which Socrates appears to have wanted to establish between self-mastery and reflection is destroyed. The irrational part of the soul remains as an irreducible element which reason can govern but not absorb. The ethical virtues, courage or justice, exist in us almost from birth; the dianoetic virtues, like prudence, are acquired only through long experience. It is also impossible to confuse the dianoetic virtues with knowledge or wisdom. Their qualities are prudence (φρόνησις), which consists in deliberating carefully—in other words, in seeking, on reflection, the best possible means of attaining an end and in prescribing the means; penetration (σύνεσις), which consists in the ability to judge others correctly by the choices they make; common sense, the faculty of judging correctly what is fitting. Whereas knowledge relates only to the universal and the necessary, all practical reflection, as we have seen, deals only with particular and contingent circumstances. The complex knowledge of the different means of attaining our ends cannot lead to universal truths (Book VI).

This same tendency to separate things that were united in the thought of Socrates and Plato is met with again in the doctrine of justice (Book V). In Plato, justice is the mainstay of the unity of the virtues; in Aristotle, it becomes a separate virtue. Not that he entirely abandons the idea that justice is the whole of virtue; in fact the just is what is prescribed by law, and the law, especially as Plato conceived it, includes a very great number of moral prescriptions, made for the purpose of encouraging virtue. It prescribes temperance, courage, and gentleness; but it is well to add that if legislation prescribes virtuous acts, its aim is not the perfection of the individual but that of society. Thus in this very general form, justice includes only one aspect of the moral life, that of our relations with others (v. 1). It also has a second form which is much more special and which itself is subdivided. This is the virtue that governs the distribution of honors or of wealth among the citizens. It enforces contracts of every kind, such as sales, purchases, and loans. In short it forbids acts of arbitrariness and violence. Aristotle, in other words, considers justice as having a distinct and irreducible function in the three forms which he finds it to have in practice; namely, the distribution of communal property among the citizens, law of contracts, and penal law. In these three kinds of justice, he finds a single principle, equality, but he understands it differently in the three cases. In distributive justice it is proportional equality, giving each his share according to his worth; the principle of contractual and penal law is arithmetical equality. The judge's function is to restore equality on behalf of the person wronged, by balancing compensations, damages, and interests, whether it is a question of a violation of contract or an act of violence. In the exchange of merchandise, this equality is made possible by the invention of the common measure, which is money.

Thus Aristotle tends to create distinct spheres in ethics each having its own principle. Furthermore, not all virtues have common conditions. When Aristotle writes so many pages on friendship (Books VIII and IX), his reason is that he considers it a condition indispensable to virtue. But only its highest form, friendship between free and equal men both moved by the love of the good, is capable of making men attain all possible perfections by imitating and correcting one another in the course of mutually serving one another. This is not like the inferior forms of friendship, the selfish friendships one finds in the aged or the pleasure-seeking friendships which join the young.

When Aristotle studies pleasure (viii, 11-14, and x, 1-5), his purpose is again to determine its highest form and to show in it a condition of moral excellence. It is indispensable to virtue that we take pleasure in what we must do and abhor what we must not do. In any case it is impossible not to tend toward pleasure, and those, like Speusippus, who declare that all pleasure is bad are refuted by universal experience which shows every sentient being seeking it as a good. It is not by hypocritical asceticism that men will be led away from injurious pleasures toward beneficial ones. The truth is that every act, whatever it is, is accompanied by pleasure when it is completed, just as the full development of a being is not devoid of beauty: pleasure is added to the act. Moreover, in encouraging the act, it completes it; a result of the act, it also becomes the cause of the perfection of this act. Consequently, pleasure can no more be sought unconditionally as an end than it can be put aside. Whatever the act is worth, so is the pleasure, in other words pleasures differ in value and also virtue cannot be perfect if it is not developed to the point of producing pleasure when it becomes actual.

Consequently, friendship and pleasure complete virtue each in their own way; but they do not give it more unity. Virtue remains dispersed in many forms. There can be no question of reducing them to one. Just as in his theory of substance Aristotle first defined substance as a general notion, including in its extension a multitude of different substances, and then passed from this general notion to that of an individual substance, God, who is pre-eminently substance, so in his ethics he passes by a very similar rhythm from the general notion of virtue, considered as the common term of human virtues, ethical and intellectual, to a virtue which is pre-eminently virtue, a virtue transcending human virtues, a divine virtue, which is the faculty of intellectual contemplation (x. 6–8). Whereas the other virtues imply the union of the soul with the body and social life, intelligence, in contemplation of truth, is isolated and self-sufficient. Whereas the rest of the moral life is a life filled with ceaseless pursuits, the contemplative life is a life of leisure, and consequently far superior, inasmuch as leisure is the end of action, and not action the end of leisure. It is, therefore, the life of what is truly divine in man, the only life which man may share with the gods who are above all thinking activities, finally the life which produces in him, together with the highest pleasure, the happiness which more than any other may be continued without fatigue.

This ethics of the contemplative man or of the student, placed far above that of the politician, again implies a separation of what Plato wanted so much to unite. Aristotle strongly felt the necessity of separating the intellectual life from the rest of social life and making it an end in itself. "All men by nature desire to know," [131] and knowledge is like an absolute which refers to nothing else. Yet we cannot say that there is any real dualism of ideals in Aristotle. For between the two lives, the practical and contemplative, there is a hierarchy and a subordination of the first to the second. The social life of a Greek city, with all the virtues it includes, is the condition in which the leisure of the contemplative wise man exists. They are two inseparable lives, in the same way in which God and the world are inseparable.

XIII *Politics*

"It is clear that a city is not simply a gathering together in order to avoid mutual wrong and to exchange services; these are certainly necessary conditions, but they do not make a city. A city is a gathering together of houses and families in order to live well, in other words to lead a perfect and independent life." [132] The first part of this passage refers to Plato, who, in defining the state by barter and division of labor, made the mistake of indicating only the material conditions and not the real nature, that is, the final cause of the state. Society makes it possible not only to live but also to live well; it is the basis of the ethical life. The science of politics will consist primarily in the examination of the conditions by which this end may be attained. But this examination consists less in theoretical constructions than in the use of observations and experiences which Aristotle multiplies and extends by extensive historical research on the constitutions of cities. The Sophists had already drawn up collections of city laws;[133] in that respect, Aristotle continued their work and he himself wrote or was responsible for the writing of the histories of various constitutions. But these histories were made only for purposes of preparing an estimate. The method here

---

[131] *Metaphysics* A. 1 (beginning).
[132] *Politics* iii. 5. 1280b 29.
[133] *Nicomachean Ethics* x. 9.

is the same as in biology; experienced facts arrange themselves in groups like sheaves, pointing in particular directions.

Moreover, the end which he assigned to the city was also to some degree the result of his experience and of his political development. He saw the basis of the moral vitality of an agrarian power, such as Sparta, in its economic independence. The independence of a city is based on the exclusion of economic relations with foreign countries. As soon as a country seeks its resources in its foreign commerce, as Athens did in the fifth century, it depends on the countries which produce grain and those which buy its products; hence, along with extensive commerce, the need for lending at interest and for banks.[134] Aristotle wholly condemned this new civilization with its concomitant of wars. He wanted to return to a natural economy. The economic unit is the family; it has all that is needed to produce what is necessary for its members' consumption; it exchanges only the surplus of this consumption. There is therefore no free and paid worker; the arrangement of slavery, with absolute power of the master (δεσπότης) over the slave, is a condition of this economic arrangement. The slave is a living tool who has no other will than his master's will and who does not participate in moral virtue; he will become useless "when the shuttles move by themselves" (i. 2). This division of humanity into masters and slaves is neither arbitrary nor violent: in obedience to finality, nature creates, in the warm climates of Asia, men with ingenious and subtle minds but without energy who are born to be slaves; only the temperate climate of Greece can produce men both intelligent and energetic, who are free by nature not by convention. In this theory which fits in so well with Aristotle's teleological orientation, one senses also an echo of the ancient struggle between Greece and the barbarians, and perhaps an attempt to justify the gigantic enterprise of universal domination by Greece, then attempted by Alexander.[135]

---

[134] Kinkel, *Die socialökonomischen Grundlagen der Staatslehre von Aristoteles* (1911), p. 92.
[135] *Politics* vii. 6. 1327b 21–23.

The family has more than an economic end. It allows the head of the family to direct imperfect souls such as those of women and children; imperfect souls, but not souls of slaves. Nor is this a matter of absolute power; the husband rules the wife as a magistrate the persons under his jurisdiction, and the father rules the children as a king his subjects (i. 5).

The family thus contains all the conditions necessary to make the city consist only in the free and the equal. In fact, all those who perform the functions of production, agricultural laborers or artisans, must be excluded from the number of citizens; these are occupations which lack nobility and which do away with "the leisure necessary to practice virtue and to engage in politics." For these functions we must employ people of another race, who think only of their work and not of revolution. The city proper has primarily military and legal functions, functions which one man can have at different ages; to these, sacerdotal functions must be added (vii. 7).

The diversity of constitutions (iv. 4 and 5) arises from the thousand ways in which these functions, always the same, may be distributed among the citizens. Democracy exists when free men without great wealth, who form the majority, are at the head of affairs; it is characterized by liberty and equality. We must distinguish further between democracies where the law rules, and democracies ruled by the mob and its ever changing votes. Oligarchy is the coming to power of the rich and the noble; it tends toward monarchy, as wealth becomes more concentrated. The diversity of governments has, therefore, one of its essential causes in the balance of wealth. Great differences in wealth inevitably give rise to oligarchy. The final goal of the city is to secure the happiness and virtue of the citizens by the rule of law. Now a rule of law is encouraged by certain economic conditions, by the development of the middle classes. "When the class of agricultural laborers and those of modest means is in control of the city, there is a reign of law; able to live only by working and having no leisure, they obey the law and hold only necessary meetings." But what if there are many citizens who are idle? Then democracy is transformed into a demagogy and "votes take the place of law." The method is clear: the problem is not to make a city but to find, in conditions effectively and historically realized, the infinitely various means, changing according to circumstances, of insuring the social good. In order to find the best constitution in a given circumstance, we must even go into geographical conditions: "The acropolis is oligarchical and monarchical, the plain is democratic" (vii. 10). Conditions are so numerous, and some of them are so much subject to change, that the constitution cannot remain stable. The desire to equal or to surpass others, the desire to grow rich, ambitions, and the increase of wealth are the principal motives which produce revolutions (v. 2).

Among these conditions, there are a great number which come from nature and of which man is not master; but there are also some which come from reflection and will, and man is master of the latter by means of education, whose purpose is to inculcate civic virtue in the child. The education which makes good citizens is that which refrains from developing one function at the expense of others and which is able to maintain the hierarchy of these functions and their proper value. Dangerous, for example, is the military education of Sparta which makes war the end of the state, whereas war and work are made only for peace and leisure; dangerous also is the abuse of gymnastics which among the Thebans makes every citizen an athlete, or the abuse of music which makes virtuosos. In reality the body must be developed for the sake of the soul; the lower part of the soul, the passions, for the sake of the higher part, the will; and finally the higher part with a view to contemplative reason (vii. 12).

The development of intellectual contemplation is, therefore, the final and only goal of which all the rest is only a condition and a consequence. In the human soul, in society as in the universe, all things tend to thought. Philosophy is perhaps less the study of thought itself, which exceeds man's grasp, than of this tendency, with its prodigiously many and varied conditions which experience teaches us. The mental universe of Aristotle is a tableau of different degrees of approximation of these conditions.[136] At the highest level, the theoretical sciences, first philosophy, physics, and mathematics study things which cannot be other than they are and whose perfection consists in their very necessity. At a lower level come the practical and productive sciences, those whose objects can be other than they are and which depend both on natural conditions furnished by fortune and on human effort. The practical sciences, ethics and politics, result in action. The productive sciences, techniques of every kind, result in products manufactured by man. But this classification does not in the least hinder the perfect continuity that makes human action, like a mathematical theorem, the result of a syllogism, and that makes rhetoric and poetry have an influence on the passions only because of the rational thought which inspires them.

xiv Peripateticism after Aristotle

The Peripatetic School, as a legal association recognized by the city, was not founded by Aristotle, who was a resident alien, but by Theophrastus, to whom he bequeathed his goods in a will which we still possess. The school became a cultural association consecrated to the Muses, possessing as common and inalienable property the houses and gardens bequeathed by Aristotle, and consisting in older members who elected the head of the school, and younger members commissioned to arrange the common meal at each new moon when they invited outsiders to the school. Philosophical work was therefore collective. Moreover, the life of the school was not easy; suspected of Macedonianism and little liked by the Athenians, it was threatened several times. When the Macedonian Demetrius of Phalera had to surrender Athens in 301, reprisals began against the Philomacedonians, directed by Demochares, the nephew of Demosthenes. They were first directed against the Peripatetics, and

---

[136] *Metaphysics* E. 1. 1025b 18–28.

Theophrastus had to leave Athens. From this time on, the ties between Peripateticism and Athens became looser. The disciples of Aristotle left willingly to work in Alexandria, whose reputation began to eclipse the glory of Athens.[137]

This affinity of the Peripatetics for the city of erudition is quite natural. It was in fact in the direction of experimental investigations that the disciples of Aristotle moved. As botanists, zoölogists, historians, they obeyed the powerful impetus for special investigations given by their master. They were Eudemus, Aristoxenus of Tarentum, and especially Theophrastus of Eresus (372–288), whose fragmentary *Metaphysics* begins by asserting an intimate contact and a kind of community between intelligible realities and the objects of physics;[138] the exaggerations of finalism in Aristotle, to which he opposes experience, also appear to have struck him (320, 12 ff.). His botanical collections, which have been preserved; his numerous physical monographs on the signs of storms, wind, water, and all kinds of geological facts;[139] his celebrated *Characters* which clearly demonstrates the tendency of Peripatetic ethics toward observation of details; his history of *Physical Opinions* which became one of the principal sources of the Greek doxographers; finally, his detailed historical investigations concerning the prytanes of Eresus; all these clearly indicate the orientation of the school. He is concerned with religion only in the manner of a historian or an anthropologist; uncertain about the nature of divinity which he sometimes sees in a mind, sometimes in the sky or the stars, he abounds in positive detail, for example in his criticism of bloody sacrifices which he shows to be backward in character and which he rejects because of the kinship between men and animals, not postulated as a dogma, but established by positive observation of the germs of reason in animals.[140] We see the same tendencies in

---

[137] Wilamowitz-Moellendorf, *Antigonos von Karystos* (1881), p. 264; Ziebarth, *Das griechische Vereinswesen* (1896), p. 71 ff.

[138] Edited by Brandis, with Aristoteles' *Metaphysics* (Berlin, 1823), p. 308.

[139] Fragment of his treatise on water discovered in the *Hibbeh Papyri* by Grenfell. Vol. I, No. 16 (ed. Blass).

[140] Selection of Porphyry in his treatise *On Abstinence*.

Clearchus of Soli who, for a purely historical purpose, collected superstitions about the future life.[141]

Aristotelianism, which many centuries later was the most rigid dogmatism possible, was at that time the most liberal of schools. In astronomy we see Clearchus of Soli abandoning the theory of spheres for that of epicycles. The fundamental principles of Aristotle's physics[142] were attacked in the theory of Strato of Lampsacus (d. *ca.* 270), who was the tutor of Ptolemy the Second at the Egyptian court from 300 to 294. In a formula exactly the reverse of Aristotle's, he taught that chance precedes nature; in fact he abandoned the doctrine of natural places and final causes, and accepted gravity alone as the one active force. Moreover, he observed the motion of falling with fresh attention and demonstrated its acceleration by showing that the force with which a heavy body hits an obstacle increases with the space traversed. From gravity alone, moreover, he deduced the relative place of the four elements from bottom to top. The lower element, compressed like a sponge, thrusts out the higher element which lodges itself at its surface; there is no ether, and the sky is of a fiery nature. Differences of weight among bodies are due to the greater or less amount of empty space they contain, and the existence of empty space is further proved by the transmission of light and heat which can be transmitted only through immaterial media. Thus a natural order (eternally the same, no doubt) can arise from a simple mechanical causality: falling, condensation, and traction explain everything. There is no other god than nature which, without sense or form, produces and engenders every being. Form no longer has the immobility which it had in Aristotle; the initial and final points of motion are born and die like the motion itself.

Let us cite further the historian Dicaearchus, who in his short history of the Greek people[143] takes up again, with a positive method, the old Hesiodic tales of the origin of history, distinguishing, as

---

[141] According to Proclus *Commentary on The Republic* (Kroll ed., II, 114).

[142] Plutarch *Concerning the Face of the Moon* chap. iv.

[143] Known by Porphyry *On Abstinence* Book iv. chap. ii.

successive ages, the golden age when men lived in leisure and peace, the nomadic age when with the domestication of animals, property, robbery, and war began, and the agricultural age, when these acts became more frequent.

Later, Critolaus, who directed the school from 190 to 150, was scarcely a Peripatetic. The supreme God becomes a reason issuing from impassive ether; the soul also is a rational ether. It is apparently Critolaus, who, in ethics, stated with precision the doctrine considered as the Peripatetic view in following centuries. According to him life in conformity with nature can only be achieved by three kinds of goods, goods of the soul, goods of the body, and external goods.

Specialization and a tendency toward a rationalism implicitly hostile to religion characterize the aging Aristotelianism, a philosophy of little popular appeal and one which succumbed rapidly before the universal success of the dogmatisms which appeared one after another following the death of Alexander. These derive not from Plato and Aristotle, but from schools of a very different kind, which had also sprung from Socraticism and of which we must now speak.

Bibliography

Works

Edition of the work of Aristotle and Commentaries (in 23 vols.) published by the Academy of Berlin, by Bekker. Vols. I and II, 1831, reprinted 1959. Vol. III: Latin translations. Vol. V, 1870: *Index aristotelicus,* by Bonitz, and *Supplementum aristotelicum,* 1885–95. *Fragments* by V. Rose, 1886; R. Walzer, Florence, 1934; W. D. Ross, Oxford, 1955.

Partial editions: *Metaphysics.* Bonitz edition, Berlin, 1848–49. Ross edition, Oxford, 1924. *Organon.* Waitz edition, 1844–46. *On the Soul.* Trendelenburg edition, 1833. *Nicomachean Ethics.* Burnet edition, 1900. *Politics.* Newman edition, 1887–92; Books III and IV translated into English with commentary by R. Robinson. Oxford, 1962. *Meteorology.* Ideler edition, 1834–36; Fobes edition, 1919. *De Coelo,* text and Italian translation by O. Longo. Florence, 1961; *Aristotle's Protrepticus: An Attempt at Reconstruction* by Ingemar Düring. Göteborg, 1961.

General Studies

O. Hamelin. *Le système d'Aristote.* 1920.

C. Piat. *Aristote.* 1903.

C. Lalo. *Aristote.* 1923.

W. D. Ross. *Aristotle.* London, 1923. French translation, 1930.

W. Jaeger. *Studien zur Entstehungsgeschichte der Metaphysik des Aristoteles.* Berlin, 1917.—*Aristoteles, Grundlegung einer Geschichte seiner Entwicklung.* 1923. English translation by R. Robinson.

E. Bignone. *L'Aristotele perduto e la formazione filosofica di Epicuro.* Florence, 1936.

F. Nuyens. *L'Évolution de la psychologie d'Aristote.* 1948.

J. Bidez. *Un singulier naufrage littéraire dans l'antiquité: A la recherche de l'Aristote perdu.* Brussels, 1943.

Le Blond. *Logique et méthode chez Aristote.* 1939.—*Eulogos.* 1939.

L. Robin. *Aristote.* Paris, 1944.

W. G. Rabinowitz. *Aristotle's "Protrepticus" and the Sources of Its Reconstruction.* I. Berkeley and Los Angeles, Calif., 1957.

R. Weil. "Etat présent des questions aristotéliciennes," *Information littéraire.* 1959. Pp. 20–31.

P. Moraux. *Les listes anciennes des ouvrages d'Aristote*. Louvain, 1951.

J. Zürcher. *Aristoteles Werk und Geist*. Paderborn, 1952.

J. Brun. *Aristote et le lycée*. Abridged. Paris, 1961.

J. Moreau. *Aristote et son école*. Paris, 1962.

See the *Actes du Congrès Budé de Lyon* (September 1958). Paris, 1960.

Special Studies

H. Maier. *Die Syllogistik des Aristoteles*. Tübingen, 1896–1900.

C. Thurot. *Études sur Aristote*. 1861.

M. Roland-Gosselin. "Les méthodes de la définition d'après Aristote," *Revue des sciences philosophiques et théologiques*, 1912.

L. Brunschvigg. *Qua ratione Aristoteles metaphysicaim vim syllogismo inesse demonstraverit*. 1897.

L. Robin. "Sur la conception aristotélicienne de la causalité," *Archiv für die Geschichte der Philosophie*, 1909 (*La Pensée hellénique des origines à Epicure*. 1942. Pp. 423–85).

P.-M. Schuhl. *Le dominateur et les possibles*. 1960.

W. and M. Kneale. *The Development of Logic*. Oxford, 1962.

Ravaisson. *Essai sur la métaphysique d'Aristote*. Vol. I, 1836. Reprinted in 1920.

L. Robin. *La théorie platonicienne des idées et des nombres d'après Aristote*. 1908. Reissued in 1962.

C. Werner. *Aristote et l'idéalisme platonicien*. 1910.

J. Bidez. *Un singulier naufrage littéraire dans l'Antiquité: A la recherche de l'Aristote perdu*. Brussels, 1943.

P. Wilpert. *Zwei aristotelische Frühschriften über die Ideenlehre*. Ratisbonne, 1959.

A. J. Festugière. "Un fragment nouveau du Protreptique d'Aristote," *Revue philosophique*, 1956.

H. D. Saffrey. Περὶ Φιλοσοφίας *d'Aristote et la théorie platonicienne des idées nombres*. Leiden, 1955.

V. Décarie. *L'objet de la métaphysique selon Aristote*. Paris, 1961.

Pierre Aubenque. *Le problème de l'Être chez Aristote, Essai sur la problematique aristotélicienne*. Paris, 1962.

Carteron. *La notion de force dans le système d'Aristote*. 1923.

Duhem. *Le système du monde de Platon à Copernic*. Vol. I, 1913. Pp. 130–214.

Pouchet. *La biologie aristotélique*. 1885.

M. Manquat. *Aristote naturaliste*. 1932.

W. Jaeger. "Pneuma im Lykeion," *Hermès*, 1913, pp. 29–74.—*Diokles von Karystos*. 1938.

L. Bourgey. *Observation et expérience chez Aristote*. Paris, 1955.

Ollé-Laprune. *La morale d'Aristote*. 1881.

A. J. FESTUGIÈRE. *Aristote: Le plaisir.* 1936.

DEFOURNY. *Aristote, théorie économique et société.* Louvain, 1914.—*Aristote et l'éducation.* 1919.—*Aristote et l'évolution sociale.* 1924.

M. GILLET. *Du fondement intellectuel de la morale d'après Aristote.*

L. COOPER and A. GUDEMANN. *A Bibliography of the Poetics of Aristotle.* New Haven, 1928.

P. MORAUX. *A la recherche de l'Aristote perdu: le dialogue sur la justice.* Louvain-Paris, 1957.

R. ROBINSON. "L'Acrasie selon Aristote," *Revue philosophique,* 1955, pp. 261–80.

R. WEIL. *Aristote et l'histoire, essai sur la Politique. Paris,* 1960.

P. AUBENQUE. *La prudence chez Aristote.* 1963.

THEOPHRASTUS. *Caractères.* Navarre edition, G. Budé collection, 1921.—*Fragments.* Teubner edition.—*Métaphysique.* W. D. Ross and Fobes edition, Oxford, 1929 (Tricot translation, Paris, 1948).

See the texts of the students of Aristotle edited by F. Wehrli after 1944 under the title: *Die Schule des Aristoteles.* I, Dicaerchus; II, Aristoxenus; III, Clearchus; IV, Demetrius of Phalerum; V, Straton of Lampsacus; VI, Lycon and Ariston of Ceos; VII, Heraclides Ponticus; VIII, Eudemus of Rhodes; IX, Phaenias of Eresus, Chamaeleon, Praxiphanes; X, Hieronymus of Rhodes, Critolaus and his pupils, General Conclusions, Index.

J. BERNAYS. *Theophrastos Schrift über die Frömmigkeit.* 1866.

BOCHENSKI. *La logique de Théophraste.* 1947.

E. BARBOTIN. *La théorie aristotélicienne de l'intellect d'après Théophraste.* Louvain, 1954.

G. RODIER. *La physique de Straton de Lampsaque.* 1891.

Studies in English

E. BARKER. *The Political Thought of Plato and Aristotle.* London, 1906.

G. GROTE. *Aristotle.* London, 1883.

WERNER JAEGER. *Aristotle: Fundamentals of the History of His Development.* Oxford, 1934.

JOHN H. RANDALL. *Aristotle.* New York.

W. D. ROSS. *Aristotle.* 2d edition; London, 1930.

———. *Aristotle's Metaphysics.* 2 vols; Oxford, 1924.

———. *Aristotle's Physics.* Oxford, 1936.

A. E. TAYLOR. *Aristotle.* New York, 1943.

INDEX

PHOENIX BOOKS
in Philosophy and Religion